"While the first edition of *Case Conceptualization* was recognized as the best training tool for learning this indispensable clinical skill, this revised edition is even better! The authors have made it not only more clinically useful but also enjoyable to read. Packed with case studies, commentaries, worksheets, and guidelines, it will continue to be the go-to text for students and practitioners."

Dr. Debbie Joffe Ellis, Adjunct Professor, Clinical and Counseling Psychology, Columbia University

Case Conceptualization

Integrating recent research and developments in the field, this revised second edition introduces an easy-to-master strategy for developing and writing culturally sensitive case conceptualizations and treatment plans.

Concrete guidelines and updated case material are provided for developing conceptualizations for the five most common therapy models: Cognitive-Behavioral Therapy (CBT), Psychodynamic, Biopsychosocial, Adlerian, and Acceptance and Commitment Therapy. The chapters also include specific exercises and activities for mastering case conceptualization and related competencies and skills. Also new to this edition is a chapter on couple and family case conceptualizations, and an emphasis throughout on trauma.

Practitioners, as well as graduate students in counseling and in clinical psychology, will gain the essential skills and knowledge they need to master case conceptualizations.

Len Sperry, MD, PhD, is a Professor at Florida Atlantic University, USA. He has taught and written about case conceptualization for 35 years. His research team has completed eight studies on case conceptualization.

Jon Sperry, PhD, is an Associate Professor of clinical mental health counseling at Lynn University, USA. He teaches, writes, and researches case conceptualization, and conducts workshops on it worldwide.

Case Conceptualization

Mastering This Competency with
Ease and Confidence

Second Edition

Len Sperry and Jon Sperry

Routledge
Taylor & Francis Group

NEW YORK AND LONDON

Second edition published 2020
by Routledge
52 Vanderbilt Avenue, New York, NY 10017

and by Routledge
2 Park Square, Milton Park, Abingdon, Oxon, OX14 4RN

Routledge is an imprint of the Taylor & Francis Group, an informa business

© 2020 Taylor & Francis

The right of Len Sperry and Jon Sperry to be identified as authors of this work has been asserted by them in accordance with sections 77 and 78 of the Copyright, Designs and Patents Act 1988.

First edition published by Routledge 2012

Library of Congress Cataloging-in-Publication Data
Names: Sperry, Len, author. | Sperry, Jonathan J., author.
Title: Core competencies: mastering this competency with ease and confidence/Len Sperry, Jon Sperry.
Other titles: Case conceptualization. | Core competencies in psychotherapy series (New York, N.Y.)
Description: 2nd edition. | New York, NY: Routledge, 2020. |
Series: Core competencies in psychotherapy | Preceded by Case conceptualization: mastering this competency with ease and confidence/ Len Sperry, Jonathan J. Sperry. 2012. | Includes bibliographical references and index. |
Summary: "Integrating recent research and developments in the field, this revised second edition introduces an easy-to-master strategy for developing and writing culturally sensitive case conceptualizations and treatment plans. Concrete guidelines and updated case material are provided for developing conceptualizations for the five most common therapy models: CBT, psychodynamic, biopsychosocial, Adlerian, and Acceptance and Commitment Therapy. Chapters also include specific exercises and activities for mastering case conceptualization and related competencies and skills. Also new to this edition is a chapter on couple and family case conceptualizations, and an emphasis throughout on trauma. Practitioners, as well as graduate students in counseling and clinical psychology, will gain the essential skills and knowledge they need to master case conceptualizations"–Provided by publisher.
Identifiers: LCCN 2020004517 (print) | LCCN 2020004518 (ebook) | ISBN 9780367251925 (hardback) | ISBN 9780367256654 (paperback) | ISBN 9780429288968 (ebook)
Subjects: MESH: Psychology, Clinical | Clinical Competence | Psychotherapy–methods
Classification: LCC RC454 (print) | LCC RC454 (ebook) | NLM WM 150 | DDC 616.89–dc23
LC record available at https://lccn.loc.gov/2020004517
LC ebook record available at https://lccn.loc.gov/2020004518

ISBN: 978-0-367-25192-5 (hbk)
ISBN: 978-0-367-25665-4 (pbk)
ISBN: 978-0-429-28896-8 (ebk)

Typeset in Times New Roman
by Deanta Global Publishing Services, Chennai, India

Contents

Foreword

I first encountered Len Sperry's work when I read his 1992 book, *Psychiatric Case Formulations*. I remember being impressed by the book's elegance and economy of style, and how Sperry and his co-authors distilled complicated ideas to their bare essentials, all while creating a practical, hands-on manual. The book shaped my views and research on case conceptualization, and I have consulted it regularly since. The first edition of *Case Conceptualization: Mastering This Competency with Ease and Confidence* continued these qualities and they are present as well in this significantly updated and timely second edition. These books fill a gap between the consensus view among experts in psychotherapy that case conceptualization competency is an essential skill, and the relative lack of formal training to assist therapists gain competence.

The essential message in the second edition is that a sound and comprehensive case conceptualization has both high explanatory and high predictive power, and for this reason contributes significantly to treatment effectiveness. Further, learning to develop such a conceptualization is readily achievable and employed in clinical practice. An explanation of the problems that have led a client to psychotherapy is not only a gift to the client in that it helps make sense of what may otherwise be a chaotic, confusing, and alienating set of experiences, but it is also a gift to the therapist, who, with the explanation in hand, has a powerful tool to guide treatment. High predictive power means that the conceptualization is forward looking. It anticipates problems in therapy before they emerge, and should lead to improved outcomes.

In a systematic and easy-to-follow manner, Sperry and Sperry aid the reader in learning how to develop compelling explanatory and highly predictive case conceptualizations. Key components of case conceptualization are described, including critical clinical information, precipitants, predisposing and maintaining factors of the client's problems, a statement of maladaptive patterns, cultural influences, and a thorough approach to planning treatment based on the foregoing information. The addition of new chapters addressing case conceptualization in couples and family therapy, in "third-wave" treatments, and in treatment for traumatized clients adds to the timeliness and utility of the book. Worksheets provided by the authors facilitate the development and organization of this information.

In reading the book, it is evident that the authors are master teachers. The style of exposition is clear and interesting, and the book abounds with case examples, client–therapist dialogue, and explanations. Conceptualizations varying in quality are contrasted and the authors explain why some provide better explanations and are more predictive. These features engage the reader and encourage the development of competency. I have learned much from reading the Sperrys' work. I commend the authors on their book and urge anyone interested in learning case conceptualization or honing their case conceptualization skills to study it well.

Tracy D. Eells
University of Louisville

Acknowledgments

We are grateful to Joshua Katz for his input on the study questions and for Gerardo Casteleiro's expertise in Acceptance Commitment Therapy as he helped us with Chapter Ten.

Introduction

Before 1990, mental health professionals and trainees seldom, if ever, talked about case conceptualizations. Not surprisingly, very few used case conceptualizations in their practice. Thirty years later, the situation is markedly different as case conceptualizations have increasingly become associated with competent, quality mental health practice. Today, the capacity to use case conceptualizations is considered an essential clinical competency, and mental health practitioners – psychotherapists, clinical psychologists, psychiatrists, substance abuse counselors, rehabilitation counselors, and school counselors – are increasingly expected to use case conceptualizations in everyday practice.

This expectation is problematic since very few practitioners have formal training in this competency, and graduate programs have only recently begun incorporating case conceptualizations in their training of mental health professionals. To complicate matters, developing and writing adequate case conceptualizations is one of the more challenging competencies for practitioners and trainees to master. If you are a mental health practitioner, you may have picked up this book in hopes of increasing your competence with case conceptualizations. If you are a trainee in a graduate mental health program, this book was likely assigned to assist you in learning this competency.

The first edition of this book addressed the challenge of learning and mastering this formidable competency. It introduced an easy-to-master *integrative case conceptualization model* for writing case conceptualizations that incorporate key elements from Cognitive-Behavioral Therapy, Dynamic psychotherapy, Adlerian psychotherapy, and the Biopsychosocial approach, as well as others. It highlighted new developments and research on case conceptualization, treatment planning, interventions, as well as cultural sensitivity. It offered detailed and compelling case examples and transcriptions that illustrate key points. Finally, it provided the reader with specific exercises for developing case conceptualization skills.

However, few could have anticipated the number of additional changes that have transpired in the eight years since the first edition was published. As a result, a new edition was proposed that was responsive to these changes. Chief among these was the addition of new chapters on Acceptance and Commitment Therapy case conceptualizations and Couple and Family case conceptualizations, as well as a brief section on case conceptualizations in Dialectal Behavioral Therapy. These additions were prompted by reader feedback, external reviewers, and requests from students and workshop participants. Given its increasing presence in everyday clinical practice, we were requested and included ways for making case conceptualizations sensitive to trauma issues. Those doing child and adolescent therapy and school counseling sought help in developing case conceptualizations geared to young clients. Accordingly, we included the case of a 13-year-old student, Katrina. Finally, we added questions for group discussion or self-study at the end of each chapter.

The organization of the book is straightforward. Chapters 1 through 5 serve as background material for the remaining chapters. Chapter 1 is an overview of case conceptualization and its components. Chapter 2 addresses diagnostic and clinical or theory-based assessment before describing the diagnostic formulation component of the case conceptualization. Chapter 3 emphasizes the clinical and cultural formulations components, while Chapter 4 emphasizes the treatment formulation component. Chapter 5 focuses on other factors and dynamics involved in developing case conceptualizations with couples and families.

These five chapters prepare the reader for the heart of the book which is Chapters 6 through 10. In these chapters, the reader is introduced to five models of case conceptualization. Each chapter provides five examples of a full-scale case conceptualization that reflects this model. In each of these chapters, the same five cases are analyzed, and a written case conceptualization is provided. Chapter 6 focuses on Biopsychosocial case conceptualizations while Chapters 7 through 10 focus on Cognitive-Behavioral case conceptualizations, Time-Limited Dynamic case conceptualizations, Adlerian case conceptualizations, and Acceptance and Commitment Therapy case conceptualizations, respectively. There is also an Appendix which includes useful worksheets, tables, and case conceptualization evaluation forms.

You may wonder if this book is necessary, easy to use, and will have real clinical value for you. Currently, there are really only two ways of constructing a case conceptualization. One is to learn and apply a structured or theory-based method, e.g., one of the CBT or Dynamic approaches. The other is to use a seat-of-the-pants method, e.g., one that a practitioner has devised by trial and error that is often little more than a case summary. A third way would be to use an *integrative case conceptualization model* which incorporates common elements from various structured methods, while allowing the unique and distinctive elements of specific methods and approaches. Unlike other books on case conceptualizations, this is the only one that presents and illustrates an integrative method of case conceptualization and provides exercises for learning it.

A word about language. The designations case conceptualizations, case formulations, clinical formulations, treatment formulations, and diagnostic formulations tend to be used synonymously. We will use the designation case conceptualizations instead of case formulations for two reasons. First, the term "case conceptualization" is now the preferred designation throughout the mental health community, and second, to avoid confusion. As noted in Part I, we breakout four components of case conceptualization: diagnostic formulation, clinical formulation, cultural formulation, and treatment formulation. For clarity of expression, we use case conceptualization to represent the process in general, and diagnostic, clinical, cultural, or treatment formulation to represent the process in particular. We will also use the general designation "practitioner" in place of terms such as psychotherapist, therapist, counselor, psychologist, psychiatrist, clinician, etc.

Finally, we would add that our professional involvement with teaching, researching, and writing about case conceptualizations is longstanding, beginning in the 1980s. The first of our many articles appeared in 1988 (Sperry, 1988) and the first book in 1992 (Sperry et al., 1992). Collectively, we have taught versions of this integrative model in continuing graduate courses, conferences, and workshops over the past 45 years. Nearly all participants have found this method easy to understand and use, and subsequently were able to master this competency and feel confident applying it to their cases, including "difficult" ones. We trust that this will also be your experience.

Len Sperry and Jon Sperry

Introduction to the Chapters in Part I

Chapters 1 through 5 of this book serve as background material for the chapters in Part II. Unlike the chapters in Part II, the chapters in Part I are largely theoretical descriptions supported by research of case conceptualization and its components and elements. However, that does not mean they are abstruse and devoid of clinical value. On the contrary, these chapters are richly illustrated with clinical case material. Chapter 1 is an overview of the structure of case conceptualization which emphasizes the clinical value and utility of a competently constructed case conceptualization. Chapter 2 addresses diagnostic and clinical- or theory-based assessment before describing the diagnostic formulation component of a case conceptualization. Chapter 3 emphasizes the clinical and cultural formulation components, while Chapter 4 highlights the treatment formulation component. Chapter 5 focuses on other factors and dynamics involved in developing case conceptualizations with couples and families.

1 Case Conceptualizations

An Overview

So, what are case conceptualizations and why is there so much interest in them today? Basically, a case conceptualization is a method for understanding and explaining a client's concerns and for guiding the treatment process. It functions like a "bridge" to connect assessment and treatment with clinical outcomes. In this era of accountability, it is not surprising that effective clinical practice presumes the competency to construct and utilize case conceptualizations. In fact, many consider case conceptualization to be the most important competency in counseling and psychotherapy, and one of the most challenging to master. This chapter introduces and overviews competency in case conceptualization.

The chapter begins by defining case conceptualization and its functions. Next, it describes and illustrates the various elements of a case conceptualization. This is followed by a discussion of the four components of a case conceptualization: diagnostic formulation, clinical formulation, cultural formulation, and treatment formulation. Then, it distinguishes three levels of sufficiency for evaluating case conceptualizations. Next, several myths about case conceptualization are discussed. Finally, it introduces background material on the five clinical cases that will be cited throughout the book and analyzed in detail in Chapters 6 through 10.

Case Conceptualization: Definition and Functions

Case conceptualizations provide clinicians with a coherent treatment strategy for planning and focusing treatment interventions in order to increase the likelihood of achieving treatment goals. While many therapists develop conceptualizations to guide their practice, not all therapists explicitly articulate these conceptualizations because they are not sufficiently confident with this competency. There are a number of reasons for developing and articulating a case conceptualization, but the most cogent reason is that a conceptualization enables therapists to experience a sense of confidence in their work (Hill, 2005). Hill (2005) believes that this confidence is then communicated to the client, which strengthens the client's trust and the belief that the therapist has a credible plan, and that therapy can and will make a difference.

Case conceptualization is defined in this book as a method and clinical strategy for obtaining and organizing information about a client, understanding and explaining the client's situation and maladaptive patterns, guiding and focusing treatment, anticipating challenges and roadblocks, and preparing for successful termination (Sperry, 2010, 2015). Case conceptualization is also a cognitive process that practitioners utilize before, during, and after sessions to understand various dynamics and therefore to determine the use of various strategies with a given client.

Definition of Case Conceptualization: Case conceptualization is a method and clinical strategy for obtaining and organizing information about a client, understanding and explaining the client's situation and maladaptive patterns, guiding and focusing treatment, anticipating challenges and roadblocks, and preparing for successful termination.

This definition highlights interrelated functions when it is understood as a clinical strategy. These five functions are:

1. *Obtaining and organizing.* The case conceptualization process begins with the first client contact and formulating tentative hypotheses about the client's presentation, expectations, and dynamics. These hypotheses are continually tested out while performing an integrative assessment guided by a search for patterns – maladaptive patterns – in the client's current and past life with regard to precipitants and predisposing and perpetuating factors.
2. *Explaining.* As the contours of the client's maladaptive pattern come into focus and hypotheses are refined, a diagnostic, clinical, and cultural formulation emerges. Within these formulations is a likely explanation of the factors that account for the client's reactions in the past, the present, and the future without treatment. This explanation also provides a rationale for treatment that is tailored to the client's needs, expectations, culture, and personality dynamics.
3. *Guiding and focusing treatment.* Based on this explanation, a treatment formulation emerges, and strategies for specifying treatment targets and for focusing and implementing treatment are developed.
4. *Anticipating obstacles and challenges.* One test of an effective case conceptualization is its viability in predicting the most likely obstacles and challenges throughout the stages of therapy, particularly those involving active engagement in and commitments to the treatment process, adherence, resistance, ambivalence, alliance ruptures, transference enactments, relapse, and termination.
5. *Preparing for termination.* The case conceptualization also assists therapists to recognize when the most important therapy goals and treatment targets have been addressed and to identify when and how to prepare for termination (Cucciare & O'Donohue, 2008). The process of terminating treatment can be quite stressful for some clients, particularly those with dependency issues, rejection sensitivity, and abandonment histories.

Therefore, an effectively constructed case conceptualization which anticipates these considerations can be immensely useful in preparing the client for termination (Sperry, 2010).

Clinically Useful Case Conceptualizations

It has been said that a clinically useful case conceptualization provides the necessary explanatory power (a compelling explanation for the presenting problem) and predictive power (anticipation of the obstacles and facilitators to treatment success) for effectively and competently planning and guiding the treatment process. So, what specifically characterizes a clinically useful case conceptualization?

Before giving our own opinion on this question, we'd like you to participate in a short experiment. Following are three case conceptualizations of the same client. They are labeled "Version 1," "Version 2," and "Version 3." Each differs in length and emphasis. Please read all three, without looking at the "commentary" that follows each. Then, ask yourself the question: "Which version (1, 2, or 3) best explains the client and best specifies a treatment plan and the likelihood of a positive outcome?" Then, feel free to go back and read the commentaries that reflect our choice and the reasons for it.

Version 1

Geri is a 35-year-old, African American female who was referred by her company's human resources director for evaluation and treatment following three weeks of depressed mood. Other symptoms include loss of energy, markedly diminished interest, insomnia, difficulty concentrating, and increasing social isolation. Of note is a family history of depression, including a maternal aunt who presumably overdosed on sleeping pills. She denies suicidal ideation and plan, now and in the past, saying that her religion forbids it. Geri meets *Diagnostic and Statistical Manual of Mental Disorders, Fifth Edition* (*DSM-5*) criteria for Major Depressive Disorder: Single Episode in the mild to moderate level. She states her health is fine, and denies the use of medication, alcohol, or recreational drugs. No previous psychiatric hospitalizations, nor individual or family therapy are reported. The clinic's psychiatrist advises that hospitalization is not indicated at this time. The treatment goals are specified as symptom reduction and return to baseline functioning. Outpatient treatment will consist of Zoloft 50 mg a day monitored by our psychiatrist, and psychotherapy (with this therapist) which will begin immediately with sessions scheduled weekly.

Commentary. This version is essentially a factual description of the case that emphasizes the DSM diagnosis and an initial treatment plan. Notable is the absence of personality, situational, and cultural dynamics. Also noteworthy is the presumption, without supporting evidence, that medication is the treatment of choice for the client. Furthermore, there is no prediction that the client will follow the generic treatment plan nor recover. It is questionable whether this version is actually a case conceptualization or not. Rather, it is basically a case summary. Unfortunately, it has virtually no explanatory or predictive power.

Version 2

Geri's increased social isolation and depressive symptoms seem to be her reaction to the news of an impending job transfer and promotion, given her history of avoiding situations in which she might be criticized, rejected, and feel unsafe. Throughout her life, she found it safer to avoid others when possible and conditionally relate to them at other times; as a result, she lacks key social skills and has a limited social network. This pattern can be understood in light of demanding, critical, and emotionally unavailable parents, strong parental injunctions against making personal and family disclosures to others, the teasing and criticism of peers, and schemas of defectiveness and social isolation. Her family history of depression may biologically predispose her to sadness and social isolation, as does the under-development of relational skills. This pattern is maintained by her shyness, the fact that she lives alone, her limited social skills, and that she finds it safer to socially isolate. The goals of treatment include reducing depressive symptoms, increasing interpersonal and friendship skills, and returning to work. Treatment will begin immediately and emphasize a reduction of her depressive symptoms and social isolation with medication prescribed and monitored by the clinic's psychiatrist. Cognitive Behavior Therapy will focus on behavioral activation strategies and cognitive restructuring of her interfering beliefs of self, others, and the world, as well as her coping strategy of shyness, rejection sensitivity, distrust, and isolation from others. In addition, collaboration with Geri's work supervisor and the human resources director will be attempted in order to accommodate Geri's return to a more tolerable work environment. Later, group therapy with a psychoeducational emphasis will be added because of her significant skill deficits in assertive communication, trust, and friendship skills. Prognosis is fair to good.

   Commentary. This version provides more explanation and implications for treatment in contrast to the descriptive focus of Version 1. Personality and situational dynamics are emphasized in this conceptualization resulting in a detailed and tailored treatment plan. The Cognitive-Behavioral perspective is evident in this version. However, cultural considerations are not addressed, nor are potential obstacles to treatment success anticipated. In short, this version has considerable explanatory power but relatively little predictive power.

Version 3

Geri's increased social isolation and depressive symptoms seem to be her reaction to the news of an impending job transfer and promotion, given her history of avoiding situations in which she might be criticized, rejected, and feel unsafe. Throughout her life, she found it safer to avoid others when possible and conditionally relate to them at other times; as a result she lacks key social skills and has a limited social network. This pattern can be understand in light of demanding, critical, and emotionally unavailable parents, strong parental injunctions against making personal and family disclosures to others, the teasing and criticism of peers, and schemas of defectiveness and social isolation. Her family history of depression may biologically predispose her to sadness and social isolation, as·

does the under-development of relational skills. Still, Geri has protective factors working for her. She has a reasonably secure attachment style with her close work friend and a strong job commitment. She also appears to qualify for job accommodations under the Americans with Disabilities Act. This means she can likely return to her current job with reduced stress.

This pattern is maintained by her shyness, the fact that she lives alone, her limited social skills, and that she finds it safer to socially isolate. Geri and her parents are highly acculturated, and she believes that her depression is the result of stresses at work and a "chemical imbalance" in her brain. No obvious indications of prejudice or conflicting cultural expectations or factors are operative. Instead, it appears that Geri's personality dynamics are significantly operative in her current clinical presentation.

The challenge for Geri is to function more effectively and feel safer while she relates to others. The goals of treatment include reducing depressive symptoms, increasing interpersonal and friendship skills, returning to work, and establishing a supportive social network there. The focus of treatment efforts will be to change her maladaptive beliefs and behaviors. The therapeutic strategy will be to utilize Cognitive-Behavioral replacement, desensitization, and social skill training to achieve these treatment goals. First, reduce her depressive symptoms with medication and desensitization, and cognitive and behavior replacement for symptoms of rejection sensitivity and isolation from others. Second, incorporate social skills training in a group therapy setting which emphasizes assertive communication, trust, and friendship skills. Collaborate with Geri's work supervisor and the human resources director will be attempted in order to accommodate Geri's return to a more tolerable work environment. Treatment will be sequenced with medication management by her physician (in consultation with the clinic's psychiatrist) and cognitive and behavioral replacement which will begin immediately in an individual treatment format.

Some obstacles and challenges to treatment can be anticipated. Ambivalent resistance is likely, given her avoidant personality structure. It can be anticipated that she would have difficulty discussing personal matters with therapists, and that she would "test" and provoke therapists into criticizing her for changing or canceling appointments at the last minute or being late, and that she might procrastinate, avoid feelings, and otherwise "test" the therapist's trustability. Once trust in the therapist is achieved, she is likely to cling to the therapist and treatment and thus termination may be difficult unless her social support system outside therapy is increased. Furthermore, her pattern of avoidance is likely to make entry into and continuation with group work difficult. Therefore, individual sessions can serve as a transition into group therapy, including having some contact with the group therapist who will presumably be accepting and non-judgmental. This should increase Geri's feeling safe and making self-disclosure in a group setting less difficult. Transference enactment is another consideration. Given the extent of parental and peer criticism and teasing, it is anticipated that any perceived impatience and verbal or non-verbal indications of criticalness by the therapist will activate this transference. Finally, because of her tendency to cling to others she trusts, increasing her capacity to feel more confident in functioning with greater independence and increasing the time between the last four or five sessions can reduce her ambivalence about termination. Assuming that Geri increases her self-confidence, relational skills, and social contacts in and outside therapy, as well as return to work, her prognosis is adjudged to be good. Otherwise, it is guarded. Treatment progress will not likely be dependent on cultural or even culturally sensitive interventions at this time. However, given her strained relationship with her father and limited involvement with men ever since, gender dynamics could impact the therapeutic relationship. Accordingly, female therapists for both individual and group therapy appear to be indicated in the initial phase of treatment.

Commentary. This version emphasizes explanation and implications for treatment instead of the descriptive emphasis of Version 1. Personality, situational, and cultural dynamics are central to this conceptualization, resulting in a tailored treatment plan that anticipates potential obstacles to treatment success. Some may consider this version too long. While it is longer and more detailed than the other two versions, these focused details add considerable explanatory and predictive power.

Table 1.1 is a visual comparison of the elements involved in each of the three versions.

Clearly, Version 3 encompasses more elements than the other two combined. While Version 2 is more detailed than Version 1, Version 3 may appear to be too detailed. Yet, it is notable that an entire group of elements are missing in Version 2, i.e., those pertaining to culture. While cultural elements do not appear to be as operative as they are in other cases, there would be no basis for making this determination without accounting for them in the case conceptualization.

Table 1.1 Comparison of Three Case Conceptualizations

Case Conceptualization Elements	Version 1	Version 2	Version 3
Presentation	x	x	x
Precipitants		x	x
Pattern: maladaptive		x	x
Predisposition		x	x
Protective Factors			x
Perpetuants		x	x
Cultural identity			x
Acculturation & stress			x
Cultural explanation model			x
Culture v. personality			x
Treatment pattern			x
Treatment goals	x	x	x
Treatment focus			x
Treatment strategy		x	x
Treatment interventions	x	x	x
Treatment obstacles			x
Treatment-cultural			x
Treatment prognosis		x	x

As we will contend throughout this book, case conceptualizations that have high explanatory power and high predictive power are more clinically useful than those that do not have high explanatory or predictive powers.

As instructors and clinical supervisors, we favor complete or full-scale case conceptualizations, i.e., those that account for all 18 elements. However, we leave it up to you to decide the number of elements that you determine are sufficient in constructing a specific case conceptualization.

Components of a Case Conceptualization

A case conceptualization consists of four components: a diagnostic formulation, a clinical formulation, a cultural formulation, and a treatment formulation (Sperry et al., 1992; Sperry, 2005, 2010). Table 1.2 lists and briefly describes each of these components.

Evaluating Case Conceptualizations

As noted previously, not all case conceptualizations are the same. Some are more clinically useful than others. We consider explanatory power and predictive power to be useful *global* criteria in evaluating a case conceptualization. Eells (2010) offers some *specific* criteria for evaluating a case conceptualization. These criteria are: To what extent is a psychological theory offered that explains the problems and symptoms? Is it sufficiently and coherently articulated? Are key components of the chosen theory included? Does it adequately account for

Table 1.2 Four Components of a Case Conceptualization

Component	Description
Diagnostic formulation	provides a description of the client's presenting situation and its perpetuants or triggering factors as well as the basic personality pattern; answers the "what" question, i.e., "What happened?"; usually includes a *DSM-5* diagnosis.
Clinical formulation	provides an explanation of the client's pattern. Answers the "why" question, i.e., "Why did it happen?"; the central component in a case conceptualization which links the diagnostic and treatment formulations.
Cultural formulation	provides an analysis of social and cultural factors; answers the "What role does culture play?" question; specifies cultural identity, level of acculturation and stress, explanatory model, and mix of cultural dynamics and personality dynamics.
Treatment formulation	provides an explicit blueprint for intervention planning; a logical extension of the diagnostic, clinical, and cultural formulations which answer the "How can it be changed?" question; contains treatment goals, focus, strategy, and specific interventions, and anticipates challenges and obstacles in achieving those goals.

the presenting problems? Are all the elements of the diagnostic and clinical formulations addressed in the treatment formulation and plan? Does the treatment
formulation and plan flow logically and coherently with the diagnostic and clinical formulations? Does the plan include explicit goals, both short-term and long-
term, and are potential red flag issues other than those the therapist can provide
considered?

Eells also offers additional criteria to evaluate the overall quality of the case
conceptualization. The criteria are: comprehensiveness, coherence, precision of
language, the degree to which formulation themes and treatment plans were elaborated, the complexity of the formulation, the link between the clinical formulation and the treatment plan, and the extent to which therapists appeared to apply
a systematic process in developing the case conceptualization (Eells, 2010). This
section provides a way of characterizing the sufficiency of case conceptualizations, including the sufficiency of each of its components. Three levels of sufficiency are described.

High-Level Case Conceptualizations

A high-level case conceptualization is recognized by the following characteristics. It addresses the "what happened" question (diagnostic formulation statement), the "why did it happen" question (clinical formulation statement), the
"what can be done about it" question (treatment formulation statement), and
the "what role does culture play" question (cultural formulation statement). In
addition, it anticipates treatment "obstacles" such as resistance, transference,
non-compliance, etc.; it specifies a clearly defined "treatment focus" and "intervention strategy"; and it serve as the basis for "tailoring" interventions. It also
serves as a guide to making and modifying treatment decisions, as the basis for
maintaining an effective therapeutic alliance, and for planning and anticipating
issues regarding termination. Finally, there is a high degree of coherence among
sections of the written report containing the various components of the case conceptualization (Sperry, 2010). Specifically, this means that the treatment formulation directly reflects the clinical formulation and the diagnostic formulation.
Finally, this conceptualization has considerable explanatory power and predictive value.

Moderate-Level Case Conceptualizations

A moderate-level case conceptualization is recognized by the following characteristics. Similar to the highly competent conceptualization, it addresses diagnostic, clinical, cultural, and treatment formulation questions. While there is also a
reasonable degree of coherence among sections of the written report containing
various components of the case conceptualization, there are missing elements that
are central to the highly competent conceptualization. Typically, while treatment
goals are included, it is less likely that a clearly identified treatment focus and a
treatment strategy are noted. Similarly, how treatment will be tailored to the client

as well as obstacles to achieving treatment targets and goals is less likely to be included. In short, these conceptualizations may have good to excellent explanatory power, but little predictive value.

Low-Level Case Conceptualizations

Low-level case conceptualizations are characterized by deficits in several respects. First and foremost, such conceptualizations tend to be an extended description of the clinical material rather than a clinically useful explanation of it because they fail to address the diagnostic, clinical, treatment, and formulation questions. As a result, treatment goals are unlikely to be sufficiently defined and focused. Because obstacles to achieving these goals are not anticipated, the clinician is likely to be surprised or dismayed with the course of treatment. Premature termination is likely because issues in the therapeutic alliance become problematic. Little or no coherence among sections of the written report containing the conceptualizations will be evident. Not surprisingly, this conceptualization has neither explanatory power nor predictive value.

Elements of a Case Conceptualization

Participants in our courses and workshops on case conceptualization agree that presenting a case conceptualization in terms of its components and elements is a painless way of understanding this competency. There are four components: diagnostic formulation, clinical formulation, cultural formulation, and treatment formulation. Each component encompasses a number of case conceptualization elements. For instance, the diagnostic formulation component consists of the elements of presentation, precipitant, and pattern-maladaptive. The topmost segment of Table 1.3 lists these three elements with brief definitions. Similarly, the other components and elements are listed and defined in the remaining parts of Table 1.3. These components and elements of the case conceptualization will be described and illustrated in considerable detail in Chapters 2 through 4.

Myths about Case Conceptualizations

A number of myths and distorted notions about case conceptualizations abound. This section attempts to dispel some of the more common ones.

Myth 1: A Case Conceptualization Is Nothing More than a Case Summary

Some consider that a case conceptualization is basically a case summary. While there are some similarities, the two are quite different. Basically, a case summary is a distillation of the facts of a case (presenting problem, developmental and social history, mental status examination, etc.). In contrast, a case conceptualization draws from those facts and constructs a story that goes well beyond a

Table 1.3 Elements of a Case Conceptualization

Presentation	presenting problem and characteristic response to precipitants
Precipitant	triggers that activate the pattern resulting in presenting problem
Pattern: maladaptive	inflexible, ineffective manner of perceiving, thinking, acting
Predisposition	factors fostering adaptive or maladaptive functioning
Protective Factors	factors that decrease the likelihood of developing a clinical condition
Perpetuants	triggers that activate one's pattern resulting in presentation
Cultural identity	sense of belonging to a particular ethnic group
Cultural stress & acculturation	level of adaptation to the dominant culture; culturally influenced stress, including psychosocial difficulties
Cultural explanation	beliefs regarding cause of distress, condition, or impairment
Culture and/or personality	operative mix of cultural and personality dynamics
Treatment pattern	flexible, effective manner of perceiving, thinking, acting
Treatment goals	stated short- and long-term outcomes of treatment
Treatment focus	central therapeutic emphasis providing directionality to treatment that is keyed to the adaptive pattern
Treatment strategy	action plan and vehicle for achieving a more adaptive pattern
Treatment interventions	specific change techniques and tactics related to the treatment strategy for achieving treatment goals and pattern change
Treatment obstacles	predictable challenges in the treatment process anticipated from the maladaptive pattern
Treatment-cultural	incorporation of cultural intervention, culturally sensitive therapy, or interventions when indicated
Treatment prognosis	prediction of the likely course, duration, and outcome of a mental health condition with or without treatment

summary of the facts of the case. It involves a high level of abstraction in drawing viable inferences that place the client's presenting problem within the context of his or her life pattern. As a result, a tailored treatment can be derived and likely obstacles and challenges can be anticipated. By contrast, case summaries have no explanatory power and little, if any, predictive power. In short, a case conceptualization is not just a case summary.

Myth 2: Case Conceptualizations Are Not Clinically Useful

It is not uncommon for some trainees and practitioners to insist that case conceptualizations are not clinically useful. In fact, research is beginning to show that using case conceptualizations is clinically useful and related to positive treatment outcomes (Kuyken, Padesdky, & Dudley, 2009). Increasingly, case conceptualization is being linked to evidence-based practice, an unmistakable indicator of clinical utility. In 2005, the American Psychological Association's Presidential Task Force on Evidence-Based Practice recognized that link (APA Presidential Task Force on Evidence-Based Practice, 2006). Others have also recognized the link and concluded that case conceptualization is essential for effective evidence-based practice.

> Case formulation is a cornerstone of evidence-based CBT practice. For any particular case of CBT practice, formulation is the bridge between practice, theory and research. It is the crucible where the individual particularities of a given case, relevant theory, and research synthesize into an understanding of the person's presenting issues in CBT terms that informs the intervention.
> (Kuyken et al., 2005, p. 1188)

Myth 3: Case Conceptualizations Are Difficult to Learn and Too Time-Consuming

It is also not uncommon for some trainees and practitioners to insist that doing case conceptualizations is too complex and time-consuming, and that learning to do them is difficult and takes a long time. Research roundly discounts this myth. It demonstrates that trainees and practitioners who participate in training sessions that are as short as two hours can and do increase their capacity to develop more accurate, precise, complex, and comprehensive clinical formulations compared to practitioners without such training (Abbas et al., 2012; Binensztok, 2019; Eells, 2015; Kendjelic & Eells, 2007; Ladd, 2015; Lipp, 2019; Smith Kelsey, 2014; Stoupas, 2016). Obviously, developing a high level of proficiency in case conceptualization takes additional time and practice. Still, the point is that even a short period of training makes a significant difference.

Myth 4: There Is Only One Type of Case Conceptualization and It Should Be Used for All Clients

It is useful and necessary to distinguish three types of case conceptualizations: provisional, full-scale, and brief case conceptualizations.

Provisional case conceptualization. This type of conceptualization is constructed during the initial evaluation of the client. It is called a provisional or a working conceptualization because inferences derived from observation, inquiry, and prior records if available, are necessarily incomplete or the inferences have not been sufficiently tested for "fit" and accuracy. As such, provisional case conceptualizations are subject to change with additional information and scrutiny.

Full-scale case conceptualization. This type of conceptualization includes most or all of the elements of the diagnostic, clinical, cultural, and treatment formulations. While it may begin as a provisional case conceptualization, the full-scale version more accurately reflects the client's story and pattern and has sufficient explanatory and predictive power to reasonably guide treatment implementation and effect change. This type of case conceptualization is indicated when clients present with symptoms and impaired functioning triggered or exacerbated by personality pathology, whose level of functioning before the current presentation was problematic. It is also indicated where histories of problems with maintaining close relationships and jobs (or school) are common, where there are limited coping resources, lower levels of resilience, and limited readiness for change.

Brief case conceptualization. This type of conceptualization includes selected elements of the diagnostic, clinical, cultural, and treatment formulations (e.g., presentation, precipitant, pattern, treatment goal(s), and treatment intervention(s)). Because fewer elements are included, it is much shorter, i.e., brief, compared to a full-scale case conceptualization statement.

Learning Exercise

Imagine you are doing initial evaluations on four young female clients whose first names are Jane. They are similar in age, education, and level of acculturation. They all complain of "feeling sad" following the breakup of an intimate relationship. Beyond these similarities are real differences. Read the following case descriptions and determine whether a full-scale or a brief case conceptualization is indicated for each case. Provide a rationale for your decision about each case.

Jane 1. This Jane meets the criteria, more or less, for Adjustment Disorder with Depressed Mood. Some avoidant and dependent features are noted. Her Level of Psychological Functioning Scale (LPFS) (American Psychiatric Association, 2013) score is rated at 1 now with 0 the highest in the past year. Previously, she has been successful in maintaining intimate relationships and a job. Her level of resilience appears to be high with readiness for change at the action stage.

Jane 2. This Jane meets the criteria for Major Depressive Disorder: Single Episode and Avoidant Personality Disorder. Her LPFS score is rated at 2 now with 1 the highest in the past year. She reports some difficulty in maintaining intimate relationships but not jobs. Her level of resilience appears to be moderate with readiness for change at the preparation stage.

Jane 3. This Jane meets the criteria for Major Depressive Disorder: Recurrent and Avoidant Personality Disorder. Her LPFS score is rated at 3 now with 2 the highest in the past year. She reports difficulty in maintaining intimate relationships and jobs. Her level of resilience appears to be low with readiness for change at the contemplative stage.

Jane 4. This Jane meets the criteria for Major Depressive Disorder: Recurrent, Dysthymic Disorder, and Post Traumatic Stress Disorder, as well as Borderline Personality Disorder. Her LPFS score is rated at 4 now with 3 the highest in the past year. She reports considerable difficulty in maintaining intimate relationships and jobs and has been on disability for three years. Her level of resilience appears to be very low with readiness for change at the precontemplative stage.

Commentary. Full-scale case conceptualizations are indicated for Jane 2, 3, and 4, while a brief case conceptualization is sufficient for Jane 1. Jane 1 has a history of being adequately resilient and sufficient coping resources to succeed with relationships and work. She has been living away from her supportive and caring family for the first time in her life. Recently, her boyfriend back home, to whom she was "practically engaged," told her that he was ending their relationship because of another woman. Not having the immediate support of her caring family, Jane sought counseling "to support me through this."

See Chapter 2 for a description of the Level of Psychological Functioning Scale.

Myth 5: All Case Conceptualizations Are Basically the Same

There are actually three different ways or methods of developing case conceptualizations. The two most common are: following a structured or theory-based method or using a seat-of-the-pants method.

Structured or standardized case conceptualizations methods. Structured methods are theory-based or standardized methods. There are several structured methods. Eleven such methods ranging from Psychodynamic to Cognitive-Behavioral methods are described and illustrated in Eells' handbook (2007). The upside of such methods is that quality and reliability can be achieved with training and experience. The downside is that these methods tend to be complex and typically require formal training and considerable experience to master.

Non-standardized case conceptualizations methods. In everyday practice, non-standardized or seat-of-the-pants methods are commonly utilized by enterprising practitioners who have improvised and developed their own idiosyncratic formulas for conceptualizing cases. Usually, these practitioners develop their approach to meet the actual or perceived requirement of third-party payers as a condition of reimbursement for services rendered. The upside of such methods is that practitioners have ownership of the way they conceptualize cases. The downside is that the quality and reliability of such methods may be absent or limited.

Integrative case conceptualization method. A Delphi polling of psychotherapy experts has predicted the development of integrative models of case conceptualization (Norcross, Hedges, & Prochaska, 2002). In his review of several current models of case conceptualization, Eells (2007) notes that overlap exists among these models. He proposes that: "Ideally, an integrative model of case conceptualization would capture these overlapping concepts... while also retaining the distinctive features of each approach. Such an integrative model could be particularly useful in psychotherapy training" (Eells, 2007, p. 428). Eells (2010) anticipates such an integrative model and provides a schematic of its features. The reader will encounter a fully articulated and user-friendly integrative model of case conceptualization in this book.

A Strategy for Increasing Competence in Case Conceptualization

Learning and mastering case conceptualization competency does not occur by chance, instead it requires having an intentional plan and strategy for increasing this essential competency. The following is a six-step, evidence-based strategy that we recommend to those we teach and supervise.

1. **Know the requisites for performing high-level case conceptualizations.**
   Several elements of case conceptualization have been introduced in this chapter. It would be wonderful if the mere inclusion of all or most of these elements in a case conceptualization was sufficient for it to be considered an excellent conceptualization. The reality is that more than just including these elements is needed. Other criteria for evaluating a conceptualization have been described, such as comprehensiveness, coherence, language precision, and the degree to which formulation themes and treatment plans are elaborated (Eells, 2010). Similarly, research reflects indicators or expertise in case conceptualizations. It shows that expert therapists produced more comprehensive, systematic, complex, and elaborate formulations than experienced therapists or trainees, although trainees produced better-quality clinical formulations than experienced therapists (Eells & Lombart, 2003; Eells et al., 2005). The Appendix includes a Case Conceptualization Evaluation Form for evaluating the quality of a case conceptualization.
2. **Dispel myths that undermine the value of case conceptualizations**.
   Earlier in the chapter, six common misconceptions of case conceptualizations were discussed and dispelled. Recognize if any of these or other myths are limiting your motivation and capacity to master this competency, and then dispel them.
3. **Engage in deliberate practice in learning this competency.**
   Deliberate practice is essential in learning and mastering the competency of case conceptualization (Caspar, Berger, & Hautle, 2004). Deliberate practice involves repetition of a specific element or case conceptualization factor until it is mastered. Ideally, deliberate practice will be incorporated into graduate training programs as a learning strategy along with systematic learning and coaching by instructors and supervisors who have sufficient expertise in constructing, implementing, and evaluating case conceptualization.
4. **Seek feedback on your case conceptualizations.**
   Providing timely and accurate feedback to trainees on an ongoing basis is essential in improving competency in case conceptualizations. Trainees need feedback that is intense and systematic, particularly when it is combined

with practice, in constructing, improving, and elaborating case conceptualizations. Because it is often lacking, such feedback needs to be intentionally incorporated into mental health training programs that are committed to this competency (Caspar, Berger, & Hautle, 2004).

5. **Study and review various case conceptualizations, particularly exemplars.**

Ongoing study of exemplar case conceptualizations can greatly aid the learning and mastery of this competency. This book includes 25 full-scale case conceptualizations which can serve as exemplars or models of high-level case conceptualizations. Read, study, discuss, question, compare, and contrast these and other examples of clinically useful case conceptualizations in order to fully understand their structure, explanatory power, and predictive power. Then model them.

6. **Learn an integrative method of case conceptualization and practice it often.**

Structured and theory-based case conceptualization methods provide unique, signature elements that can add or reduce the explanatory and predictive power of a particular case. The challenge for the trainee and the practitioner is to determine which structured conceptualization elements are the best "fit" in a particular case. Developing expertise in the full utilization of several structured methods limits the fullest use of these methods. On the other hand, an integrative method that can incorporate the key elements (i.e., predisposition, treatment focus, treatment strategy, and treatment interventions) of specific structured methods, such as the Cognitive-Behavioral, Dynamic, or Adlerian, can increase the resulting case conceptualization's explanatory and predictive power over a non-integrative method. As noted in the Preface, the integrative nature of the method described and illustrated here is the unique contribution and clinical value of this book.

Five Clinical Cases

This section contains background information on five clinical cases that will be referred to and analyzed in subsequent chapters. The cases represent clients of different ages, genders, ethnicities, patterns, and presenting problems. Chapters 2 through 4 will cite certain of these cases to illustrate various points. Chapters 6 through 10 present capsule versions of all five cases followed by detailed case conceptualizations of each case from various perspectives: Biopsychosocial, Cognitive Behavior, Dynamic, Adlerian, and Acceptance and Commitment Therapy. These chapters also provide exercises so that readers can practice constructing key elements of case conceptualization from these various perspectives.

Geri

Geri R. is a 35-year-old, female administrative assistant of African American descent. She is single, lives alone, and was referred by her company's human resources director for evaluation and treatment following a three-week onset of depressed mood. Other symptoms included loss of energy, markedly diminished interest, insomnia, difficulty concentrating, and increasing social isolation. She had not shown up for work for four days prompting the referral. The planned addition of another senior executive led Geri's supervisor to discuss a promotion wherein Geri would be transferred out of a relatively close-knit work team where she had been for 16 years – and had been an administrative assistant for six years – to become the new senior administrative assistant for the newly hired vice president of sales. She reports that her parents are alive and that she has a younger brother. She insists that her brother was favored and spoiled by her parents, and she recalls being criticized by her parents and made fun of by her peers and her brother. She reports that for years she has had little or no contact with her parents or her brother, has never been in a long-term relationship or been married, and has worked at the same company since graduating from a local community college. She acknowledged that it was difficult to trust others and that she had only one real friend whom she trusted. This was an older woman at her company who was very supportive and never judgmental. She denies any individual or family therapy and indicates that this is her first meeting with a mental health professional.

Antwone

Antwone is an African American Navy seaman in his mid 20s. An otherwise talented seaman, he has a short temper and recently lashed out at crew members at the slightest provocation. After his most recent fight, which Antwone claimed was racially motivated, his commander fined and demoted him and then ordered him to undergo counseling from the base psychiatrist. Antwone initially resisted working with the psychiatrist, but after a period of testing him, Antwone agreed to cooperate. He recounted a painful early childhood in which his father was killed by an irate girlfriend, and his mother – another of his father's girlfriends – gave birth to him in prison. She was convicted of drug dealing. Afterward, he was placed in foster care with an African American family where he was alternately neglected and then abused (emotionally, verbally, and physically) by his foster mother and sexually abused by her adult daughter. Antwone was one of three foster boys in the home. Their foster mother condescendingly called the three "niggers" and demanded that they meet her every demand. At one point, the foster mother beat him unconscious. Thereafter, he assumed a flight mode and would cower in fear whenever she was around. She despised his best friend Jesse, in part because after episodes of sexual abuse, Antwone would run to Jesse who would emotionally calm and support him. When he was 15, however, as the foster mother began to berate him, he could no longer endure her tyranny and he grabbed the shoe with which she was beating him and threatened her. She responded by throwing him out to live on the streets. Subsequently, he lashed out at perceived injustices. By base policy, treatment at the mental health clinic was short, with a maximum of three sessions. During their third session, the psychiatrist indicated that treatment would be ending and encouraged Antwone to find his real family. He emphasized that this was an important step for Antwone to get closure on his issues. An infuriated Antwone lashed out, yelling that everyone in his life had abandoned him, including Jesse and now the psychiatrist. Antwone recounted that he was an innocent bystander when Jesse was shot while robbing a convenience store. For the first time, Antwone was able to admit his anger at being abandoned by Jesse as well as the psychiatrist. He realized that finding his family was necessary. With much effort and persistence, he finds and meets both his father's family and his mother as well as confronting his foster mother and her daughter. The person described here is actually Antwone Fisher who is now an accomplished poet, writer, playwright, and film producer. The case information is from his autobiography and the film *Antwone Fisher*.

Richard

Richard is a 41-year-old, Caucasian male who is being evaluated for anxiety, sadness, and anger about his recent divorce. This was his first marriage to a professional woman with two children from a previous marriage. He is handsome and engaging and his charming manner has allowed him to move in professional circles even though he is a high school dropout. He currently lives on his own, is employed as a machine operator, and frequents night clubs where he "is on the lookout for the perfect woman." He reported that he and his former wife had "communication problems" and that she complained that he embarrassed her by his contrarian viewpoints when they were at social events. After the most recent episode, she informed him that she wanted a separation and thereafter filed for divorce. He has held four jobs over the past six years and was fired from his last job because he smashed his fist through a wall after being confronted by a female coworker. He is an only child of alcoholic parents whom he describes as "fighting all the time." He has had some individual counseling and while he reports having some insight into his issues, there has been no appreciable change in his interpersonal behavior.

Maria

Maria is a 17-year-old, second-generation Mexican American female who was referred for a psychological evaluation by her parents concerned with her mood swings over the past two to three months and concerned about her alcohol use. Maria described her basic concern as a conflict between going away to college in the fall and staying home to attend to her mother who is terminally ill. While her parents want her to stay home, her Anglo friends are encouraging her to go to college. She reports being pulled in two different directions and "stuck in the middle" and feeling "down" and "pressured" regarding this decision. She also feels guilty that she may fail to measure up to what a "good daughter" should be and may lose her parents' acceptance and approval. Her family is extremely important to her and "I have an obligation to my parents." Yet, she also wants to expand her horizons; however, "If I stay with my family my whole life, I'll be a failure... I'll have wasted all my potential." She has tried to talk with her parents but they seem unable to understand her. She's conflicted, yet she does not want to "disappoint" or "make the wrong decision I'll regret it forever." While she did admit to a single episode of alcohol use to make herself feel better, she denies any other alcohol or substance use.

Maria is the younger of two daughters. Her older sister dropped out of high school, has a history of drug usage, and has minimal contact with the family. Her parents immigrated from Mexico some 12 years ago, although her extended family remains there. She lives with her parents in a largely Mexican community in a major metropolitan area where they own a small dry cleaners and lead "traditional Mexican-American lives." Reportedly, they unfairly compare Maria to her sister and believe that if Maria does anything wrong she'll end up just like her sister. But while they are overly strict with her, Maria believes "it is because they care." Maria speaks Spanish, has both Anglo and Mexican friends, and has not experienced anti-immigrant discrimination in the past five years as she and her family did when they first arrived in the United States. She believes her problems are due to a "lack of faith in God" and she says that she prays every day to be "delivered from darkness." Maria's mother's illness has also affected her father who is convinced that without a caretaker – such as Maria – she will not live long.

Katrina

Katrina is a 13-year-old female of mixed ethnicity. She was referred for counseling by her guidance counselor due to recent depressive symptoms, poor academic performance, and oppositional behavior and fighting with other students at school. Her aggressive behavior and academic challenges increased after Katrina overheard a conversation between her mother and aunt in which she found out that her father had an affair for eight years. She was shocked to learn that this resulted in two births. Other difficulties include several fights with other students in the classroom, frequent conflict with her mother, skipping 15 days of school over the past six months, and diminished interest in her academic work. While she had previously excelled academically, she now displayed a marked loss of interest in activities that used to give her pleasure, such as drawing and reading. Katrina's father is currently living in Puerto Rico and has no contact with the family. Katrina lives in a small apartment with her mother and younger brother near her school. She reported being frustrated with the lack of space, since they had to downsize from the single-family home they lived in before her father left the family one year ago.

Because Katrina was a minor, it was necessary for the school guidance counselor to speak with Katrina and her mother together during the initial session. Katrina's mother, Julia, stated that she believes that Katrina will not talk to most people about her problems because she does not trust anyone. During the first meeting, Katrina reported that she does not trust anyone and that she is not interested in attending counseling sessions if the practitioner is going to tell her what to do. Self-disclosure was very difficult for Katrina during the initial interview and Julia answered the majority of the questions that were asked, in some cases speaking for Katrina when she made efforts to speak. Julia reported that Katrina's father was highly critical and also emotionally withdrawn throughout Katrina's childhood. Katrina also stated, "I don't really have a dad, since real fathers are supposed to take care of their families." She said she was tired of her teachers and her mother always forcing her to do things that she doesn't want to do.

Support of Professional Organization and the Realities of Training and Practice

Professional accrediting organizations, such as the American Psychological Association (APA) and the Council for Accreditation of Counseling and Related Educational Programs (CACREP), broadly support case conceptualization in training programs and everyday practice. For example, the APA states that case conceptualization is essential "for the effectiveness of psychological practice and enhancement of public health" ("APA Task Force," 2006, pp. 271–285). CACREP also requires that counseling students learn "a systems approach to conceptualizing clients" (Section 2: F.1.b., CACREP Standards, 2016, p. 12) as well as "essential interviewing, counseling, and case conceptualization skills" (Section 2: F.1.g., CACREP Standards, 2016, p. 13).

In the past decade, the research, training, and practice of case conceptualization have increased considerably and there are now several models of case conceptualization. Still, clinicians and clinicians-in-training may find the prospect of developing and using case conceptualizations difficult or even overwhelming. Today, trainees typically learn to conceptualize cases in one of three ways: (1) in a didactic graduate course; (2) in a clinical graduate course, i.e., a university-based practicum or internship seminar; or (3) at a practicum or internship training site (Berman, 2015). In some graduate counseling programs, such as at Florida Atlantic University and Lynn University, students learn case conceptualization in all three ways.

However, some have noted a discrepancy between the expectations of such professional organizations' standards and the state of training programs regarding the effective use of case conceptualization in counseling practice (Ridley, Jeffrey, & Roberson, 2017). For example, case conceptualization is an under-developed skill in many clinicians and is consequently practiced inconsistently (Sperry, 2010; Johnstone & Dallos, 2014). Others argue that due to the multitude of case conceptualization models, there is inconsistency in case conceptualization supervision, and that site supervisors' tendency to advise their supervisees to use the method of case conceptualization preferred by their supervisor has created a "case conceptualization crisis" (Ridley & Jeffrey, 2017, p. 354). They also contend that lack of standardized approaches to case conceptualization has led to case conceptualization protocols that are either too simple or too complicated. This has resulted in fragmentation and lack of consistency in the practice of case conceptualization (Ridley et al., 2017; Berman, 2015).

It is noteworthy that Tracy Eells, an esteemed researcher on case conceptualization, does not agree with much of this "crisis" characterization (Eells, 2017).

Fortunately, the integrative model of case conceptualization that informs both the first and second edition of this book, provides a way of incorporating all approach-based case conceptualization models. This and other integrative models reduce most of these "crisis" characterizations. Nevertheless, the matter of lack of standardization and how site supervisors teach case conceptualization to supervisees remain a concern.

History of Case Conceptualizations and Terminology

The matter of terminology should be addressed before closing this chapter. In courses, workshops, case conferences, articles, and books, you might hear or read about case conceptualizations, case formulations, clinical formulations, treatment formulations, and diagnostic formulations. Most often, these designations are used synonymously. It is not uncommon for the designations "case formulation" and "case conceptualization" to be used in the same paragraph, or to have a section of a book chapter titled "case conceptualization," and yet that designation is never to be found again in that section. Instead, the designation "case formulation" is used.

Historically, "case formulation" was the preferred and commonly used term or designation. In fact, the designation "case conceptualization" does not seem to have entered professional parlance until 2000. Articles, book chapters, and books on psychiatry and clinical psychology exclusively used the designation "case formulation" until recently. In contrast, "case conceptualization" has been used almost exclusively in the counseling and psychotherapy literature for quite some time. Today, case conceptualization seems to be gaining ascendency in all mental health disciplines. Accordingly, we will use the designation "case conceptualization" when describing and discussing this competency in general terms, while reserving the terms "diagnostic formulation," "clinical formulation," "cultural formulation," and "treatment formulation" as specific components of a case conceptualization.

Concluding Comment

Case conceptualization is among the most important competencies that mental health professionals are increasingly expected to master. In the past, some professionals justified and excused their unwillingness to develop this competency on the grounds that case conceptualizations were not clinically useful, and that learning to do them was too complex and time-consuming. As indicated earlier in this chapter, neither clinical lore nor emerging research support this sentiment. In fact, research shows that case conceptualizations are clinically useful, represent evidence-based practice, and positively influence treatment outcomes. Likewise, research on expertise and training in case conceptualization supports the value of formal training. Incorporating competency in case conceptualization in a graduate program provides trainees with the opportunity to demonstrate the capacity to integrate theory and practice, which may be the most elusive programmatic goal of therapy training.

It is encouraging to note that mastering competency in case conceptualization is becoming a high priority in many counseling, psychiatry, and psychotherapy training programs, and that reluctance to using case conceptualizations is decreasing as trainees and practitioners realize that it is one of the most valuable clinical competencies necessary for effective clinical practice (Falvey, 2001).

CHAPTER 1 QUESTIONS

1. Explain how personality, situational, and cultural dynamics, and other factors can increase both the explanatory power and the predictive power of case conceptualization in the three versions of the case of Geri at the beginning of this chapter.
2. Describe the four main components of case conceptualization – diagnostic, clinical, cultural, treatment – and highlight some of the key components and their importance in developing an appropriate treatment plan.
3. Discuss the elements of presentation, precipitant, pattern, predisposition, and perpetuants, and their role in developing a high-level case conceptualization.
4. Explain how dispelling the myths of case conceptualization is necessary in developing a "high-level case conceptualization."
5. Compare some of the strategies provided for increasing competency in case conceptualization and which of these you would find most helpful and why.

References

Abbas, M., Walton, R., Johnston, A., & Chikoore, M. (2012). Evaluation of teaching an integrated case formulation approach on the quality of case formulations: Randomised controlled trial. *The Psychiatrist, 36*(4), 140–145.

American Psychological Association Presidential Task Force on Evidence-Based Practice. (2006). Evidence-based practice in psychology. *The American Psychologist, 61*(4), 271–285.

Berman, P.S. (2015). *Case conceptualization and treatment planning: Integrating theory with clinical practice* (3rd ed.). New York, NY: Pearson.

Binensztok, V. (2019). *The influence of reflective practice on the case conceptualization competence of counselor trainees* (Doctoral dissertation). Florida Atlantic University, Boca Raton, FL.

Caspar, F., Berger, T., & Hautle, I. (2004). The right view of your patient: A computer-assisted, individualized module for psychotherapy training. *Psychotherapy: Theory, Research, Practice, Training, 41*(2), 125–135.

Council for Accreditation of Counseling & Related Educational Programs 2016 Standards. (2016). 2016 CACREP standards. Retrieved from http://222.cacrep.org/for-programs/2016-cacrep-standards/.

Cucciare, M., & O'Donohue, W. (2008). Clinical case conceptualization and termination of psychotherapy. In M. O'Donohue & W. Cucciare (Eds.), *Terminating psychotherapy: A clinician's guide* (pp. 121–146). New York, NY: Routledge.

Eells, T. (2007). Comparing the methods: Where is the common ground? In T. Eells (Ed.), *Handbook of psychotherapy case formulation* (2nd ed., pp. 412–432). New York, NY: Guilford.

Eells, T. (2010). The unfolding case formulation: The interplay of description and inference. *Pragmatic Case Studies in Psychotherapy, 6*(4), 225–254.

Eells, T.D. (2015). *Psychotherapy case formulation.* Washington, DC: American Psychological Association Books.

Eells, T.D. (2017). Thematic mapping maps much territory but needs stronger evidence-based coordinates: A commentary. *Journal of Clinical Psychology, 73*(4), 425–438.

Eells, T., & Lombart, K. (2003). Case formulation and treatment concepts among novice, experienced, and expert cognitive-behavioral and psychodynamic therapists. *Psychotherapy Research, 13*(2), 187–204.

Eells, T., Lombart, K., Kendjelic, E., Turner, L., & Lucas, C. (2005). The quality of psychotherapy case formulations: A comparison of expert, experienced, and novice cognitive-behavioral and psychodynamic therapists. *Journal of Consulting and Clinical Psychology, 73*(4), 579–589.

Falvey, J. (2001). Clinical judgment in case conceptualization and treatment planning across mental health disciplines. *Journal of Counseling and Development, 79*(3), 292–303.

Hill, C. (2005). Therapist techniques, client involvement, and the therapeutic relationship: Inextricably intertwined in the therapy process. *Psychotherapy: Theory, Research, Practice, Training, 42*(4), 431–442.

Johnstone, L., & Dallos, R. (Eds.). (2014). Introduction to formulation. In *Formulations in psychology and psychotherapy: Making sense of people's problems* (2nd ed., pp. 1–17). New York, NY: Routledge.

Kendjelic, E., & Eells, T. (2007). Generic psychotherapy case formulation training improves formulation quality. *Psychotherapy: Theory, Research, Practice, Training, 44*(1), 66–77.

Kuyken, W., Fothergill, C.D., Musa, M., & Chadwick, P. (2005). The reliability and quality of cognitive case formulation. *Behaviour Research and Therapy, 43*(9), 1187–1201.

Kuyken, W., Padesdky, C., & Dudley, R. (2009). *Collaborative case conceptualization: Working effectively with clients in cognitive-behavioral therapy.* New York, NY: Guilford.

Ladd, C. (2015). *The effect of case conceptualization on counselor competence and the influence of self-efficacy* (Doctoral dissertation). Florida Atlantic University, Boca Raton, FL.

Lipp, S.L. (2019). *The effects of case conceptualization training and deliberate practice coaching on counselor competence* (Doctoral dissertation). Florida Atlantic University, Boca Raton, FL.

Norcross, J., Hedges, M., & Prochaska, J. (2002). The face of 2010: A Delphi poll of the future of psychotherapy. *Professional Psychology: Research and Practice, 33*(3), 316–322.

Ridley, C., & Jeffrey, C. (2017). Thematic mapping in case conceptualization: An introduction to the special section. *Journal of Clinical Psychology, 73*(4), 353–358.

Ridley, C.R., Jeffrey, C.E., & Roberson, R.B. (2017). Case mis-conceptualization in psychological treatment: An enduring clinical problem. *Journal of Clinical Psychology, 73*(4), 359–375.

Smith Kelsey, E. (2014). *The effect of case conceptualization training on competence and its relationship to cognitive complexity*. Boca Raton, FL: Florida Atlantic University. doi:UMI No. 3647556.

Sperry, L. (2005). Case conceptualization: A strategy for incorporating individual, couple, and family dynamics in the treatment process. *The American Journal of Family Therapy*, *33*(5), 353–364.

Sperry, L. (2010). *Core competencies in counseling and psychotherapy: Becoming a highly competent and effective therapist*. New York, NY: Routledge.

Sperry, L. (2015). Diagnosis, case conceptualization, and treatment. In L. Sperry, J. Carlson, J.D. Sauerheber & J. Sperry (Eds.), *Psychopathology and psychotherapy* (3rd ed., pp. 36–50). New York, NY: Routledge.

Sperry, L., Blackwell, B., Gudeman, J., & Faulkner, L. (1992). *Psychiatric case formulations*. Washington, DC: American Psychiatric Press.

Stoupas, G. (2016). *The effects of case conceptualization training over time and its relationship to practitioner attitudes towards evidence-based practice* (Vol. 78). Florida Atlantic University, Boca Raton, FL. Retrieved from http://search.ebscohost.com/lo gin.aspx?direct=true&db=psyh&AN=2017-23164-046&lang=es&site=ehost-live.

2   Assessment and Diagnostic Formulation

Assessment is a prerequisite to developing a case conceptualization, and a comprehensive assessment is essential in developing a competent and clinically useful case conceptualization.

Assessment organizes the content of the case conceptualization, focuses treatment goals, clarifies expectations about what can and what needs to change, and then defines the client's and the clinician's roles in the change process (Sim, Gwee, & Bateman, 2005). The diagnostic formulation is one of the four components of a case conceptualization. It is basically an appraisal of the client's presentation, precipitants, and pattern. It describes the client's situation and answers the "What happened?" question. The diagnostic formulation reflects both a diagnostic assessment and a clinical assessment.

This chapter emphasizes the diagnostic formulation which is based on an adequate diagnostic assessment and clinical assessment. The chapter begins with a description of both diagnostic and clinical assessments. Then, it describes and illustrates the diagnostic formulation.

Finally, the centrality of pattern in the Integrative Case Conceptualization model is described. In this and subsequent chapters, the assumption is that while assessment influences all components of the case conceptualization, the case conceptualization influences and guides the assessment process.

Diagnostic Assessment and Clinical Assessment

Consider the following scenario:

A practitioner evaluates two clients who manifest high levels of social anxiety and avoidance. Neither communicates well with others, and both prefer to be alone rather than engage socially. A diagnostic assessment indicates that both clients meet the criteria for the same *Diagnostic and Statistical Manual of Mental Disorders, Fifth Edition (DSM-5)* disorder. But, beyond this shared diagnosis, they have very different treatment plans. The reason is that the clinical assessments, in this instance, a Cognitive-Behavioral assessment, provided very different results. One client has few social skills. He speaks quietly and haltingly, is a poor listener, and others tend to ignore or make negative remarks about the way he speaks. The clinical assessment reveals significant behavioral deficits. Accordingly, the treatment plan has a more behavioral focus and emphasizes social skills training. In contrast, the other client listens well, can communicate adequately, and others tend to respond favorably to him. His problem is not that he has skill deficits but rather that he believes that he lacks social skills. As a result, he experiences anticipatory fears of saying the wrong things and being humiliated, and so he is likely to discount positive comments from others. This treatment plan has a more cognitive focus and emphasizes the client's maladaptive beliefs. After 12 sessions of tailored treatment, both clients are symptom-free and have increased their capacity for social relatedness.

Had treatment for both clients been based primarily on their common *DSM-5* diagnosis – the way many treatment planning books and software programs are based – positive treatment outcomes might not have been achieved. The point is that diagnostic assessment and clinical assessment differ considerably, and that effective and competent practitioners assume that every client is unique and multifaceted. Accordingly, they carefully assess and conceptualize clients and then tailor interventions that target their uniqueness.

Diagnostic Assessment

A diagnostic assessment is a focused assessment of the client and the current and developmental context influencing the client. The purpose of this assessment is to discover the answer to the question: What accounts for the client's concerns, distress, and/or diminished functioning for which the client seeks therapeutic assistance? A relatively complete diagnostic assessment interview can often be accomplished within the first 30–40 minutes of the initial session between client and practitioner. However, the timeframe necessary to complete such an evaluation may take considerably longer depending on the client's previous history and treatment, sense of ease and trust in the practitioner, language facility, and other psychological and cultural factors.

The focus of the diagnostic assessment is to gather information about the client that is relevant to the treatment process and outcomes. This includes data on the client's current problems; current functioning and mental status; social, cultural, developmental, and medical history and health behaviors; and, particularly, the expectations and resources the client brings to therapy. Since cultural factors such as cultural identity, level of acculturation, and cultural explanatory model can influence the treatment process, it is imperative that these factors be identified.

The value of the diagnostic assessment cannot be underestimated. It aids the practitioner with immediate clinical considerations: Is the client's presentation primarily psychotic, non-psychotic, or personality disordered, and is the client's presentation so acute and severe as to require immediate intervention such as hospitalization? Essentially, the diagnostic assessment is a phenomenological description and a cross-sectional assessment of the client in terms of diagnostic criteria.

Level of Psychological Functioning Scale (LPFS)

The Level of Psychological Functioning Scale is a *DSM-5* measure for quickly and accurately determining the presence of a personality disorder. It assesses the four components of personality functioning in the Alternative *DSM-5* Personality Disorders model: identity, self-direction, empathy, and intimacy. Impairment in these four elements of personality functioning is rated along a continuum of five levels of functioning and impairment where 0 = little to no impairment; 1 = some impairment; 2 = moderate impairment; 3 = severe impairment; and 4 = extreme impairment. Moderate or greater impairment is required for the diagnosis of a personality disorder (Sperry, 2016). This scale is included on pages 775–778 in Section III of the *DSM-5* (American Psychiatric Association, 2013).

Clinical Assessment

While the diagnostic assessment is useful in establishing a diagnosis based on a client's symptoms and behaviors which match the *DSM-5* criteria, a diagnosis does not provide an in-depth understanding of the client. A standard diagnostic assessment will not identify the personality dynamics nor the relational dynamics that activated that particular set of symptoms. Nor will it specify why or how these symptoms began when they did, nor what maintains them. On the other hand, a clinical assessment can provide such an understanding. Accordingly, the clinical assessment, also known as theory-based assessment, is a valuable component of a comprehensive assessment strategy. Five such assessments are described below.

Biopsychosocial Assessment

Biopsychosocial assessment focuses on the identification of relevant biological, psychological, and social factors. A factor is relevant to the extent to which it offers an explanation for the client's symptoms and functioning. Biological factors include health history, health status, substance use: alcohol, illicit drugs, nicotine, caffeine. Psychological factors include adaptive and maladaptive beliefs, emotions and emotion regulation, behavioral excesses and deficits, as well as skill deficits. Social factors include family dynamics, friends, social support, environmental factors, and work demands.

Cognitive-Behavioral Assessment

The type of information gathered in a theory-based assessment differs depending on the specific theoretical orientations. For instance, Cognitive Behavior Therapy (CBT)-based assessment emphasizes cognitions and behaviors. It focuses on questions such as: What particular maladaptive thoughts or beliefs lead to the client's specific emotional and behavioral problems? How do problematic emotions and behavior feed back into the maintenance of maladaptive thoughts and beliefs? (Ledley, Marx, & Heimberg, 2005). Assessing such clinical information is essential in developing a CBT-based case conceptualization.

Dynamics Assessment

In dynamically oriented approaches, such as Time-Limited Dynamic Psychotherapy, the focus of inquiry is more likely to be on eliciting a story or a narrative of recurrent maladaptive interpersonal patterns that reflect dysfunctional mental working models and their reenactment in the therapeutic alliance (Binder, 2004; Binder & Betan, 2013). Accordingly, identifying the cyclic maladaptive pattern is essential to the dynamic case conceptualization as well as providing a treatment focus (Levenson, 1995).

Adlerian Assessment

In Adlerian assessment, the focus is primarily on the identification of lifestyle convictions, i.e., maladaptive beliefs and schemas, and on family patterns and dynamics. This can be accomplished with such assessment devices as the elicitation of early recollections, family constellations, and other indicators of lifestyle convictions (Dinkmeyer & Sperry, 2000). Such information is essential in constructing an Adlerian case conceptualization.

Acceptance Commitment Therapy (ACT) Assessment

Assessment in Acceptance and Commitment Therapy involves evaluating the client's psychological flexibility through six processes. Present moment awareness, values, committed action, self as context, defusion, and acceptance comprise the model of psychological flexibility. For instance, while assessing for present moment awareness, a therapist evaluates the client's ability to relate and function in the present moment, without being "hooked" by their unchangeable past or unknowable future. On the other hand, within the process of defusion, the therapist assesses the client's ability to observe their thoughts and feelings, rather than behaving "from" their thoughts and feelings.

Integrative, Pattern-focused Assessment

Finally, in the integrative model, the basis for this book, assessment is pattern focused. This means that the principal focus of clinical assessment is pattern identification while the primary treatment outcome is pattern change (Sperry, Blackwell, Gudeman, & Faulkner, 1992; Sperry, 2005, 2010). By identifying the sequence of the client's presenting symptoms or concerns, their precipitants or triggers and pattern when activated, result in the client's response. The heart of the case conceptualization is the client's pattern, and treatment endeavors to shift the client's maladaptive pattern to a more adaptive pattern.

Diagnostic Formulation

The diagnostic formulation is a descriptive appraisal of the client's presentation and precipitants, and reflects the client's pattern. It answers the "What happened" question. It is a phenomenological description as well as a cross-sectional assessment of the client's unique situation and pattern. This formulation is based on both a diagnostic assessment and a clinical assessment.

Key Elements of the Diagnostic Formulation

1. **Presentation**

     Presentation refers to the client's characteristic response to precipitants. Presentation, also called the presenting problem, includes the type and severity of symptoms, personal and relational functioning or impairment, and its history and course. It also includes medical and DSM diagnoses.

2. **Precipitant**

     Precipitants refer to the triggers or stressors that activate the pattern resulting in the presenting problem or concern. Another way of saying this is that precipitants are antecedent conditions that coincide with the onset of symptoms, distressing thoughts, or maladaptive behaviors. A precipitant can be identified by considering the factors present at the onset and first manifestation of the problem or concern: where did it occur, at what time, who was there, what was said and done, what happened next, and so on.

3. **Pattern**

     A pattern is a succinct description of a client's characteristic way of perceiving, thinking, and responding. It links the client's presentation with the precipitant and makes sense of the situation. Patterns are driven by the client's predispositions and reflect the client's perpetuants. A pattern can be adaptive or maladaptive. An adaptive pattern reflects a personality style that is flexible, appropriate, and effective, and is reflective of personal and interpersonal competence. In contrast, a maladaptive pattern tends to be inflexible, ineffective, and inappropriate, and causes symptoms, impairment in personal and relational functioning, and chronic dissatisfaction. If the maladaptive pattern is sufficiently distressing or impairing, it can be diagnosed as a personality disorder.

     A pattern may be situation specific or longitudinal. A situation-specific maladaptive pattern is an explanation that is unique to the current situation only. On the other hand, a longitudinal pattern is an explanation that is common to the current as well as to previous situations. In other words, it reflects a lifelong pattern which can provide a reasonable explanation or set of reasons for the client's situation (Sperry et al., 1992; Sperry, 2005, 2010).

The following case illustrates the distinction between these types of patterns.

Jack is a 13-year-old, African American male who has displayed extreme angry outbursts and disrespect toward his mother over the past three months. This has included physically threatening his mother on two occasions after which the court ordered anger management counseling and family counseling. Both had little impact on his behavior. His mother was understandably concerned and asked the court to commit Jack to a residential treatment program. Before acting on the mother's request, the judge referred Jack to a clinical psychologist for a comprehensive Biopsychosocial evaluation. The evaluation identified a situation-specific pattern wherein the primary precipitant for Jack's threatening behavior was his mother's rummaging through his room looking for drugs and tearing up musical scores that Jack had composed, claiming "I don't want you to turn out like your brother." His brother is a rock musician who was in state prison for selling and distributing cocaine. Jack wants to be a lead guitarist and write music like his brother.

However, Jack neither used, experimented with, nor had drugs in his room or anywhere else. His stepfather sides with his mother in denigrating Jack's music writing efforts and refuses to pay for private music lessons. Otherwise, Jack is reasonably respectful to his parents, is doing relatively well in school, and no other acting out behaviors have been noted with peers or school staff, nor the clinician. Noteworthy is that Jack's outbursts have been selective – only his mother – despite the taunts of older adolescents in the school and neighborhood, where Jack has been able to control his anger. In other words, there is no indication of an ongoing and pervasive pattern of angry outbursts. Given the situation-specific pattern, a conservative treatment strategy was planned. It involved two sessions with the parents in which they were apprised of the situation-specific nature of Jack's pattern and were coached on eliminating the precipitant, i.e., rummaging through Jack's room and ripping up his music. The psychologist also assisted the parents in finding ways of engaging Jack in a less provocative, more nurturing, but firm manner. Without such triggers their relationship would be more like those that Jack experiences in school. If this proved effective, no further individual or family treatment would be needed, at the present time. If this was not sufficiently effective, other interventions would be considered. In fact, the parental coaching was effective.

Commentary. This case demonstrates the distinction between situation-specific and ongoing pervasive patterns and the importance of performing a comprehensive evaluation in arriving at a clinically useful case conceptualization. It demonstrates the importance of accurately specifying the key elements of the diagnostic formulation (presentation, precipitant, and pattern). In addition, it illustrates how a treatment plan was based on the diagnostic formulation and how reducing and eliminating the precipitant (the mother's provocative actions) led to a reduction of the presentation (Jack's predictable acting out).

Figure 2.1 visually represents the relationship among precipitant, pattern, and presentation, and Table 2.1 lists and briefly defines the elements of a diagnostic formulation.

Precipitant ------------------------------> [Pattern] --------------------------> Presentation

Figure 2.1 Relationship of Precipitant, Pattern, and Presentation

Table 2.1 Elements of the Diagnostic Formulation

Presentation	presenting problem and characteristic response to precipitants
Precipitant	triggers that activate the pattern resulting in a presenting problem
Pattern-maladaptive	inflexible, ineffective manner of perceiving, thinking, acting

Constructing a Diagnostic Formulation: Case of Geri

This section illustrates how a competent practitioner begins to construct a case conceptualization during an initial interview. The case of Geri was introduced in Chapter 1. Briefly, Geri is a 35-year-old, single, African American who was referred for therapy because of an extended absence from work. Segments of the transcript that follows are from the first session. This session involved both a diagnostic assessment (to specify a diagnosis, identify safety concerns, and discern treatment considerations) and a clinical assessment (to identify the maladaptive pattern and construct a diagnostic assessment). The reader will note that the practitioner's line of inquiry was guided by the case conceptualization in that the practitioner asked and elicited information on the diagnostic formulation elements.

Pr: I understand that Ms Hicks, the director of human resources at your company referred you to me. What's your understanding of why we're meeting today?
Cl: She wanted me to see you because I haven't been feeling too well lately.
Pr: In what way haven't you been feeling well?
Cl: Over the past three weeks, I've been feeling pretty sad. And, I guess it's been affecting my work a lot. I've got no initiative, no desire to get involved with anything.

So far, the **presentation** is known, or at least part of it. The practitioner then focuses on identifying a **precipitant** or triggering event.

Pr: So this all started about three weeks ago?
Cl: Yeah.
Pr: What was going on that time?
Cl: Well, my supervisor said there was an opening for a senior administrative assistant in the vice president of sales' office. She said she recommended me for the job and I should be ready to move to the executive suite in a week. (pause) The last thing I would ever do is to switch to another office and work for someone I don't know. (exhales and sighs) Even if there's a promotion and raise that goes with it.

Pr: It sounds like that news deeply affected you.
Cl: Yeah. It's like the bottom fell out of my world right then.
Pr: What did it mean for you?
Cl: Feeling safe is more important for me than a promotion and a raise.

The practitioner is momentarily taken back by what he hears. Whereas many would be happy with the prospect of a promotion and a raise, this client experiences just the opposite; she becomes depressed and isolative. At this point, there is a **presentation** (depression and withdrawal) and a precipitant (talk of a promotion). From these two elements, the practitioner derives a tentative **pattern**, i.e., she "withdraws when she perceives she is unsafe." The pattern is tentative and is subject to modification based on additional information. Additional inquiry can also determine whether this pattern is situational or longstanding.

Commentary. Here is how the practitioner came to specify Geri's pattern. His questions and inquiry were guided by an understanding of the clinical value of identifying the elements of the diagnostic formulation. In the process of eliciting them, he recognized that Geri's interpersonal direction or movement was *away from* others. Avoidance and withdrawal are very common forms of moving away from others. She also said that "feeling safe is more important." Then, he put the two ideas together, "withdrawing to feel safe." Next, he put the pattern together with the precipitant and presentation: talk of a promotion which is a significant stressor for her leads to withdrawal and depression in an individual who appears to have a pattern of withdrawing when she feels unsafe, i.e., talk of working for a new boss in a new location, both of which she perceives as very threatening and unsafe.

Diagnostic Formulation for Geri

Table 2.2 summarizes the key elements of the diagnostic formulation for Geri.

Pattern and the Integrative Case Conceptualization Model

Two basic premises are useful in understanding the Integrative Case Conceptualization model. The first premise is an understanding about personality development, psychopathology, and psychotherapy. It assumes that individuals unwittingly develop a self-perpetuating, maladaptive pattern of functioning and

Table 2.2 Diagnostic Formulation: Case of Geri

Presentation	increased social isolation and depressive symptoms
Precipitant	her reaction to an impending job promotion and transfer out of a close-knit work group
Pattern-maladaptive	withdraws when she perceives she is unsafe
[*DSM Diagnoses* Major Depressive Disorder and Avoidant Personality Disorder]	

relating to others (personality development). Inevitably, this pattern underlies a client's presenting issues (psychopathology). Effective treatment always involves a change process in which the client and practitioner collaborate to identify this pattern, break it, and replace it with a more adaptive pattern. At least two outcomes result from this change process: Increased well-being and resolution of the client's presenting issue (Psychotherapy).

The second premise is that pattern change is at the heart of the case conceptualization process. Pattern is the predicable, consistent, and self-perpetuating style and manner in which individuals think, feel, act, cope, and defend themselves (Sperry, Brill, Howard, & Griscom, 1996; Sperry, 2006). Pattern change involves three processes: (1) identify the maladaptive pattern, (2) relinquish the maladaptive pattern and replace it with a more adaptive pattern, and (3) maintain the adaptive pattern (Beitman & Yue, 1999). Figure 2.2 depicts this model.

Pattern and Case Conceptualization

The pattern change process will be reflected in a clinically useful case conceptualization. Pattern identification is the process of elucidating the client's maladaptive pattern and is the realm of the *diagnostic formulation*. Explaining how the maladaptive pattern developed and is maintained is the realm of the *clinical formulation* and *cultural formulation*, while a plan for replacing it with a more adaptive pattern is the realm of the *treatment formulation*.

Relational Styles, Personality Styles, and Patterns

Some time ago, Alfred Adler and Karen Horney observed that all behavior can be understood as movement in social contexts. Four kinds of movement are possible: toward, away from, against, or ambivalent, e.g., toward and against (Sperry, 2011). These types of movement can be thought of as relational styles. They are also representative of distinct personality styles. Personality styles are enduring patterns of perceiving, relating to, and thinking about oneself and others that are exhibited across a wide range of personal and social contexts. When these patterns are flexible and adaptive they are called personality styles, but when they are inflexible, maladaptive, and result in considerable impairment and distress they are called personality disorders. Since patterns, relational styles, and personality styles are integrally related, knowing a client's movement or relational style is indicative of their personality style or disorder.

Clients' names from the five cases – introduced in Chapter 1 and appearing throughout the rest of the book – are listed in Table 2.3 along with corresponding relational styles and personality styles.

Pattern Identification -> PatternChange: —> Pattern Maintenance

Figure 2.2 Model of the Pattern Change Process

Table 2.3 Relational and Personality Styles of the Five Case

Case	Relational Style	Personality Style/Disorder
Geri	moves away	avoidant
Antwone	moves against	narcissistic/paranoid
Maria	moves toward	dependent
Richard	moves against	narcissistic
Katrina	Ambivalent – away and against	paranoid

The Centrality of Pattern in the Integrative Case Conceptualization Model

Pattern and pattern change are central constructs in the Integrative Case Conceptualization model. In fact, the five case conceptualizations methods highlighted in this book all emphasize the construct of pattern or are receptive to it. For example, the "cyclic maladaptive pattern" is a central construct in the Time-Limited Dynamic approach, and the "schema-driven pattern" is a key part of the Cognitive-Behavioral approach (Young, Kloske, & Weishaar, 2003). In the Adlerian approach, the designation life plan or pattern is used synonymously with the lifestyle, and in the Acceptance and Commitment Therapy approach, committed action and valued-based behaviors represent the adaptive pattern. Finally, the hallmark of the Biopsychosocial approach is that it is sufficiently pluralistic to incorporate constructs from all theoretical approaches (Sperry et al., 1992). Clearly, this includes "pattern."

Concluding Comment

An accurate and productive comprehensive assessment is critical in constructing and utilizing a case conceptualization. Such an assessment involves both a diagnostic assessment and a clinical or theory-based assessment. While many trainees conduct an initial assessment by asking a long list of predetermined questions, a more productive comprehensive assessment is one that is informed by the case conceptualization, particularly the diagnostic formulation. We illustrated how the case conceptualization can effectively guide the assessment process in eliciting the elements of the diagnostic formulation. The case conceptualization also guides the construction of the clinical formulation and the cultural formulation. Both of these components of the case conceptualization are the focus of the next chapter.

CHAPTER 2 QUESTIONS

1. Compare a diagnostic assessment to a clinical assessment and point out the key components of each.
2. Discuss how combining a diagnostic and a clinical assessment makes for a stronger case conceptualization. Provide an example.

3. Explain some of the key elements that distinguish the six theory-based assessments presented in this chapter (Biopsychosocial, Cognitive-Behavioral, Dynamic, Solution Focused, Adlerian, Acceptance and Commitment Therapy, and Integrative).
4. Describe the key elements (presentation, precipitant, pattern) of the diagnostic formulation placing emphasis on an expanded discussion of pattern, and how this element ties into the entire case conceptualization.
5. Discuss some of the relational styles of movement and the common personality styles or disorders with which they may correspond.

References

American Psychiatric Association. (2013). *Diagnostic and statistical manual of mental disorders* (5th ed.). Arlington, VA: American Psychiatric Association Press.

Beitman, B., & Yue, D. (1999). *Learning psychotherapy*. New York, NY: Norton.

Binder, J. (2004). *Key competencies in brief dynamic psychotherapy: Clinical practice beyond the manual*. New York, NY: Guilford Press.

Binder, J.L., & Betan, E.J. (2013). *Core competencies in brief dynamic psychotherapy: Becoming a highly effective and competent brief dynamic psychotherapist*. New York, NY: Guilford.

Dinkmeyer, D., & Sperry, L. (2000). *Counseling and psychotherapy: An integrated, individual psychology approach*. Upper Saddle River, NJ: Prentice Hall.

Ledley, D., Marx, B., & Heimberg, R. (2005). *Making cognitive-behavioral therapy work*. New York, NY: Guilford.

Levenson, H. (1995). *Time-limited dynamic psychotherapy*. New York, NY: Basic Books.

Sim, K., Gwee, K., & Bateman, A. (2005). Case formulation in psychotherapy: Revitalizing its usefulness as a clinical tool. *Academic Psychiatry, 29*(3), 289–292.

Sperry, L. (2005). Case conceptualization: A strategy for incorporating individual, couple, and family dynamics in the treatment process. *The American Journal of Family Therapy, 33*(5), 353–364.

Sperry, L. (2006). *Cognitive behavior therapy of DSM-IV-TR personality disorders* (2nd ed.). New York, NY: Routledge.

Sperry, L. (2010). *Core competencies in counseling and psychotherapy: Becoming a highly competent and effective therapist*. New York, NY: Routledge.

Sperry, L. (2011). Personality disorders: A quick and reliable strategy for screening and diagnosing axis ii disorders. In H. Rosenthal (Ed.), *Favorite counseling and therapy techniques* (2nd ed., pp. 291–298). New York, NY: Routledge.

Sperry, L. (2016). *Handbook of diagnosis and treatment of DSM-5 personality disorders* (3rd ed.). New York, NY: Routledge.

Sperry, L., Blackwell, B., Gudeman, J., & Faulkner, L. (1992). *Psychiatric case formulations*. Washington, DC: American Psychiatric Press.

Sperry, L., Brill, P., Howard, K., & Grissom, G. (1996). *Treatment outcomes in psychotherapy and psychiatric interventions*. New York, NY: Brunner/Mazel.

Young, J., Klosko, J., & Weishaar, M. (2003). *Schema Therapy: A practitioner's guide*. New York, NY: Guilford.

3   Explanations and Clinical and Cultural Formulations

As noted in Chapter 2, a clinical formulation is one of the four components of a case conceptualization. It provides an explanation of the client's presentation, and offers a rationale for the client's symptoms, concerns, level of functioning, and maladaptive relational pattern. It answers the "why" question. The cultural formulation likewise provides an explanation for the client's presentation but from a different perspective than the clinical formulation. It describes the impact of cultural factors on the client and answers the "what role does culture play" question. The cultural formulation provides a cultural explanation of the client's presentation as well as the impact of cultural factors on the client's personality and level of functioning. This chapter focuses on both these dimensions of the case conceptualization. It describes the clinical formulation and its key elements and illustrates these with case material. Then, it describes the cultural formulation and its key elements and illustrates these with case material. As a prelude to this discussion, we briefly describe explanations and explanatory power and the reasoning processes involved in constructing case conceptualizations. The chapter concludes with a discussion about the importance of incorporating a trauma-informed perspective in the case conceptualization process.

Explanations and Explanatory Power

Explanations are central to the conceptualization process. An explanation is the practitioner's hypothesis (or set of hypotheses) and best guess for understanding a client's maladaptive pattern and the cause or causes of a client's presentation. The value of a case conceptualization, particularly the clinical formulation component of it, is the degree to which the clinical formulations offer an accurate and compelling explanation of why clients act, think, perceive, and feel the way they do. The degree to which formulations sufficiently explain a pattern is referred to as its explanatory power. Explanatory power can range from "poor" to "highly compelling." It does not seem to be a function of a particular approach, which means that there is no theoretical approach that best explains the patterns and presentations of all clients.

As trainees and practitioners become more competent and confident in constructing case conceptualizations, they realize that not every case conceptualization is as compelling as others. Another way of saying this is that a case conceptualization can have varying degrees of explanatory power ranging from low to very high. At a case conference, when trainees are asked: "Does this case conceptualization offer an adequate explanation for the 'Why' question?" and the response is: "Not really," it would be reasonable to discuss the explanatory power of the case conceptualization and if it is low, how it can be increased.

Explanatory power is a function of the accuracy and "fit" of the clinical formulation between the explanation offered and data from a particular case. Although some therapeutic approaches may state or imply the superiority of their case conceptualization method over other methods, the reality is that because individuals and the contexts in which they live and relate are sufficiently unique and complex, no single case conceptualization method can provide the best explanations for all cases. Nevertheless, a given case conceptualization method may provide a fuller and more compelling explanation, and thus more explanatory power, than another case conceptualization model.

Reasoning Processes in Case Conceptualization

Generating viable explanations involves two reasoning processes that are central in completing an assessment and a case conceptualization (Sperry, 2005). They are deductive and inductive reasoning, and forward and backward reasoning.

Deductive Reasoning Process

Deductive reasoning involves reasoning from the general to the specific. This reasoning process is essential in completing a diagnostic assessment as well as completing the diagnostic formulation component of the case conceptualization. Accordingly, arriving at a *Diagnostic and Statistical Manual of Mental Disorders, Fifth Edition* (*DSM-5*) diagnosis is an example of deductive reasoning. It is a process that involves collecting data about symptomatic distress and impaired functioning, ordering this data into criteria, and matching these criteria to a single diagnostic category. In other words, the diagnosis (the general) provides order and meaning to symptoms matching criteria (the specifics). For instance, a client who presents with specific symptoms and who meets the following criteria would qualify for the diagnosis of Social Anxiety Disorder: (1) marked fear of exposure to the possible scrutiny of others; (2) avoidance of situations in which such scrutiny may occur; (3) marked fear of exposure to unfamiliar people; (4) responds with intense anxiety or panic when facing such exposure; (5) recognition that their fear is excessive and irrational; and (6) become socially isolated as a consequence of this fear (American Psychiatric Association, 2013). In short, the deductive reasoning process proceeds from the general to the specific.

Inductive Reasoning Process

In contrast, inductive reasoning involves reasoning from the specific to the general. This reasoning process is essential in the process of recognizing patterns and developing the clinical, cultural, and treatment formulation components of a case conceptualization. The more data that is available, i.e., symptoms, social and developmental history, etc., the more complex and difficult it can be to develop and feel confident about a clinical formulation. The reason is that deriving a clinical formulation requires inductive reasoning. Unlike deductive reasoning, the inductive reasoning process involves synthesizing and drawing inferences from a group of seemingly unrelated bits of data about symptoms, functioning and history, a single unifying concept, theme, or pattern that connects all that disparate data into an explanation of why the client is experiencing these particular problems in this particular context at this particular time.

Imagine that you are playing a mind game that involves speculation. You will be given a series of clues – in the guise of items – and will be asked to offer a series of guesses as to what they ultimately represent. First, you are given an iPod and a phone charger. You speculate their link or commonality is "electronic devices." Then, you are given a book of crossword puzzles. Finding a commonality is a bit more challenging, but after a moment's reflection you conclude: "things that entertain and pass the time." Next, you receive a map and a bottle of water. The task has become much more difficult, but you infer a more abstract guess or formulation, "they are all inanimate objects." Two other clues are then given: two parents and three children. It then occurs to you that the concept that links all these items together is "family trip"; however, instead of saying this out loud, you look for other information that could confirm, deny, or modify this inference. Ten other clues are given, including snacks, sunglasses, and hand wipes. Each of these adds to your tentative inference of a "family trip," because in each instance the clues are consistent with or confirm your guess. You now confidently voice your answer: "family trip" and win the game! For many, the prospect of finding a common meaning among 15 or more discrete pieces of data might be daunting and even maddening. That is why having a clinical theoretical framework aids the process of developing a clinical formulation. Not only does a theoretical framework provide a way of meaningfully linking collected data together, but it also provides a map for eliciting and attending to selected pieces of data while "ignoring" other data. For instance, imagine that the theoretical framework of practitioner #1 (an acknowledged master therapist) would have her elicit four pieces of data: parents, child, car, and map, for which the linking theme is "family trip." Compare this to practitioner #2 (a beginning practicum student) who, guided by no theoretical framework, collects all 15 pieces of data in no particular order. As is often the case, students and practitioners with little or no training and experience in deriving clinical formulations tend to engage in premature closure. They might take the first three pieces of data presented and arrive at and verbalize "things that entertain" as their answer, an inference that is only partially accurate.

Forward Reasoning

Another way in which experts differ from trainees and practitioners in constructing case conceptualizations is in the use of forward and backward reasoning processes. Forward reasoning involves moving from data to one or more hypotheses until a solution is achieved. This form of reasoning is more commonly utilized by experts. A case conceptualization statement demonstrating this type of reasoning might read: The client reports that she became angry at her boyfriend and notes that as a child she was quite close to her father who is described as affectionate and passive. Thus, she may expect other men to act like her father, and becomes confused and angry when they do not. This statement begins with data provided by the client and draws an inference based upon it (Eells et al., 2011).

Backward Reasoning

In contrast, backward reasoning involves moving from a solution on the basis of a hypothesis to finding supporting data. This form of reasoning is more commonly utilized by trainees. A case conceptualization statement demonstrating this type of reasoning might read: He probably is borderline personality disordered, and so it is likely that he was emotionally and sexually abused while growing up. This statement begins with an inference that the client has a personality disorder and then speculates about a possible cause (Eells et al., 2011). In short, forward reasoning is characterized by facts-to-inference reasoning while backward reasoning is characterized by inference-to-facts reasoning.

Reasoning Processes and Training

The task of synthesizing and drawing inferences from seemingly disparate pieces of data into a cohesive pattern and then into a clinically useful case conceptualization is one that often seems beyond the capacity of many trainees. While it is true that individuals with a talent for analytic thinking and synthesis tend to approach the case conceptualization process with ease, such ability, while necessary, is not sufficient. Instruction and practice, ongoing practice, are essential. Case conceptualization, particularly clinical formulation, is the requisite skill for effective treatment planning (Eells & Lombart, 2003). Optimally, this competency is best acquired through didactic instruction, supervision, and continued practice. However, this competency can also be acquired and mastered with self-instruction, practice, and commitment. This involves ongoing study of exemplary case conceptualizations and deliberate practice in modeling the requisite skills of focused inductive reasoning, inference making, forward reasoning, pattern recognition, and then drafting versions of the diagnostic, clinical, cultural, and treatment formulations until a sufficient level of explanatory and predictive power is achieved. The next section focuses on the clinical formulation.

Clinical Formulation

The clinical formulation is the central component in a case conceptualization and, along with the cultural formulation, serves to link the diagnostic and treatment formulations. The key element of the clinical formulation is the *predisposition* which provides an explanation for the client's maladaptive pattern and links *precipitant* with *presentation*. This section defines the key elements of the clinical formulation and their relationship to key elements of the diagnostic formulation.

Elements of Clinical Formulation

Essentially, the clinical formulation is an appraisal of the client's predispositions, protective factors, and perpetuants and provides an explanation for the client's pattern and presenting problem (Sperry, 2010). Predisposition and perpetuants are described and their relationship to pattern, presentation, and precipitant is visually depicted.

1. Predisposition

Predisposition, also called etiological or predisposing factors, is all the possible factors that account for and explain the client's pattern and presenting issues. Eells (2010) refers to it as the "origins" of the formulation. The predisposition is derived largely from the developmental, social, and health histories which provide clues about likely predisposing factors, and reflect the client's biological, psychological, and social vulnerabilities. Biological vulnerabilities include medical history, current health status, medications, as well substance use. They also include treatment history such as a personal or family history of suicide and substance abuse or dependence. Psychological vulnerabilities include intrapsychic or intrapersonal, interpersonal, and other psychological factors including intelligence and personality dynamics such as personality style, maladaptive beliefs and schemas, automatic thoughts, intermediate beliefs, resilience, self-concept, self-control, and character structure. They also include all behavioral deficits and excesses, other symptom disorders, and self-management, problem-solving, communication, relational, negotiation, and conflict resolution skills. Social vulnerabilities include family dynamics, such as parental and sibling characteristics, interaction styles, family secrets, educational achievements, religious training, sexual experiences, and early neglect and abuse, be it verbal, emotional, physical, sexual, or financial. They also include the family level of functioning, family stressors, separation, divorce, peer relations, job stressors, support systems, and environmental factors. For example, it would be important to identify vulnerabilities to depression, impulsivity, or to specific social and environmental factors such as drinking friends, living in poverty, or working in a hostile environment.

2. Protective Factors

Protective factors are factors that decrease the likelihood of developing a clinical condition. These include: a secure attachment style, resilience, effective coping skills, a positive support system, as well as leaving an abusive relationship. Protective factors are actually the mirror opposite of risk factors which are factors that increase the likelihood of developing a clinical condition. These include remaining in an abusive relationships, self-harm, and suicidal ideation. Similar to protective factors are strengths which are psychological processes that enable one to think and act in ways that benefit themselves and others. These include mindfulness, self-control, and self-confidence.

3. Perpetuants

Perpetuants are also called maintaining factors. Essentially, perpetuants are processes in which a client's pattern is reinforced and confirmed by both the client and the client's environment. Perpetuants serve to "protect" or "insulate" the client from symptoms, conflict, or the demands of others. For example, individuals who are shy and rejection-sensitive may gravitate toward living alone because it reduces the likelihood that others will criticize or make interpersonal demands on them. Because the influence of these factors seems to overlap, at times it can be difficult to specify whether a factor is a predisposition or a perpetuant. These might include skill deficits, hostile work environment, living alone, negative responses of others, etc. Other times, predisposing factors function as maintaining factors. For instance, an individual with an avoidant style (predisposition) tends to engage in social isolation. By repeatedly distancing themselves from others in order to be safe, that individual is unlikely to develop the social skills necessary for making friends, developing assertive communication and intimate relationships, or engaging in conflict resolution. As a result of feeling lonely and ineffective in relating to others, the individual may unwittingly confirm her core belief that she is defective or unlovable.

The relationship among predisposition, pattern, perpetuants, precipitant, and presentation are indicated in the visual diagram in Figure 3.1. See also Table 3.1.

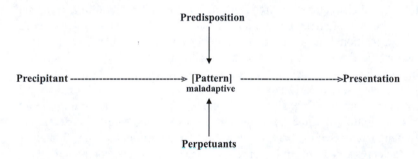

Figure 3.1 Relationship Among Predisposition, Pattern, Perpetuants, Precipitant, and Presentation

Table 3.1 Elements of a Clinical Formulation

Predisposition	factors fostering adaptive or maladaptive functioning
Protective Factors	factors that decrease the likelihood of developing a clinical condition
Perpetuants	triggers that activate one's pattern resulting in presentation

Table 3.2 depicts the predisposition elements from the clinical formulations for the case of Geri for three different therapeutic approaches: Biopsychosocial, Cognitive-Behavioral, and Time-Limited Dynamic approaches. Note the different emphasis for each of these three approaches. While the Cognitive-Behavioral model limits the focus of its explanation to maladaptive behaviors and cognitions, the Biopsychosocial and Dynamics models have a much broader focus. For example, the psychological dimension of the Biopsychosocial model is broad enough to encompass the maladaptive behaviors and cognitions of the Cognitive-Behavioral model, as well as other psychological factors, such as resilience, and self-control. But while the Time-Limited Dynamic model is broad like the Biopsychosocial

Table 3.2 Clinical Formulations of Geri: Biopsychosocial, Cognitive-Behavioral, and Dynamics

Biopsychosocial **Predisposition**	*biological*: family history of depression *psychological*: shy, avoidant, non-assertive *social*: current: avoids situations in which she might be criticized, rejected, or otherwise harmed; past: experienced demanding, critical, emotionally unavailable parents, and teasing and criticism of peers
Cognitive-Behavioral **Predisposition**	*maladaptive cognitions*: views herself as inadequate and frightened of rejection, and views the world as rejecting and critical but wants safe relationships; *maladaptive schemas*: defectiveness and social isolation *maladaptive behaviors*: history of being teased, criticized, rejected, and otherwise harmed in early life; demonstrates shyness and avoidance behavior in situations she perceives as unsafe and prefers social isolation to engagement with others
Time-Limited Dynamics **Predisposition**	*Acts of the Self*: feels depressed and worried about job promotion *Acts of Others toward the Self*: her parents, her brother, and friends were critical of her as a child; she has a close friend who is supportive *Expectations of Others' reaction*: she expects coworkers, friends, and family members to be judgmental, critical, and demanding of her; she expects her new supervisor to be critical of her work performance *Acts of the Self toward the Self (introject)*: she believes that she is inadequate and is very self-critical *interactive countertransference*: practitioner felt pulled toward her while also feeling pushed away

model, it is more specific in its emphasis on interpersonal relations and introjects, or beliefs about self.

Evaluating the Explanatory Power of a Clinical Formulation

While this book describes four of the most common theoretical-therapeutic methods (Cognitive-Behavioral, Time-Limited Dynamic, Adlerian, and Acceptance and Commitment Therapy), many practitioners utilize the Biopsychosocial method, or some variant of it, as the basis for conceptualizing cases. An often-cited reason why practitioners use a non-theoretical method, such as the Biopsychosocial method, is that their clinical formulation can remain close to the actual data of the case, i.e., clients' own words, ideas, and "explanations," and because the formulation can be more "integrative" and include insights from one or more theoretical-therapeutic method. In other words, a practitioner can keep adding predisposing factors to build a theory of the case that has a reasonably high explanatory power.

The case of Antwone can be useful in evaluating the explanatory power of a clinical formulation component of a case conceptualization. You may recall that Antwone's presentation involved enraged outbursts and anger that was retaliatory in nature. Various precipitants are noted in his current and past history. These include peers who taunt him, particularly authority figures who make what he considers unreasonable or arbitrary demands. He was also racially taunted and teased about his lack of sexual experiences. Other precipitants include the loss or abandonment of important persons such as his only close friend, Jessie, and the anticipation that he may be abandoned by his Navy psychiatrist. Another way of saying this is that his maladaptive pattern was to strike back when taunted or faced with an actual or anticipated loss.

Here is how a practitioner might think through the clinical formulation process with the goal of constructing a formulation with a reasonably high explanatory power. The practitioner begins by considering what is perhaps the most obvious predisposing factor: Antwone's pervasive, early childhood abuse history. Unfortunately, one cannot explain Antwone's enraged outbursts, his retaliation, or fighting simply on the basis of this abuse history. The reason is that many individuals with such abuse histories who experience the same or similar precipitants do not consistently and predictably respond to others' provocations with aggression and rage. Nor does a second predisposing factor, his abandonment experience, increase the explanatory power by much. The reason is that many individuals with similar abandonment experiences do not react vengefully when provoked. Similarly, a third predisposing factor, observing and modeling his foster mother's abusive behavior does not offer a reasonably compelling explanation since many other abuse victims have observed abusiveness but have not modeled it. The practitioner notes that all three of these predisposing factors share a commonality: they are external and historical descriptors.

The practitioner then looks for internal factors. A fourth predisposing factor is different in that it reflects an internal disposition that is ongoing. It is Antwone's capacity to strike back and the experience of striking back and seeking to avenge a perceived wrong. The practitioner recalls that after 15 years of meekly "stuffing" his foster mother's abuse, Antwone reversed his pattern, pushed her back, and threatened harm if she abused him again.

Along with the first three, this factor provides a more compelling explanation for Antwone's behavior, as it does for the one-third of abused individuals who then become abusers. Together, the explanatory power of these four predisposing factors is higher. The practitioner considers an additional predisposing factor, core maladaptive beliefs or schemas from the Cognitive-Behavioral model. The practitioner reasons that someone with the schemas of defectiveness (belief that one is inferior, bad, and unwanted), abuse-mistrust (belief that others can abuse and humiliate), and punitiveness (belief that others should be harshly punished) is likely to strike back and avenge others who abuse and have made him feel defective. In eliciting information on schemas, the practitioner concludes that these three sets of schemas or maladaptive core beliefs are present and that Antwone's experience of being abused and abandoned, along with his capacity to and experience of striking back at others, plus the core beliefs that others must be punished for abusing or taunting him further increases the explanatory power.

This case illustrates how a practitioner evaluates a provisional clinical formulation and elicits additional material on predisposing factors to construct a clinical formulation that has more explanatory power. Noteworthy is that the practitioner initially utilized the Biopsychosocial method and then turned to the Cognitive-Behavioral method to guide his efforts to increase the explanatory power of his developing clinical formulation.

Cultural Formulation

The cultural formulation is the third of the four components of a case conceptualization.

Given the prominent role that cultural beliefs, values, attitudes, and practices can play in the lives of clients, highly effective practitioners are sensitive to and routinely seek to learn additional cultural information on their clients. Such information helps practitioners better understand their clients' personal coping and social resources, as well as helping them explore the various cultural issues that contribute to clients' suffering and distress (Hayes, 2016; Ridley & Kelly, 2007).

How effective are practitioners and trainees in developing and using cultural formulations in their practice? In a study of practitioners, most believed that effective practice was aided by the use of cultural formulations. However, very few actually developed or used these formulations to guide their clinical practice (Hansen et al., 2006). Trainees seem to share a similar fate (Neufield et al., 2006). At a time when cultural sensitivity is becoming the norm in the mental health professions, developing this essential competency is no longer optional for trainees and practitioners; it has, or will soon, become mandatory. This section defines cultural formulations and describes four elements useful in specifying such formulations. Then, two case examples illustrate these four elements of a cultural formulation and their treatment implications.

Definition of a Cultural Formulation

A cultural formulation supports the clinical formulation and can inform treatment focus and the type of interventions chosen. The cultural formulation is a systematic review of cultural factors and dynamics that have been described in the "Social History and Cultural Factors" section of a clinical case report. It answers the "What role does culture play?" question. More specifically, the cultural formulation statement describes clients' cultural or ethnic identity, their level of acculturation, and their cultural explanatory mode (Sperry, 2010). It provides a cultural explanation of the client's condition as well as the impact of cultural factors on the client's personality and level of functioning. Furthermore, it forms the basis for anticipating if cultural elements may impact the relationship between the individual and the practitioner, and whether culturally sensitive treatment is indicated (GAP Committee on Cultural Psychiatry, 2002).

Elements of a Cultural Formulation

The cultural formulation is based on four key cultural elements: cultural identity, cultural stress and acculturation, cultural explanatory model, and the impact of cultural vs. personality dynamics.

1. Cultural Identity

The cultural formulation begins to take shape during the diagnostic assessment. As part of the "Social and Cultural History" of that assessment, the practitioner presumably elicits information on the client's cultural identity, i.e., sense of being defined by membership in a cultural or ethnic group. This identification is not a demographic fact, rather it is the individual's self-appraisal and an indicator of their affirmation and sense of belonging to a particular ethnic group, whether it is their original ethnic group or to the mainstream culture. It is noteworthy that some adolescents who come from mainland China to attend private high schools in the United States quickly assume American names and identities, claiming that their mainstream peers will have difficulty pronouncing their Chinese names. Or, a light-skinned, Haitian American client identifies herself as a "Caucasian American" to distance herself from what she perceives as negative stereotypes of Haitians and African Americans. This contrasts with a Cuban American client who states with pride that he remains loyal to his Cuban customs, language, and food preferences. Such attitudes influence an individual's stated ethnic or cultural identity.

In terms of cultural competence in counseling practice, D'Andrea and Daniels (2001) articulated a multicultural framework which includes a list of cultural factors in their RESPECTFUL model:

RESPECTFUL

Religious values
Economic/class issues
Sexual identity issues
Psychological developmental issues
Ethnic/racial identity issues
Chronological
Trauma and threats to well-being
Family issues
Unique physical issues
Language and location of residence issues

Likewise, Hays (1996, pp. 332–334) established a model that outlines a similar cultural framework in her ADDRESSING model:

ADDRESSING

Age/generational
Disability (developmental)
Disability (acquired)
Religion
Ethnicity/race
Social status
Sexual orientation
Indigenous heritage
National origin
Gender

Both models provide a framework that practitioners can use to guide the assessment process as well as a system for practitioners to complete their own self-assessment to assess their own biases, power, and privilege, and to examine how these dynamics can and do influence the counseling process. These cultural factors were highlighted by the American Counseling Association (Arrendondo & Perez, 2006) and the American Psychological Association (2003) because of their historical neglect.

2. Cultural Stress and Acculturation

Acculturation is the process of adapting to a culture different from one's culture of origin. It is a known stressor and risk factor that can affect the health and behavior of immigrants. This contrasts with enculturation which is the process of learning one's own culture of origin including its language, values, and rituals (Barry, 1997). Adapting to another culture can be problematic and stressful and is called acculturative stress. Acculturative stress is defined as stress rooted in acculturation. It differs from more everyday life stress in that it involves acculturation-specific issues such as ethnic identity, discrimination, cultural values, and cultural and second language competence which result in psychosocial distress (Berry & Annis, 1974; Wu & Mak, 2012). Such stress is not uncommon in the acculturation process. It can be as blatant as racial remarks about skin color or more subtle discrimination resulting from stares over an accent or dialect when asking for directions or ordering food in a restaurant. It is also evident in generational differences in acculturation level such as when children of immigrant parents are more acculturated than their parents. Not surprisingly, this disparity in acculturation levels can give rise to conflicts over expectations for language usage, dating, curfews, career plans, and overall adherence to the rituals and values of the family's culture of origin.

Research indicates that psychological maladjustment is associated with higher levels of acculturation and that sociocultural adaptation or competence serves to modulate the effects of acculturative stress (Wu & Mak, 2012). Such sociocultural competence can be increased by language proficiency, effective social interaction, and communication competence, which includes knowledge and skills in intercultural communication styles, rules, and social norms.

The level of acculturation can be estimated with a self-rating or practitioner-rating instrument. One that is commonly used is the *Brief Acculturation Scale* (Burnam, Hough, Karno, Escobar, & Telles, 1987). This scale consists of three items rated on a five-point scale: client's language (native vs. English), generation (first to fifth), and social activities (preference for friends – native vs. mainline friends). It measures three levels of acculturation: low, medium, and high, and is practitioner rated based on interview data.

Cultural stress describes any cultural psychosocial event or dynamic that is problematic to an individual who identifies from a cultural group. Some examples of stressors include oppression, discrimination, microaggressions, or racially motivated workplace bullying (mobbing). Examples of vulnerable populations that are likely to experience cultural stressors include individuals from lower socioeconomic groups (SES), individuals living with disabilities, individuals who are minorities from non-dominant races and/or ethnicities, children and elderly individuals, and individuals who do not identify as heterosexual or cisgender.

3. Cultural Explanation

A client's explanation for the reason they believe they are experiencing their problem or concern is very revealing as are the words and idioms used to express their distress (Bhui & Bhugra, 2004). Practitioners should routinely elicit a cultural explanation or explanatory model, i.e., clients' beliefs regarding the cause of their distress, condition, or impairment such as "nerves," possessing spirits, somatic complaints, inexplicable misfortune, testing or punishment from God, etc. In addition, eliciting clients' expectations and preferences for treatment and,

Table 3.3 Elements of a Cultural Formulation

Cultural identity	sense of belonging to a particular ethnic group
Cultural stress and acculturation	level of adaptation to the dominant culture; stress rooted in acculturation including psychosocial difficulties
Cultural explanation	beliefs regarding cause of distress, condition, or impairment
Culture and/or personality	operative mix of cultural and/or personality dynamics

if indicated, past experiences of healing in their culture provide useful information in treatment planning decisions.

4. Culture and/or Personality

Another consideration in developing a cultural formulation is identifying the extent of the influence and impact of cultural dynamics and personality dynamics on the presentation or presenting problem. Personality dynamics include the client's personality style. The practitioner's task is to estimate the operative mix of cultural dynamics and personality dynamics.

When the acculturation level is high, cultural dynamics may have relatively little impact on the presenting problem while personality dynamics may have a significant impact. When the acculturation level is low or cultural stress is high, cultural dynamics may have a significant impact. Sometimes, both personality and cultural dynamics have a similar impact. This is particularly common in cultures that expect females to be dependent and subordinate to males, and where female clients also exhibit a pronounced dependent personality style. The importance of determining the mix of cultural and personality dynamics is critical in decisions about the extent to which culturally sensitive treatment may be indicated. It can be helpful for trainees to quantify the level of influence of cultural and personality dynamics on the presenting issues. One such system is listing the amount of influence from each dynamic on a 1–100 scale. For example, a client with significant cultural stress and a healthy personality structure might be 90:10, in which 90% of the variance of the case is culturally influenced and only 10% is from personality factors. A client with significant cultural stress and significant personality dynamics (such as a personality disorder) may have a ratio of 55:45. Table 3.3 summarizes these elements.

Constructing a Cultural Formulation: Illustrations

Constructing a clinically useful cultural formulation is based on the preceding four elements. For this reason, an accurate and complete assessment of this information is essential. Two cases illustrate differences in cultural formulation.

In the case of Geri, the four elements of her *cultural formulation* are:

- identifies as a middle-class African American with limited ethnic ties
- highly acculturated with no obvious acculturative stress, i.e., prejudice, while gender roles in her family system favor men over women

- believes her depression results from job stress and a chemical imbalance in her brain
- personality dynamics are significantly operative

In contrast, in the case of Antwone, the four elements of his *cultural formulation* are:

- identifies as African American
- highly acculturated with considerable acculturative stress
- believes his problems result from racial degradation and abuse from his African American foster family and racial provocations by white peers and superiors
- both personality *and* cultural factors are operative

In short, although both Geri and Antwone appear to have high levels of acculturation, there are obvious differences in their cultural stress as well as in their explanatory models, and the mix of personality and cultural dynamics. Presumably, culturally sensitive treatment considerations would be prominent in working with a client like Antwone but not necessarily with a client like Geri.

Trauma and Case Conceptualization

Mental health practitioners frequently encounter clients who present for treatment and have experienced a recent or childhood traumatic event. Unfortunately, many practitioners feel unprepared and ill-equipped to therapeutically work with these particular individuals and are unable to integrate trauma-informed principles into their treatment (SAMHSA, 2014b). While various definitions of trauma exist, the Substance Abuse and Mental Health Services Administration (SAMHSA) definition will be presented here:

> Individual trauma results from an event, series of events, or set of circumstances that is experienced by an individual as physically or emotionally harmful or life threatening and that has lasting adverse effects on the individual's functioning and mental, physical, social, emotional, or spiritual well-being.
>
> (2014, p. 7)

Trauma-informed principles are well suited to integrate within the integrated case conceptualization framework presented in this book. Harris and Fallot (2001) identified five trauma-informed principles: safety, trust, choice, collaboration, and empowerment. Similarly, the SAMHSA's six trauma-informed principles are: safety; trustworthiness and transparency; collaboration and mutuality; peer support; empowerment; voice and choice; and cultural, historical, and gender issues (SAMHSA, 2014b).

Trauma-informed care principles provide a framework for understanding and conceptualizing the symptoms and challenges of clients who have experienced traumatic events in all aspects of the mental health care delivery system (Harris & Fallot, 2001). While the trauma-informed approach does not assume that every client has experienced trauma, it does recognize that trauma is prevalent among many who seek counseling services. One of the most significant studies to examine the effects of early childhood trauma that influenced the awareness of the widespread prevalence of trauma is the Adverse Childhood Experiences (ACE) study that followed 17,000 participants longitudinally and found that ACEs were directly correlated with early death (Felitti et al., 1998).

A recent study found that adverse childhood experiences were significantly associated with poorer health outcomes including coronary heart disease, obesity, chronic obstructive pulmonary disease, and depression (Merrick et al., 2019). In that study, one in six adults (15.6%) reported at least four ACE and 60.9% reported at least one ACE. Similarly, in another study carried out in the United States, 61% of men and 51% of women reported experiencing at least one trauma or adverse experience in their lifetime (Kessler et al., 1999), while 90% of clients in public mental health settings have been exposed to at least one traumatic event (Goodman, Rosenberg, Mueser, & Drake, 1997; Mueser et al., 1998).

Trauma-informed principles are easily integrated into the integrated case conceptualization model covered in this book. First off, trauma-informed case conceptualization (TF-CC) is essential to use with clients who are reporting exposure to acute trauma and even adverse childhood events. Below, you will find a list of trauma-informed principles and considerations applied to the case conceptualization formulations covered in this book (SAMHSA, 2014a):

Diagnostic formulation:

- Adequate trauma history assessment is essential for the diagnostic formulation. The ACE assessment is available in the public domain.
- Practitioners need to understand various types of trauma and events (natural disasters, terrorism, relational trauma, developmental trauma, etc.) that can precipitate and perpetuate trauma responses.
- Be aware of immediate and delayed reactions to trauma.
- Common diagnostic considerations include Acute Stress Disorder, Post Traumatic Stress Disorder (PTSD), dissociative disorders, depressive disorders, and Borderline Personality Disorder.
- Assess if the client has a history of other psychiatric disorders or current disorders that are co-occurring (such as Substance Use Disorder) with a PTSD presentation.

Clinical formulation:

- This formulation is ultimately responsible for understanding the impact of trauma on a client.
- Trauma-related symptoms can be conceptualized through various theories. Some theories understand the behavioral responses of trauma (avoidance of a feared stimulus) as an adaptation to the traumatic event. Behavioral responses to trauma are often in the service of reducing discomfort and emotional flooding.

- If trauma-related symptoms are the focus of treatment, it is important to understand the client's personal meaning of the event.
- Consider how Biopsychosocial risk factors influence the current symptoms and distress. For example, does the client have a family history of depression and also several generations of domestic violence relationships in their family?

Cultural formulation:

- The cultural formulation is used to consider how cultural factors can be risk factors or protective factors within the case conceptualization and treatment planning process.
- Assess if the client was a victim of a hate crime and if they are a member of a vulnerable or marginalized population. Determine if they were a victim of a cultural trauma (e.g., war, genocide, government oppression, torture, or terrorism).
- Determine how symptoms of PTSD and other trauma-related disorders may manifest differently in the client's culture.
- Assess cultural beliefs about trauma and their expectations of what psychological treatment should or should not include.
- Assess cultural resources and protective factors such as church support, local support groups, and culturally bound healing practices.

Treatment formulation:

- A trauma-informed treatment formulation is essential to use when working with clients who have experienced recent or past traumatic events because it focuses on the use of specific interventions and the timing of therapeutic processes.
- Before formal treatment strategies are utilized, the practitioner will work to foster a strong collaborative relationship that emphasizes safety, support, empowerment, and choice.
- The use of grounding strategies and self-soothing strategies is paramount in preparing the client for the therapy process.
- Practitioners should strive to avoid re-traumatization during the therapy process by monitoring the client's non-verbal communication during a session, not insisting that they talk about their trauma, and providing a safe and confidential meeting space.
- Work to identify their triggers and coping responses to these triggers.
- Incorporate strengths, protective factors, and resiliency into the treatment process. For example, many victims of trauma report increased bonding with family and community, a redefined sense of purpose in life, and an increased desire to volunteer or give to charitable causes that positively impact victims of trauma.
- Despite your theoretical orientation, you can normalize trauma-related symptoms by providing psychoeducation about the common responses to recent or

historical trauma, such as the fact that hyperarousal, sleep disturbance, avoidance, increased alcohol consumption, and nightmares are common.

- Connect clients to trauma-informed peer support groups when appropriate.
- A non-exhaustive list of treatment modalities includes acute approaches such as Psychological First Aid, and ongoing treatments such as Trauma-Focused Cognitive Behavior Therapy (TF-CBT), Cognitive Processing Therapy (CPT), Exposure Therapy, Eye Movement Desensitization and Reprocessing (EMDR), Narrative Therapy, and Stress Inoculation Training (SIT).

Concluding Comment

This chapter has described and illustrated both the clinical formulation and the cultural formulation components of the case conceptualization. Both provide an explanation for the client's presenting problems as well as their pattern. With the increasing value placed on practitioners' sensitivity to diversity and cultural issues, it should not be surprising that practitioners are increasingly expected to construct and implement case conceptualizations that are culturally sensitive. Accordingly, this chapter has emphasized the cultural formulation and its relationship to the clinical formulation and has highlighted the importance of integrating a trauma-informed perspective into the case conceptualization process. A basic premise of this book is the more accurate and compelling the clinical and cultural explanations, the more clinically useful the case conceptualization. Chapter 4 emphasizes the importance and clinical utility of the clinical formulation and cultural formulation to the treatment formulation. See Hayes (2016) for a wealth of information about the interplay of cultural considerations and psychological conditions.

CHAPTER 3 QUESTIONS

1. Describe how using a deductive and an inductive reasoning process can help formulate explanations in completing an assessment and case conceptualization.
2. Compare forward and backward reasoning in the case conceptualization process. What methods of training help in building this competency and which are attributed to experts?
3. Explain how the key element of predisposition of the clinical formulation relates to pattern and how this links precipitant with presentation in a well-written case conceptualization.
4. Why would the use of a non-theoretical method such as Biopsychosocial be so commonly used in a clinical formulation? Are there any advantages, and what alternatives are also incorporated?
5. Describe the four key elements of a cultural formulation and discuss the importance of including this information as it relates to the overall case conceptualization.
6. Why is trauma-informed awareness important in the case conceptualization process?

References

American Psychiatric Association. (2013). *Diagnostic and statistical manual of mental disorders* (5th ed.). Arlington, VA: American Psychiatric Association Press.

American Psychological Association. (2003). Guidelines on multicultural education, training, research, practice, and organizational change for psychologists. *American Psychologist, 58*, 377–402.

Arrendondo, P. & Perez, P. (2006). Historical perspectives on multicultural guidelines and contemporary applications. *Professional Psychology: Research and Practice, 37,* 1–5. http://dx.doi.org/10.1037/07355-7028.37.1.1

Berry, J. (1997). Immigration, acculturation, and adaptation. *Applied Psychology: An International Review, 46*(1), 5–34.

Berry, J., & Annis, R. (1974). Acculturative stress. *Journal of Cross-Cultural Psychology, 5*(4), 382–405.

Bhui, K., & Bhugra, D. (2004). Communication with patients from other cultures: The place of explanatory models. *Advances in Psychiatric Treatment, 10*(6), 474–478.

Burnam, M., Hough, R., Karno, M., Escobar, J., & Telles, C. (1987). Acculturation and lifetime prevalence of psychiatric disorders among Mexican Americans in Los Angeles. *Journal of Health and Social Behavior, 28*(1), 89–102.

D'Andrea, M., & Daniels, J. (2001). RESPECTFUL counseling: An integrative model for counselors. In D. Pope-Davis & H. Coleman (Eds.), *The interface of class, culture and gender in counseling* (pp. 417–466). Thousand Oaks, CA: Sage.

Eells, T. (2010). The unfolding case formulation: The interplay of description and inference. *Pragmatic Case Studies in Psychotherapy, 6*(4), 225–254.

Eells, T., & Lombart, K. (2003). Case formulation and treatment concepts among novice, experienced, and expert cognitive-behavioral and psychodynamic therapists. *Psychotherapy Research, 13*(2), 187–204.

Eells, T., Lombart, K., Salsman, N., Kendjelic, E., Schneiderman, C., & Lucas, C. (2011). Expert reasoning in psychotherapy case formulation. *Psychotherapy Research, 21*(4), 385–399.

Felitti, V.J., Anda, R.F., Nordenberg, D., Williamson, D.F., Spitz, A.M., Edwards, V., & Marks, J.S. (1998). Relationship of childhood abuse and household dysfunction to many of the leading causes of death in adults: The adverse childhood experiences (ACE) study. *American Journal of Preventive Medicine, 14*(4), 245–258.

GAP Committee on Cultural Psychiatry. (2002). *Cultural assessment in clinical psychiatry.* Washington, DC: American Psychiatric Press.

Goodman, L., Rosenberg, S., Mueser, K., & Drake, R. (1997). Physical and sexual assault history in women with serious mental illness: Prevalence, correlates, treatment, and future research directions. *Schizophrenia Bulletin, 23*(4), 685–696.

Hansen, N., Randazzo, K., Schwartz, A., Marshall, M., Kalis, D., Fraziers, R., Burke, C., Kerscher-Rice, K., & Norvig, G. (2006). Do we practice what we preach? An exploratory survey of multicultural psychotherapy competencies. *Professional Psychology: Research and Practice, 337*(1), 66–74.

Harris, M., & Fallot, R. D. (Eds.). (2001). *New directions for mental health services. Using trauma theory to design service systems.* San Francisco, CA: Jossey-Bass.

Hayes, P.A. (2016). *Addressing cultural complexities in practice: Assessment, diagnosis, and therapy* (3rd ed.). Washington, DC: American Psychological Association.

Hays, P. A. (1996). Addressing the complexities of culture and gender in counseling. *Journal of Counseling & Development, 74*(4), 332–338. https://doi.org/10.1002/j.1556 -6676.1996.tb01876.x

Kessler, R.C., Sonnega, A., Bromet, E., Hughes, M., Nelson, C.B., & Breslau, N.N. (1999). Epidemiological risk factors for trauma and PTSD. In R. Yehuda (Ed.), *Risk factors for PTSD* (pp. 23–59). Washington, DC: American Psychiatric Press.

Merrick, M.T., Ford, D.C., Ports, K.A., Guinn, A.S., Chen, J., Klevens, J., ... Ottley, P. (2019). Vital signs: Estimated proportion of adult health problems attributable to adverse childhood experiences and implications for prevention: 25 states, 2015–2017. *MMWR: Morbidity and Mortality Weekly Report, 68*(44), 999–1005.

Mueser, K., Goodman, L., Trumbetta, S., Rosenberg, S., Osher, F., Vidaver, R., Anciello, P., & Foy, D. (1998). Trauma and Posttraumatic Stress Disorder in severe mental illness. *Journal of Consulting and Clinical Psychology, 66*(3), 493–499.

Neufield, S., Pinterits, E., Moleiro, C., Lee, T., Yang, P., & Brodie, R. (2006). How do graduate student therapists incorporate diversity factors in case conceptualizations? *Psychotherapy: Theory, Research, Practice, Training, 43*(4), 464–479.

Ridley, C., & Kelly, S. (2007). Multicultural considerations in case formation. In T. Eells (Ed.), *Handbook of psychotherapy case formulation* (2nd ed., pp. 33–64). New York, NY: Guilford.

Sperry, L. (2005). Case conceptualization: A strategy for incorporating individual, couple, and family dynamics in the treatment process. *The American Journal of Family Therapy, 33*(5), 353–364.

Sperry, L. (2010). *Core competencies in counseling and psychotherapy: Becoming a highly competent and effective therapist*. New York, NY: Routledge.

Substance Abuse and Mental Health Services Administration. (2014a). *SAMHSA's concept of trauma and guidance for a trauma-informed approach*. Retrieved from https://s3 .amazonaws.com/static.nicic.gov/Library/028436.pdf

Substance Abuse and Mental Health Services Administration. (2014b). *Trauma-Informed Care in Behavioral Health Services. Treatment Improvement Protocol (TIP) Series, No. 57*. Center for Substance Abuse Treatment. Rockville, MD: Substance Abuse and Mental Health Services Administration. Retrieved from https://www.ncbi.nlm.nih.gov/ books/NBK207201/

Wu, E., & Mak, W. (2012). Acculturation process and distress: Mediating roles of sociocultural adaptation and acculturative stress. *The Counseling Psychologist, 40*(1), 66–92.

4   Treatment Planning and Treatment Formulations

Two of the most common concerns that trainees have in working with clients are reflected in the questions: "What do I say?" and "What do I do?" While logical, these questions can quickly get trainees lost and off track, which is common when trainees lack an accurate cognitive map to guide them. To develop accurate cognitive maps to guide the treatment process, trainees must first become competent at *focusing*, which means knowing where to focus one's attention when listening and observing. One of the most useful questions that trainees can ask themselves and their supervisor is: "What should I be noticing and listening for when I talk with this client?" The apparent magic that distinguishes master practitioners from average ones lies in what each attends to and focuses on. The better trainees get at focusing, the better practitioners they will become. Because highly effective practitioners continually develop and refine this art and competency over their careers, trainees should not expect to master this competency right away. Case conceptualization is the technical term for the therapeutic art and competency of focusing, including an "assessment focus" which is central to pattern recognition in the diagnostic formulation, and a "treatment focus" on pattern change which is central to the treatment formulation and treatment process.

This chapter addresses the treatment formulation component of a case conceptualization. The elements of the treatment formulation are first described. Treatment focus and treatment strategy are then emphasized, and seven basic treatment strategies are highlighted. Then, guidelines for developing a treatment formulation for specifying tailored treatment are presented. Since tailored treatment should reflect cultural sensitivity, three types of culturally sensitive treatments are described. Finally, guidelines for selecting such treatments are presented.

Treatment Formulation

This section describes the elements of the treatment formulation with an emphasis on treatment focus and treatment strategy.

Elements of the Treatment Formulation

1. Treatment Goals

Treatment goals are specific outcomes clients expect to achieve in their treatment. Also called therapeutic objectives and treatment targets, treatment goals form the basis for the work a practitioner and the client do together. Clinically useful treatment goals are measurable, achievable, and realistic, and are effective to the extent they are mutually agreed upon and the client understands them, commits to them, and believes that they are attainable. Goals can be short term or long term. Typical short-term goals are symptom reduction, increased relational functioning, return to baseline functioning, and return to work. For example, the goals may be to reduce and eventually eliminate depressive symptoms or compulsive checking and counting behaviors. A common long-term goal is pattern change, including personality change. Long-term change that focuses on personality and pattern features is also called second-order change. In short, treatment goals are the stated outcome of treatment. In terms of the journey metaphor, treatment goals would represent the destination.

2. Treatment Focus

Treatment focus refers to the central therapeutic emphasis that provides directionality to treatment and aims at replacing a maladaptive pattern with a more adaptive pattern. Today, treatment focus is increasingly important as the directionality of treatment has shifted from the non-directive dictum of "follow the client's lead" to the accountability based dictum of "demonstrate positive treatment outcomes." "There is a convincing body of empirical evidence indicating that therapist ability to track a treatment focus consistently is associated with positive treatment outcomes" (Binder, 2004, p. 23). Treatment focus not only provides direction to treatment, but it also "serves as a stabilizing force in planning and practicing therapy in that it discourages a change of course with every shift in the wind" (Perry, Cooper, & Michels, 1987, p. 543). Unlike most trainees and many practitioners, highly competent and effective practitioners excel at establishing and maintaining a productive treatment focus.

In our integrative case conceptualization model, treatment focus is a key element. In the journey metaphor, treatment focus is represented by a map or Global Positioning System (GPS) directions of the best route or track. Establishing a treatment focus symbolizes "getting on track" while maintaining the treatment focus represents "staying on track." This treatment focus metaphor is clinically very useful because it reminds the practitioner to keep answering the question: "What is the best therapeutic direction to take right now?"

When working with a client's situation, the practitioner can take at least three different directions or tracks: (1) ask a string of factual questions in hopes of finding the "right" direction; (2) free-form it and go wherever the conversation leads – called "following the client's lead"; or (3) head toward the destination, i.e., the treatment goal. Trainees commonly take the first or second track or both, and seldom take the third track in which they therapeutically process the situation and effect change.

A common scenario for trainees is to get lost or sidetracked in an unproductive discussion with clients. For example, a client reports that she had intended to do the mutually agreed-upon homework assignment but ended up doing something else instead. The trainee then asks several factual questions about the circumstances. While collecting more data about the situation, the trainee has unwittingly colluded with the client's maladaptive pattern of making excuses instead of taking action. After running out of excuses, the client shifts to another topic and says she was really depressed (or anxious) yesterday after which the trainee proceeds again down the first or second track. Soon, the session comes to an end and no progress has been made and no change has been affected.

However, trainees and practitioners can take the third track. If they are guided by a specific therapeutic approach, the "direction" question has already been answered and specific guidelines given for how to therapeutically process a situation. For instance, in working with a client who has failed to do agreed-upon homework, the Cognitive-Behavioral approach is clear about directionality: focus on troublesome situations which are triggered or exacerbated by the client's maladaptive beliefs or behaviors. Here, the practitioner recalls from the case conceptualization that the client's core belief is that she is inadequate and worthless, and that one of her intermediate beliefs is that if she tries and fails, she will feel worthless, so she does not try. Thus, it is not a surprise that the client did not do the assignment and instead makes excuses. Informed by the case conceptualization, the practitioner can therapeutically process the maladaptive beliefs that were activated by the homework situation. The practitioner knew there was a treatment focus to follow. However, the practitioner still must decide whether or not to follow that directive.

Table 4.1 identifies the treatment focus directive for the five therapeutic approaches addressed in this book.

3. Treatment Strategy

Treatment strategy is the action plan for focusing specific interventions to achieve a more adaptive pattern. The plan involves relinquishing and replacing the maladaptive pattern with a more adaptive pattern, and then maintaining that pattern. In terms of the journey metaphor, treatment strategy represents selecting an appropriate route and a vehicle that can reach the destination in a safe and timely fashion. For example, selecting a town car or a sedan and taking an

Table 4.1 Treatment Focus in Five Therapeutic Approaches

Biopsychosocial	troublesome situations triggered or exacerbated by biological, psychological, and/or sociocultural vulnerability(ies)
Cognitive-Behavioral	troublesome situations triggered or exacerbated by maladaptive beliefs and/or behavior
Dynamic (Time-Limited)	troublesome interpersonal situations triggered by the cyclic maladaptive pattern
Adlerian	troublesome situations triggered or exacerbated by mistaken beliefs and/or discouragement
Acceptance and Commitment	to decrease persistent avoidance and psychological rigidity by exploring flexibility processes and expanding behavioral repertoire

interstate route is better suited for driving from New York to Los Angeles in three days than attempting that same journey with a motorcycle or a small sports car and taking county highways.

The most common treatment strategies are interpretation, cognitive restructuring, replacement, exposure, social skills training and psychoeducation, support, medication, and corrective experiences. Ordinarily, one or more of these treatment strategies is associated with a given therapeutic approach. For example, insight and corrective emotional experience are associated with the Dynamics approaches, while cognitive restructuring, exposure, and skill building are associated with the Cognitive Behavior approaches. However, some advocate that a range of treatment strategies can be utilized to achieve treatment goals. For instance, Binder (2004) indicates that treatment strategies associated with the Cognitive Behavior approaches might be useful and necessary in achieving treatment goals with some clients in Dynamic psychotherapy.

Interpretation. An interpretation is a hypothesis or guess about the connection between a client's thoughts, behaviors, or emotions and his or her unconscious emotions or thoughts. Interpretation can focus entirely on the present situation, called a dynamic interpretation, or it may suggest a link between the present and the past, called a genetic interpretation (Greenson, 1967). In either instance, the client can gain a new frame of reference and a deeper understanding of themselves and their lives. They go beyond the client's overt words and offer new meaning or explanation (Beitman & Yue, 1999). Insight is central to psychoanalytic psychotherapy and insight is achieved with the sequence: clarification → confrontation → interpretation → clarification → confrontation → interpretation, and so on. "Working through" is the process of repeating the sequence until the interpretation is accepted and internalized. Clearly, interpretation is central to this sequence. While interpretation is primarily associated with the Dynamics approaches, interpretations are also used in various other approaches including Jungian Therapy, Existential Therapy, Feminist Therapy, and Adlerian psychotherapy. While interpretation in the Dynamics approach suggests a causal connection between the past and the present, in the Adlerian view of interpretation the practitioner links the "past and present to indicate the continuity of the maladaptive life-style, not to demonstrate a causal connection" (Mosak, 2005, p. 74).

Cognitive restructuring. Cognitive restructuring is one of the basic cognitive strategies for helping clients identify, challenge, and modify maladaptive and distorted beliefs so they become more adaptive (Meichenbaum, 1977). Cognitive restructuring is often considered the first step when using Cognitive-Behavioral strategies. It assists clients in becoming aware of automatic thinking patterns and their influence on self and others; changing the way they process information and behavior; and learning to modify their beliefs about self, others, and the world. Various techniques are utilized in restructuring such beliefs, including guided discovery, Socratic questioning, examining the evidence, cognitive disputation, reattribution, i.e., modifying the attributional style, and cognitive rehearsal (Wright, Basco, & Thase, 2006).

Replacement. An alternative to restructuring maladaptive beliefs (and modifying maladaptive behaviors) is to replace maladaptive or unhelpful thoughts or interpretations and behaviors with more adaptive and helpful ones, i.e., thoughts and behaviors which are more likely to achieve the client's desired outcomes. Use of the replacement strategy is so common that most practitioners are unlikely to recognize using it. For example, with insufficient time in the session to process a new issue with cognitive disputation, a practitioner might say "The next time when no one is calling you to do something and you are starting to feel sorry for yourself and telling yourself that nobody cares about you, what could you do instead?" The practitioner is asking the client to come up with a replacement behavior ("I'll get on the phone and call Fred or Jack") and/or a replacement thought ("Because when I talk to them I'll realize that others really do care about me"). For many clients who are not responsive to cognitive restructuring interventions such as cognitive disputation, replacement can be an effective intervention. While it is the principal treatment strategy in Cognitive Behavior Analysis System of Psychotherapy (McCullough, 2000; McCullough, Schramm, & Penberthy, 2014), replacement is common across several therapeutic approaches, most notably in Cognitive Therapy, Solution-Focused Therapy, and Adlerian psychotherapy.

Exposure. Exposure is a treatment strategy that involves intentional and prolonged contact with a feared object combined with actively blocking undesirable avoidance behaviors. The exposure strategy involves the process of habituation. Habituation is a form of learning wherein an individual will stop responding or attending to a stimulus (e.g., thought, object, place, people, or action) as a result of repeated exposure. During exposure treatment, the client is confronted with a stimulus which has previously elicited an unwanted behavior or emotional response. Even though the client will experience increased anxiety in the short term, in the long term, repeated and incremental exposure to that feared stimulus in vivo (live) or in the client's imagination, anxiety and the avoidance response are extinguished because of the principle of habituation. A variety of exposure techniques can be employed including systematic desensitization, guided imagery, flooding, and implosion (Goldfried & Davison, 1994).

Support. This strategy assists clients to function better by providing safety, acceptance, and caring (Winston, Rosenthal, & Pinsker, 2004). The practitioner provides a supportive environment for clients to reflect on their life situation and feel safe and cared for while relieving symptoms or assists clients to live with them rather than attempting a personality or pattern change. It reinforces adaptive patterns of thoughts and behaviors in order to reduce stress and conflicts. This supportive relationship is critical in helping clients cope better, even if they cannot change the problems they are facing. It helps clients to cope with the challenges of daily life and is especially useful for dealing with long-term problems that are difficult to change. This strategy integrates psychodynamic, cognitive-behavioral, and interpersonal techniques, and is part of a therapeutic approach known as Supportive Therapy (Winston et al., 2004).

Psychoeducation and social skills training. Psychoeducation is a broad treatment strategy of educating and training individuals experiencing psychological disturbance to increase their knowledge, coping capacity, and skills required to solve their presenting problems. Skill deficits may be noted in areas such as assertiveness, problem-solving, communications, friendship skills, feeling identification and expression, empathy, negotiation, and conflict resolution (Goldfried & Davison, 1994). There are various means by which clients can be helped to learn new and more adaptive interpersonal skills patterns such as assertive communication. Skills training can occur in both individual and group therapeutic contexts and typically employs a mix of interventions including instruction, role playing, modeling, feedback, social reinforcement, and practice (Alberti, 1977; Goldfried & Davison, 1994). Common interventions utilizing the skills training strategy include assertiveness training, problem-solving training, and communication skills training.

Medication. Medication for psychiatric conditions is referred to as psychotropic medication. Psychotropic medication is a chemical substance that influences several brain functions including perception, pain, mood, consciousness, cognition, and behavior. Basically there are four classes of such medication: anxiolytics which target anxiety symptoms; antidepressants which primarily target depressed moods and secondarily anxiety and other symptoms; anti-manics which target mania; and antipsychotics which target psychotic symptoms. Used alone, such medication can effectively reduce symptoms but is seldom a cure. Because medications produce side effects and long-term usage can result in medical complications and conditions such as diabetes, heart disease, and obesity, medication monitoring is essential. The use of psychotropic medication is increasing largely because insurers and health maintenance organizations consider medication to be more cost-effective than psychotherapy alone. However, recent research indicates that the combination of medication and psychotherapy may be more cost-effective over the long run. For example, several studies have found that when antidepressant medication is used in conjunction with Cognitive Behavior Therapy (CBT), the combination is more effective than either strategy alone in the long-term treatment of depression (Arnow & Constantino, 2003). Psychotherapy can be provided by the prescriber or, more commonly, by a practitioner who works in collaboration with the prescriber.

Corrective emotional experience. The treatment strategy of corrective emotional experience is based on the assumption that insight alone is insufficient to effect a change in a client's behavior. Instead, true change is more likely to occur when insight is followed with a corrective experience. Corrective emotional experience involves re-exposing a client, under more favorable circumstances, to emotional situations which she could not handle in the past (Alexander & French, 1946). Historically, corrective emotional experience referred specifically to the positive effects of experiencing the discrepancy between how clients expected a practitioner to react to them regarding an important life issue or event, e.g., critical, and how the practitioner actually responded to them about the issue or event, e.g., supportive. Today, corrective experience has a more general meaning. It refers to all aspects of the therapeutic process that allow clients to experience an unexpected form of relational interaction than can help in healing a previously maladaptive pattern. Practitioners can employ one or both of these understandings of the corrective emotional experience in therapy, i.e., they can foster a corrective experience by actively processing clients' specific relational expectations or, in a more general way, they can foster a caring, positive therapeutic alliance (Levenson, 1995). The value of this more general understanding should not be underestimated. Experiencing a practitioner's caring, empathy, concern, and unconditional acceptance may be the first and most important corrective emotional experience in the lives of many clients. This experience can continue to occur throughout the therapeutic process as practitioners respond to their clients in a manner that is respectful, accepting, and caring; often the opposite of their own parents or parental figures. Furthermore, corrective emotional experiences can occur outside therapy as clients begin to discover that, because of their corrective experiences with their practitioners, others respond to them differently than in the past. In short, the genuine relationship between clients and practitioners, and its constancy, often serve as an ongoing corrective emotional experience which can generalize to others.

4. Treatment Interventions

A treatment intervention is a therapeutic action designed to positively impact a client's issue or problem. Treatment interventions are selected based on the treatment targets and the willingness and capacity of the client to proceed with the intervention. While there are hundreds of treatment interventions, effective treatment outcomes involving pattern change require the selection of interventions that operationalize the treatment strategy. With regard to the journey metaphor, treatment interventions represent trip provisions such as the right grade of fuel; tires that are appropriate for the terrain; and sufficient food, water, and money.

5. Treatment Obstacles and Challenges

There are many obstacles and challenges to treatment. Such obstacles may originate from the client, practitioner, client–practitioner, or factors in the treatment process itself. A full discussion of these factors is beyond the scope of this chapter; the interested reader can consult chapters 4 through 7 of Sperry (2010). Anticipating obstacles and challenges to the implementation of the treatment plan is indispensable in achieving treatment success. The test of an effective case conceptualization is its viability in predicting the obstacles and challenges throughout the stages of therapy, particularly those involving resistance, ambivalence, transference enactments, and issues that complicate maintaining treatment gains and preparing for termination (Sperry, 2010).

Knowledge of the client's personality style and maladaptive pattern is invaluable in anticipating obstacles. For example, a client with dependent and avoidant features can be anticipated to have difficulty discussing personal matters and "test" and provoke practitioners into criticizing them for changing or canceling appointments or being late. It is likely that the client will procrastinate, avoid feelings, and otherwise "test" the practitioner's trustability. However, once trust is achieved, the client is likely to cling to the practitioner, making termination difficult unless their social support system is increased. In terms of the journey metaphor, treatment obstacles and challenges are represented as anticipated route closures, detours, accidents, weather, and terrain. In contrast, clients with a passive-aggressive pattern or a high level of reactance might demonstrate ambivalence or resistance when certain expectations are communicated. Also considered would be the client's early relational conflict or trauma and the likelihood that transference enactments will occur. Clients who have never experienced success in making small personal changes suggest failure-proneness, which will likely be operative in therapy, unless these failure-prone dynamics are directly addressed. Furthermore, clients who have difficulty saying goodbye or have experienced unexpected loss of significant others will likely find termination most difficult.

6. Treatment-Cultural

Informed by the cultural formulation, the practitioner can decide whether cultural factors are operative and whether culturally sensitive treatment is indicated. If culturally sensitive treatment is indicated, the practitioner must then select among cultural intervention, Culturally Sensitive Therapy, or culturally sensitive interventions and then plan how these interventions can be incorporated with other interventions specified in the treatment plan. A subsequent section of this chapter discusses guidelines for incorporating culturally sensitive treatments.

7. Treatment Prognosis

Treatment prognosis is a prediction of the likely course, duration, severity, and outcome of a condition or disorder with or without treatment. A prognosis can be given before treatment begins, to allow the client the opportunity to weigh the benefits of different treatment options. Some practitioners also offer a prognosis based on whether anticipated treatment obstacles and challenges are surmounted. Prognoses range from excellent, good, fair, guarded, to poor.

In terms of the journey metaphor, the prognosis is the likelihood of safe arrival at a destination within the anticipated timeframe.

Table 4.2 summarizes these seven elements.

Relationship of Treatment Formulation Elements

These seven elements may initially appear to be discrete entities in the treatment process. The reality is that they are closely related. To the extent that they are perceived as disconnected and unrelated, a treatment plan of the treatment formulation will reflect this view. An objective third party who reviews a trainee's or a practitioner's treatment formulation with such a disconnected view is likely to find disconnects in the treatment plan of the treatment formulation. There may be a disconnect between the treatment goals and the diagnosis and diagnostic formulation, or there may be a disconnect between what was an otherwise coherent and reasonably compelling clinical formulation and the treatment focus and strategy. Probably, the most common disconnect is between the treatment pattern and the treatment goals and interventions. While a rather standard treatment goal for a

Table 4.2 Elements of a Treatment Formulation

Treatment pattern	flexible, effective manner of perceiving, thinking, acting
Treatment goals	the stated short- and long-term outcomes of treatment
Treatment focus	the central therapeutic emphasis providing directionality to treatment that is keyed to a more adaptive pattern
Treatment strategy	the action plan and vehicle for achieving a more adaptive pattern
Treatment interventions	specific change techniques and tactics related to the treatment strategy for achieving treatment goals and pattern change
Treatment obstacles	predictable challenges in the treatment process anticipated from the maladaptive pattern
Treatment-cultural	the incorporation of cultural intervention, Culturally Sensitive Therapy, or interventions when indicated
Treatment prognosis	a prediction of the likely course, duration, and outcome of a mental health condition with or without treatment

client with a diagnosis of depression may be reducing depressive symptoms is listed and matched with treatment interventions of medication referral and behavioral activation, the treatment goal and interventions may have little or nothing to do with achieving the adaptive treatment pattern.

To the extent that these treatment formulation elements are understood as interrelated, and this is reflected in the specifics of the treatment plan, there is increased likelihood that tailored treatment will be planned and implemented. Figure 4.1 visually depicts relationships among these elements.

Adaptive Patterns, Pattern Change, and Orders of Change

Pattern change involves three steps. The first step involves modifying the client's maladaptive pattern by first reducing its intensity and frequency, and the second step involves developing more adaptive patterns and increasing their intensity and frequency. The third step is maintaining the adaptive pattern (Beitman & Yue, 1999).

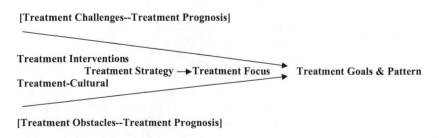

[Treatment Challenges--Treatment Prognosis]

Treatment Interventions
        Treatment Strategy →Treatment Focus   Treatment Goals & Pattern
Treatment-Cultural

[Treatment Obstacles--Treatment Prognosis]

Figure 4.1 Relationship of Treatment Formulation Elements

It can be clinically useful for trainees to conceptualize the change process in terms of orders of change. While originating in the family therapy literature, similar orders of change are being described in the psychotherapy literature (Fraser & Solovey, 2007). The basic assertion of this perspective is that when therapy is effective, a transformation of current efforts is needed to effect change in contrast to therapy that produces stability. For example, an unemployed client with a diagnosis of social anxiety disorder might take medication that effectively reduces his anxiety symptoms but does not replace his maladaptive pattern of fearfulness and avoidance. Thus, he might fill out a job application online, but out of fear decides he cannot tolerate the prospect of a job interview when it is offered. If medication reduces his symptoms, a degree of stability has been achieved. This represents first-order change. However, if the client is helped by the practitioner to learn to face his fears and avoidance behavior directly so that he can be interviewed, offered, and start the job, a more adaptive pattern is achieved. These actions that reflect a more adaptive pattern represent second-order change. If this same client is able to disengage from excessive fearful and anxious feelings without the assistance of a practitioner, he has achieved third-order change. This represents the ultimate goal of therapy wherein client's function "as their own therapists."

In our own clinical and supervisory experience, we can add another order of change. Zero order of change, if we can call it that, represents situations when no change is affected for any number of reasons. This situation is particularly common when trainees, often to reduce their own anxiety about how to proceed, employ the tactic of continually asking factually oriented questions rather than processing the client's issues or adequately engaging the client. Unfortunately, the unspoken message of this tactic is that "I don't know what to do and I don't expect you will get better." Or, practitioners are unable to establish and maintain a treatment focus, and mutually engage the client in the change process. The result is that clients may continue to experience symptoms, become demoralized about their situation ever improving, or not improve because they may not want to face the responsibilities that come with getting better, such as finding a job, returning to work, or making a relationship work. Table 4.3 summarizes the orders of change.

Table 4.3 Four Orders of Change in Treatment

Order	Description
Zero	no change effected and may negatively impact the treatment process
First	assist clients to make a small change or reduce symptoms or achieve stability
Second	assist clients to alter their pattern
Third	clients learn to recognize and change patterns on their own; "become their own therapists"

Readiness to Change and Treatment Planning and Formulation

Prochaska, DiClementi, and Norcross (1992) found that individuals who change their behaviors, on their own or with a counselor's help, typically proceed through five stages of change. The stages are: precontemplation, contemplation, preparation, action, and maintenance. Movement through these stages is not necessarily a linear process, rather clients may vacillate between various stages throughout treatment. Relapse is common among various psychological conditions. This model is quite useful in understanding and predicting client change across a wide array of client concerns in counseling as well as in the treatment formulation process.

A preliminary assessment of readiness for change can be extremely valuable and useful in treatment planning. Since most clients cycle in and out of these stages several times before achieving their goals, it is helpful to gauge the current stage during the initial session, and to monitor movement within these stages. Ideally, the client enters therapy at the preparation or action stage, which means that treatment outcomes will be predictably positive. When the client enters at the precontemplative or contemplative stage, the counselor's primary task is to tailor treatment in order to move the client toward the action stage while still finding the balance between the client's own self-determination and their overall well-being.

Readiness is typically assessed through observation or ongoing assessment. Asking a client, "On a scale of 1-to-10, how motivated are you feeling about working towards this particular goal?" can be a simple scaling question used to examine the client's readiness and motivation to engage in the counseling process. Markers, by stage, to elicit or observe when assessing readiness include:

Precontemplation	The client does not consider his or her behavior to be a problem and does not currently consider making any change.
Contemplation	The client considers that his or her behavior may be a problem but they do not commit to any change.
Preparation	The client has made a commitment to change a behavior considered problematic and intends to make the change in the near future. The client may have identified steps toward change in this stage.
Action	The client is actively making changes and is not returning to pre-treatment behavior/thought patterns.
Maintenance	The client has maintained change for over six months. (Prochaska et al., 1992)

After evaluating hundreds of treatment formulations since the first edition of this book, it is clear to us that many experienced therapists do not consider the client's readiness to change when considering treatment formulation and planning. This is a very simple factor to overlook, so we strongly urge readers to clearly assess the client's readiness to change and reflect the treatment formulation accordingly. In the cases where a client remains in the precontemplation stage of change in the first three therapy sessions, practitioners can continue to focus efforts on building a relationship with the client, using empathic responding skills and utilizing motivational interviewing or related strategies, until the client commits to treatment change and actively collaborates in setting treatment goals.

Guidelines for Developing a Treatment Formulation

The following are some guidelines for developing a treatment formulation and a treatment formulation statement.

1. **Review the diagnostic and clinical formulations noting the operative pattern, and consider severity and acuity regarding the treatment mode, as well as the client's treatment expectations, level of readiness and engagement, etc.**

   The first decision involves choosing an initial treatment mode: inpatient, intensive outpatient, partial hospitalization, residential, or outpatient treatment. If there is any indication of self-harm or harm to others, this must be addressed immediately. Then, proceed to review any biological aspects in any of the factors, including the predisposing factors. For instance, if caffeine, nicotine, or other xanthine use seem to be triggering or exacerbating the client's condition and symptoms, reduce or remove them. If a medical evaluation or a medication evaluation is indicated, consider making an appropriate referral and/or arrangements for collaboration. Evaluate the extent to which social–environmental predisposing factors are operative that are beyond the ken of therapeutic influence and consider options. If relational or family factors are operative, consider couples or family consultation or therapy. If the client's treatment expectations are potentially problematic or readiness is not at the action stage, address these and other related matters.

2. **If there is a situational pattern, meaning that there is no ongoing maladaptive pattern, consider addressing *presentation* and *precipitating* factors as the initial mode of treatment.**

   It may well be that symptomatic distress, suicidal ideation, conflict resolution, or other presentations might be directly reversed by eliminating the precipitating stressor or trigger. When this is not possible or sufficiently effective, response prevention techniques might reduce or stop the *presentation*, be it symptom, conflict, or impaired functioning. Presumably, resolution will occur. If, however there is a reoccurrence, it may suggest that there is an ongoing maladaptive pattern which was not identified. If so, proceed to the third guideline.

3. **If an ongoing maladaptive pattern is operative, specify treatment targets which reflect treatment goals and specify a treatment focus.**

   Specifying treatment targets related to operative *predisposing* and *perpetuating* factors is a common way of proceeding in therapy, perhaps in most therapies when there is no immediate change from eliminating triggers or when blocking responses is not sustainable. Thus, decisions about selecting support, interpretation, cognitive restructuring, or exposure strategies are typically based on client receptivity and capacity to respond to an intervention in addition to considerations such as client resources, need, dynamics, explanatory model, and expectations.

The *treatment focus* serves as a guide or an action plan for the practitioner to achieve the treatment goal. Typically, it is based on a conceptual map informed by the practitioner's theoretical orientation. For example, in interpersonally oriented dynamic therapies the focus is usually the client's maladaptive interpersonal style or pattern, while in Cognitive-Behavioral therapies the focus is usually on maladaptive thinking and behaviors.

4. **Consider how interventions might be tailored and sequenced.**

Decisions about tailoring and sequencing are important and cannot be left to chance. Accordingly, consider how factors such as severity, level of functioning, level of acculturation, skill sets, and personality dynamics could foster or impede specific interventions. Also, consider client expectations. Decisions about sequencing are based on several factors such as access to specific treatment resources, success in achieving a particular treatment goal, or situation-specific considerations. For example, if the *pattern* is determined to be situation specific, begin by addressing *precipitating* factors, and only consider other factors if there is little or no response.

5. **Anticipate potential obstacles and challenges to treatment**

Review the client's story – including the developmental and social history – looking for potential obstacles specifically related to the therapeutic alliance, personality dynamics, or the stage of therapy, and, in general, to treatment progress. Typically, these will involve resistances, ambivalence, transference enactments, and alliance ruptures, but they could include predictions of difficulty with certain treatment modalities or even termination. Knowledge of such potential obstacles allows the practitioner time to plan how these challenges will be met, if and when they arise.

6. **Write an integrative treatment formulation statement**

This statement incorporates the psychological and social treatment goals and interventions, and the biological goals and interventions, if applicable.

Culturally Sensitive Treatments

Three types of culturally sensitive treatment are described in this section. Thereafter, guidelines for determining when and if to incorporate such treatments are provided.

1. Cultural Intervention: An intervention or healing method or activity that is consistent with the client's belief system regarding healing and potentially useful in effecting a specified change. Some examples are: healing circles, prayer or exorcism, and involvement of traditional healers from that client's culture. Sometimes, the use of cultural interventions necessitates collaboration with or referral to such a healer or other expert (Paniagua, 2005). Still, a practitioner can begin the treatment process by focusing on core cultural values, such as *respito* and *personalismo*, in an effort to increase the "clinician's achieved credibility," i.e., the client's perception that the practitioner is trustworthy and effective.

2. Culturally Sensitive Therapy: Culturally Sensitive Therapy is a psychotherapeutic intervention that directly addresses the cultural characteristics of diverse clients, i.e., beliefs, customs, attitudes, and their socioeconomic and historical context (La Roche & Christopher, 2008). Because they utilize traditional healing methods and pathways, such approaches are appealing to certain clients. For example, Cuento Therapy addresses culturally relevant variables such as *familismo* and *personalismo* through the use of folk tales (*cuentos*) and is used with Puerto Rican children (Costantino, Malgady, & Rogler, 1986). Likewise, Morita Therapy which originated in Japan and is now used throughout the world for a wide range of disorders, from shyness to schizophrenia (Li & He, 2008). These kinds of therapy appear to be particularly effective in clients with lower levels of acculturation.

3. Culturally Sensitive Intervention: A Western psychotherapeutic intervention that has been adapted or modified to be responsive to the cultural characteristics of a particular client. Because of their structured and educational focus, Cognitive Behavior Therapy interventions are acceptable to many cultures and are the most often modified to be culturally sensitive (Hays & Iwanasa, 2006). For example, particularly in culturally diverse clients with lower levels of acculturation, disputation and cognitive restructuring of a maladaptive belief are seldom the CBT intervention of choice, whereas problem-solving, skills training, or cognitive replacement interventions (Sperry, 2010) may be more appropriate.

Guidelines for Selecting Culturally Sensitive Treatments

The following are four guidelines for deciding if culturally sensitive treatments are indicated. The guidelines assume that the client's cultural identity, level of acculturation, explanatory model, and treatment expectations have been elicited and that a cultural formulation was developed.

1. If a client identifies (cultural identity) primarily with the mainstream culture and has a high level of acculturation and there is *no* obvious indication of prejudice, racism, or related bias, consider conventional interventions as the primary treatment method. However, the practitioner should be aware that a culturally sensitive treatment may (also) be indicated as the treatment process develops.
2. If a client identifies largely with the mainstream culture and has a high level of acculturation and there *is* an indication of prejudice, racism, or related bias, consider culturally sensitive interventions or cultural interventions for cultural aspects of the client's concern. In addition, it may be useful to utilize conventional interventions for related non-cultural concerns, i.e., personality dynamics.
3. If a client identifies largely with their ethnic background and their level of acculturation is low, consider cultural interventions or Culturally Sensitive

Therapy. This may necessitate collaboration with or referral to an expert and/or an initial discussion of core cultural values.

4. If a client's cultural identity is mainstream and their acculturation level is high, but that of their family is low, such that the presenting concern is largely a matter of cultural discrepancy, consider a cultural intervention with the client and the family. However, if there is an imminent crisis situation, consider conventional interventions to reduce the crisis. After it has been reduced or eliminated, consider introducing cultural interventions or Culturally Sensitive Therapy.

Illustration of the Treatment Formulation

The elements of Geri's treatment formulation are summarized in Table 4.4. The reader will note that the adaptive pattern element is also included since it is central to constructing the treatment formulation.

Concluding Comment

Most mental health professionals consider the treatment formulation of the case conceptualization to be the most important component. After all, the actual clinical value of a case conceptualization is whether the treatment plan is sufficiently directed and focused to achieve the expected change and result in positive treatment outcomes. This chapter ends the theoretical and research-based discussion of case conceptualization and its components. In the remaining chapters (Chapters 6 through 10), the emphasis shifts to the application of theory to practice, and the learning of case conceptualization competencies.

TREATMENT FORMULATION ACTIVITY

Watch a counseling video for approximately five minutes. Stop the recording and attempt to answer the following questions:

1. What techniques and counseling skills was the practitioner utilizing?
2. Why did they select those specific techniques/skills? What was their intention?
3. If you are aware of the theoretical orientation, did the practitioner use skills that were outside of their declared theoretical orientation?

   Note: All the questions and techniques used stem from the overarching treatment focus. For example, Aaron Beck (Cognitive Therapy) asks questions about thoughts and the impact of those thoughts on a person's emotions, while Carl Rogers (Person-Centered Therapy) engaged clients through the use of reflections, empathy, and therapeutic presence. This activity is designed to highlight the intentionality of specific counseling interventions within a particular treatment focus.

Table 4.4 Treatment Formulation Element in the Case of Geri

Pattern-adaptive	Connect while feeling safe	
Treatment goals	Targets	Interventions
	a. reduce symptoms	a. medication monitoring (physician); individual therapy
	b. reduce avoidant pattern	b. individual therapy (replacement strategy)
	c. enhance social network on and off the job	c. collaborate with work supervisor; skill-oriented group therapy
	d. increase IP skills/trust	d. skill-oriented group therapy; assertive communication and friendship skills
Treatment focus	increase connectedness and decrease avoidant pattern	
Therapeutic strategy & interventions	support; replacement; skills training (interventions noted above)	
Treatment obstacles	*ambivalence*: anticipate: – procrastination, feeling avoidance, "testing" practitioner's trustability – clinging to practitioner after trust is achieved – likely resistance to group interventions because of avoidant style – difficulty with termination *transference–countertransference enactment:* "impatience" and "criticalness" → transference dynamics	
Treatment-cultural	gender may be an issue so assign supportive female practitioners; gender roles from her family of origin should be examined	
Treatment prognosis	good, provided she can increase relational skills and social contacts, and return to work	

CHAPTER 4 QUESTIONS

1. In developing a comprehensive treatment formulation, Table 4.1 highlights these elements. Describe their importance to the overall treatment focus.
2. Discuss the importance of understanding the four orders of change in treatment from Table 4.3 and how this relates back to the three steps of pattern change in a comprehensive treatment plan.
3. Explain how to modify a treatment formulation and statement based on the guidelines presented in this chapter. What are some of the more common adjustments that might need to be made?
4. Describe the three types of culturally sensitive treatments. Name a few appropriate to specific cultures, and which is used more broadly and why.
5. When is it appropriate to incorporate culturally sensitive treatment? Provide some specific examples.

References

Alberti, R. (1977). *Assertiveness: Innovations, applications, and issues*. San Luis Obispo, CA: Impact Publications.

Alexander, F., & French, T. (1946). *Psychoanalytic therapy: Principles and applications*. New York, NY: Ronald Press.

Arnow, B., & Constantino, M. (2003). Effectiveness of psychotherapy and combination treatment for chronic depression. *Journal of Clinical Psychology, 59*(8), 893–905.

Beitman, B., & Yue, D. (1999). *Learning psychotherapy*. New York, NY: Norton.

Binder, J.L. (2004). *Key competencies in brief dynamic psychotherapy: Clinical practice beyond the manual*. New York, NY: Guilford Press.

Costantino, G., Malgady, R., & Rogler, L. (1986). Cuento therapy: A culturally sensitive modality for Puerto Rican children. *Journal of Consulting and Clinical Psychology, 54*(5), 639–645.

Fraser, S., & Solovey, A. (2007). *Second order change in psychotherapy*. Washington, DC: American Psychological Association.

Goldfried, M., & Davison, G. (1994). *Clinical behavior therapy* (expanded edition). New York, NY: Wiley.

Greenson, R. (1967). *The technique and practice of psychoanalysis* (Vol. 1). New York, NY: International Universities Press.

Hays, P., & Iwanasa, G. (Eds.). (2006). *Culturally responsive cognitive-behavioral therapy: Assessment, practice, and supervision*. Washington, DC: American Psychological Association.

La Roche, M., & Christopher, M. (2008). Culture and empirically supported treatments: On the road to a collision? *Culture and Psychology, 14*(3), 333–356.

Levenson, H. (1995). *Time-limited dynamic psychotherapy: A guide to clinical practice*. New York, NY: Basic Books.

Li, C., & He, Y. (2008). Morita therapy for schizophrenia. *Schizophrenia Bulletin, 34*(6), 1021–1023.

McCullough, J. (2000). *Treatment for chronic depression: Cognitive behavioral analysis system of psychotherapy*. New York, NY: Guilford.

McCullough, J., Schramm, E., & Penberthy, K. (2014). *CBASP as a distinctive treatment for persistent depressive disorder: Distinctive features.* New York, NY: Routledge.

Meichenbaum, D. (1977). *Cognitive behavior modification: An integrative approach.* New York, NY: Plenum.

Mosak, H. (2005). Adlerian psychotherapy. In R. Corsini & D. Edding (Eds.), *Current psychotherapies* (7th ed., pp. 52–95). Belmont, CA: Brooks/Cole-Thomson.

Paniagua, F. (2005). *Assessing and treating culturally diverse clients: A practical guide.* Thousand Oaks, CA: Sage.

Perry, S., Cooper, A., & Michels, R. (1987). The psychodynamic formulation: Its purpose, structure, and clinical application. *The American Journal of Psychiatry, 144*(5), 543–551.

Prochaska, J.O., DiClemente, C.C., & Norcross, J.C. (1992). In search of how people change: Applications to the addictive behaviors. *American Psychologist, 47*, 1102–1114. PMID: 1329589.

Sperry, L. (2010). *Core competencies in counseling and psychotherapy: Becoming a highly competent and effective therapist.* New York, NY: Routledge.

Winston, A., Rosenthal, R., & Pinsker, H. (2004). *Introduction to supportive psychotherapy.* Washington, DC: American Psychiatric Press.

Wright, J., Basco, M., & Thase, M. (2006). *Learning cognitive-behavior therapy: An illustrated guide.* Washington, DC: American Psychiatric Press.

5   Case Conceptualizations
Individual, Couple, and Family

For most clinicians, case conceptualization means formulating a case for a specific client, i.e., an individual case conceptualization. While individual case conceptualizations are useful, they provide only a partial formulation when clinicians work with a couple or a family or when the individual client's concerns reflect relational dynamics. Therefore, the ability to identify and incorporate such couple and family dynamics in the case conceptualization is essential. Even if an individual partner or parent is engaged in individual therapy and the focus is on his or her individual maladaptive pattern, therapists who can also identify relational and family interaction patterns are most likely to achieve optimal treatment outcomes with that client.

Accordingly, this chapter briefly describes two additional forms of case conceptualization: couple case conceptualization and family case conceptualization. Since pattern is the basis for case conceptualization, all three types of case conceptualizations are described in terms of their underlying patterns. A clinical example illustrates these three case conceptualizations.

Patterns in Individuals, Couples, and Families

Just as the case conceptualization is considered the heart of evidence-based practice, a basic premise of this book is that pattern is the basis for case conceptualization irrespective of whether the client is an individual, a couple, or a family. Just as the maladaptive pattern is essential in understanding an individual client and planning and implementing treatment, with couples, each partner's behavior reflects both their personal maladaptive pattern and their relational interaction pattern. Similarly, each family member's behavior reflects both their personal pattern and the family interaction pattern.

Individual (Partner) Patterns

Individuals run the risk of bringing their maladaptive patterns and problems into their everyday lives, particularly their couple and family relationships. Not surprisingly, the maladaptive pattern of a partner or parent can and often does impact the other partner and other family members. Typically, the pattern of each partner is complementary and accounts for much of their initial attraction to each other, and these individual patterns influence both relational and family interaction patterns. As noted at the outset of this chapter, therapists who provide individual therapy would do well to identify the individual's pattern as well as the influence of their relational pattern and family pattern in order to optimize treatment outcomes.

Students and clinicians whom we have taught and supervised find it convenient and clinically valuable to frame individual patterns in terms of personality styles, i.e., movement and purpose. The following 11 personality styles styles – of which 10 are related *Diagnostic and Statistical Manual of Mental Disorders, Fifth Edition (DSM-5)* personality disorders. It should be noted that the passive aggressive personality disorder no longer appears in the current DSM yet is common in clinical practice. These 11 styles/disorders seem to encompass most individual patterns.

Histrionic	maladaptive pattern in which the individual actively moves toward others to get attention but pays a high price or becomes compromised
Dependent	maladaptive pattern in which the individual passively moves toward others to enlist their help by pleasing and meeting their needs, but not meeting their own sufficiently
Narcissistic	maladaptive pattern in which the individual moves against others to get special treatment by elevating themselves while using or belittling others
Paranoid	maladaptive pattern in which the individual actively moves against others by anticipating harm and retaliating, believing that they will be harmed by others
Antisocial	maladaptive pattern in which the individual actively moves against others to harm them and protect themselves; they are not law-abiding but live by their own internal code
Avoidant	maladaptive pattern in which the individual passively moves away from others to avoid harm and feel safe, while isolating from and avoiding others
Schizoid	maladaptive pattern in which the individual actively moves away from others to avoid involvement with them; they have limited need for companionship
Schizotypal	maladaptive pattern in which the individual actively moves away from others by acting differently, being indifferent to social convention and wary of unfamiliar people
Obsessive compulsive	maladaptive pattern in which the individual moves actively but ambivalently toward self and others, being over conscientious and perfectionistic while emotionally distant
Passive	maladaptive pattern in which the individual moves passively but ambivalently toward aggressive others but resists their demands; will say they will do something, but will not do it
Borderline	maladaptive pattern is a decompensated version of the dependent, passive-aggressive, or histrionic style with intense/unstable personal and relational behavior under stress

Relational Interaction Patterns

Each partner plays a role in the relationship, as each displays one or two habitual and cyclical patterns of relating that each has learned over time in order to cope. In the couples therapy literature, these patterns are referred to as couples interaction patterns or relational patterns. None of the negative patterns described below results in both partners growing and thriving. At best, they allow the relationship to survive, at least for a while. Presumably, couples therapy can break and replace these patterns with more adaptive ones. The following section provides brief descriptions of five of the most common negative relational patterns and one positive pattern. Given that each partner assumes a role in the relationship, each typically displays one or two cyclical patterns, habitually. These patterns have been learned over time in order to cope. These patterns are referred to as interaction or relational patterns in the couples therapy literature. Of the negative patterns described below, none results in both partners growing and thriving. The best possible outcome for these patterns is that the relationship survives. Couples therapy presumes to interrupt and replace these patterns with more adaptive patterns. In the following section, a brief description will be provided for the four most common negative relational patterns. Additionally, one positive pattern will be described.

Demand/Withdraw

This pattern includes behaviors that demonstrate blaming, accruing, criticizing, or demanding [demand] change from the other partner. The result from the other partner is characterized by giving in, deferring, surrendering, or complying [submit] (Christensen & Shenk, 1991). Other designations that describe these patterns are pursuer-distancer, engulfment-abandonment, closeness-distance, or affiliation-independence (Christensen & Shenk, 1991). This type of pattern is the most common and the most researched pattern among couples. Some indications of this pattern are: partner aggression and hostility, negative emotion, dissatisfaction in the relationship, and divorce. The demand/withdraw pattern has recently been researched as a predictor of depression (Knobloch-Fedders et al., 2014; Holley, Haase, Chui, & Bloch, 2018). The following negative relational patterns are its variants.

Demand/Submit

This type of pattern surfaces when one partner criticizes, blames, or demands [demand] change from the other partner. The other partner's response is to avoid, become defensive, fail to respond, or refuse to discuss the issue [submit]. Although it has not received as much research as the demand/withdraw pattern, this is a common interaction pattern.

Withdraw/Withdraw

This pattern is a typical result of exhaustion caused by the demand/withdraw pattern. Both partners begin to withdraw in the face of conflict because they are hesitant to engage emotionally. When hopelessness seeps in, they begin to give up. Additionally, the pursuer in these cases may be a "soft" pursuer, who despite strong anxious energy does not show their levels of overload. Therefore, despite being a pursuer, they give up easily. On the other hand, a "burnt out" pursuer is typically a result of a partner who has given up trying to reach out to the other partner. Withdrawal can then indicate the beginning of the process of grieving and detaching in a relationship.

Attack/Attack

This pattern occurs when an attack is met with an attack. Therefore, it is no surprise that it includes escalation of discord in the relationship. In this pattern, also a variant of the demand/withdraw pattern, the withdrawer is likely to fall back on withdrawing following the escalation. That is, until that partner feels sufficiently provoked once again. Another common designation for a couple with this pattern is the "high conflict couple" (Fruzzetti, 2006).

Reactive Demand/Withdraw

Usually, this pattern is born out of a reversal in a previous long-standing pattern. This occurs when there is a change in the role of one of the partners. For instance, a husband who is demanding [demand] surrenders and begins to limit his relationship investment. He may begin to distance and withdraw himself [withdraw]. With a withdrawing partner, the other partner may at first fail to notice the change, which will typically prompt an interruption in the relationship or incite a breakup or divorce. As a result, the initially withdrawing partner assumes a role of pursuer and begins to demand a fix. This can push the withdrawing partner even further. Essentially, this pattern is a modification and response of a long-standing pattern.

Constructive Engagement

This pattern is characterized by the ability of both partners to express issues in a "non-attacking way that accurately reflects what they feel, think, or want, including accurate expression of primary emotions. The other partner listens, brings curiosity, tries to understand, and communicates understanding, even if he or she disagrees" (Fruzzetti & Payne, 2015, p. 609). The result of this pattern is both the ability to problem solve and foster mutual validation. However, this pattern requires awareness of emotions and the ability to communicate and regulate emotions in both partners.

Other Ways of Characterizing Couple Interaction

Based on her extensive clinical experience with couples, Susan Johnson (2008) described three negative patterns of communication that keep couples stuck. These three types of communication are referred to as the "Demon Dialogues," in a book meant to serve as a tool for couples undergoing couples therapy. Each of the "Demon Dialogues" denotes a pattern of communication that is a roadblock to relating healthily to one another. She noted that they surface when couples are incapable of connecting with each other. The dialogues match the withdraw/withdraw, demand/withdraw, and attack/attack patterns (Johnson, 2008).

On the other hand, based on his extensive research with couples, John Gottman (2014) developed a different method for categorizing relationships. He developed a typology based on relational behavior, rather than specifying the cyclical relational patterns. The five types specified are: Conflict-Avoiding, Volatile, Hostile, Hostile-Detached, and Validating (Gottman, 2014). While the first four types are negative, the Validating type is positive and results in satisfaction and growth in the relationship.

Whether adaptive or maladaptive, relational patterns are typically learned by each individual partner through modeling prior to meeting. These patterns are typically reflected in the parents of each individual and they can be a component of the attraction process for the couple. These patterns are born out of the patterns of personality for each partner. Explaining the couples' relationship and how these factors operate are the functions of an effective case conceptualization. The maladaptive patterns that the individuals demonstrate can be reflected in all aspects of the relationship: type of communication, intimacy and sex, problem-solving and conflict resolution, and others. It logically follows that relational patterns can predict relationship outcomes.

Regrettably, to couples, these patterns can make it seem that the situation they are in is hopeless, even while their differences may be marginal. This is exacerbated by the polarizing nature of the maladaptive patterns. This can make partners perceive each other as standing on opposite sides of a spectrum. On the other hand, maladaptive patterns can serve as safeguards and insulators, preventing partners from reaching closeness or intimacy.

Family Interaction Patterns

Similar to individual case conceptualizations, family case conceptualizations focus "on the unique contexts, needs, and resources of the individual family members and the system as a whole" (Bitter, 2009, p. 374). Therefore, the relational interactions of the family must be described. The value in conceptualizing the relational patterns in families has been demonstrated over the past 40 years in both research and clinical experience with the Beavers Systems Model of Family Functioning (Beavers, 1981; Hampson & Beavers, 2012).

Two main dimensions – family competence and style – are used to conceptualize families in the Beavers Systems Model of Family Functioning. The competence dimension ranges from optimal to severely dysfunctional (optimal, adequate, midrange, borderline, severely dysfunctional). On the other hand, in lower-functioning families, style dimensions range from centripetal (internalizing and clinging) to centrifugal (demanding, attacking, externalizing). Combined, these two dimensions result in nine family types. Of these, the last six types are sufficiently problematic to warrant clinical intervention.

1. **Optimal Families**

   These families are characterized by highly effective relational functioning. As such, members of the family are aware of their influence and effect on others. Using a multitude of approaches, they are able to solve their problems easily. They also seek and achieve intimacy. Boundaries between family members are respected, and the parents are able to share power flexibly. When conflict surfaces, it tends to be immediately addressed and quickly resolved.

2. **Adequate Families**

   These families are characterized by moderately effective relational functioning. The parents can often struggle for power. They also exhibit diminished ability for achieving intimacy and trust. They are also less happy and spontaneous. The family members may experience some distress, pain, and loneliness. However, they are typically capable of sufficiently coping.

3. **Midrange Centripetal Families**

   These families are characterized by somewhat impaired relational functioning. Direct control and hostility are employed, but they are able to express caring. There is a lack of spontaneity, while authority and rules are accentuated. They work hard, pay their bills, develop transference, and keep their struggles hidden from their neighbors.

4. **Midrange Centrifugal Families**

   These families are characterized by somewhat impaired relational functioning. Indirect control, manipulation, blame, and intimidation are often used while seldomly expressing warmth or care. Family members develop contempt for authority both within and outside the constraints of the family. Typically, the parents spend minimal time at home and, earlier than the norm, the children transition onto the streets and into communities.

5. **Midrange Mixed Families**

   These families are characterized by somewhat impaired relational functioning. They exhibit alternating patterns of centripetal and centrifugal behavior. The behavioral variants of these families in the interview range from dominant or submissive to petty bickering and blaming. The children, on the other hand, alternate between resisting and accepting control from their parents.

6. **Borderline Centripetal Families**

   These families are characterized by moderately impaired relational functioning, and engage in verbal rather than behavioral chaos. The battles for control are intense but not overt. The family rules do not allow for open rebellion or covertly expressed rage. Therefore, clients from these families can become severely obsessional and anorectic.

7. **Borderline Centrifugal Families**

These families are characterized by moderately impaired relational functioning, and are likely to openly express anger. The parental relationships can be riddled with battles and conflict, while being generally non-supportive. The children in these families learn manipulation and utilize it on their parents. This sometimes results in a borderline personality disorder diagnosis.

8. **Severely Dysfunctional Centrifugal Families**

These families are characterized by severely impaired relational functioning and are viewed by others as strange. The parents typically set unclear rules and expectations, while denying ambivalence. The children are denied opportunities to find their individuality and function independently. It is not unusual for schizoid personality or schizophrenia to be present in one or more family members.

9. **Severely Dysfunctional Centripetal Families**

These families are characterized by severely impaired relational functioning and are openly hostile and contemptuous. Nurturing and tenderness are seldom provided by the parents. On the other hand, ambivalence is denied and there is an expectation of negative feelings. The relational and emotional development of the children is stunted and can result in antisocial personalities. Commonly found in these families are drug abuse, child abuse, and sexual deviance.

Individual, Couples, and Family Case Conceptualizations

Individual (Partner) Case Conceptualizations

It is suggested that three case conceptualizations be prepared when working with couples. These are: an individual case conceptualization for each partner, and a third for the relationship. The personality style/disorder and maladaptive pattern should be included in each case conceptualization, at minimum, for each partner. For instance, an individual who demonstrates attention-seeking behavior will typically reflect a histrionic personality disorder or style. On the other hand, a partner who exhibits overly conscientious traits and a perfectionistic pattern of behavior may reflect an obsessive-compulsive personality disorder or style.

Couple Case Conceptualizations

For individual clients, most therapeutic approaches include their own unique method of case conceptualization. However, in working with couples, the couples case conceptualization is influenced largely by the relational interaction pattern. "Specifically, therapists focus on identifying the problem interaction cycle around the presenting problem. Typically, couples … have one or two basic patterns of interaction that characterize the presenting problem" (Gehart, 2017, p. 256). Therefore, the couple's relational pattern or patterns are emphasized in the couple case conceptualization in order to explain the presenting problem in the context of the relationship we find it useful to specify one of the five relational patterns described above.

Family Case Conceptualizations

Family case conceptualizations are case conceptualizations that incorporate family or systemic dynamics. Surprisingly, family case conceptualizations have only recently entered the family therapy literature (Sperry, 2004, 2005; Carlson, Sperry, & Lewis, 2006). Similarly, family therapy textbooks have only now begun to discuss the concept of family case conceptualization (Bitter, 2009; Gehart, 2010; Reiter, 2013). Gehart contends that a family case conceptualization is the first step in providing competent family therapy, in which therapists "conceptualize the situation with the help of theory" (2010, p. 1).

As with individual case conceptualizations, the most useful family case conceptualizations "focus on the unique contexts, needs, and resources of the individual family members and the system as a whole" (Bitter, 2009, p. 374). Not surprisingly, such case conceptualizations are based on a detailed assessment of family system dynamics. These include couple, parental, and sibling subsystem dynamics. More specifically, it includes the capacity for negotiation, power sharing, and intimacy, as well as family resources, strengths, and the family narrative (Sperry, 2016).

Case Example: Jessie and Jeffrey

Jessie and Jeffrey Lehman have recently begun relational counseling because of increasing conflict and relational dissatisfaction. Jessie is a 29-year-old, second-generation Latina female with a history of bipolar disorder. She has been married to Jeffrey for six years and the couple do not have any children. Jessie sought out couples therapy due to relational dissatisfaction and recurrent anger. She admits that she has considered divorce particularly when her husband seems uninterested in her despite her flirtatiousness and threats to leave him. Nevertheless, her desire is to mend her marriage. Jeffrey is a 34-year-old, Caucasian engineer. Jeffrey is very successful, but he is proper, emotionally distant, rigid, and not disposed to compromise. Five years prior to coming to therapy, Jessie was diagnosed with Bipolar II disorder and histrionic personality disorder. She reported that individual therapy had been helpful in dealing with her bipolar symptoms but reported a poor response to medication trials. Jessie stated that Jeffrey has been "obviously concerned" for her and her symptoms throughout their marriage but complained that "he doesn't really show it." Jessie is financially dependent on Jeffrey because her mental condition precludes her from seeking or maintaining full-time work.

One of her chief complaints is that Jeffrey does not pay any attention to her when he returns from work. "No hugs, no kisses, no greeting. He doesn't even ask me how I'm doing or tell me how his day went," she stated. She described that he spends most of his time in front of the TV, reading the newspaper, or playing games in his "man cave." Seeking to engage and have more contact with him, Jessie gets "all dolled up" before Jeffrey gets home. She expects to be hugged and kissed, and she wants to have a conversation during dinner and thereafter. Jessie's strategy to get Jeffrey's attention includes following him around and attempting to engage with him right when he gets home. In return, Jeffrey responds with anger at first, followed by silence and withdrawal. There are times when he skips dinner in lieu of spending more time in his man cave. The results of these circumstances exacerbate feelings of anger and rejection in Jessie. She perceives herself as unloved, unnoticed, and rejected, which reinforces her loneliness.

A diagnostic evaluation reveals the following: Jessie meets *DSM-5* Diagnoses for (296.89) Bipolar Disorder II, moderate severity and exhibits histrionic personality traits. Jeffrey meets the criteria for (301.4) Obsessive-Compulsive Personality Disorder. The couple's relational issues would be classified as in *DSM-5* (V61.0) Relationship Distress.

Individual (Partner) Case Conceptualization

Central to Jessie's case conceptualization is her maladaptive histrionic pattern in which she demands attention from others. Her pattern is predictably triggered when she feels inadequate and unloved. It reinforces her needs and demands for ongoing attention. She identifies as Cuban-American of middle-class upbringing and status and is highly acculturated. Her cultural explanation is that there are vast "personality differences between me and my husband." Therefore, culturally sensitive treatment does not appear to be indicated at this time.

Central to Jeffrey's case conceptualization is his obsessive-compulsive pattern in which he overworks, avoids feelings, and distances himself from others. His pattern is triggered by demands for closeness and emotional expression particularly from Jessie. Instead, he becomes increasingly conscientious and perfectionistic. He identifies as a third-generation "upper middle class white male of privilege."

Couples Case Conceptualization

This couple demonstrates a demand-withdraw pattern. This pattern is understandable given each partner's case conceptualization. Jessie's strategies to achieve her needs for attention and love exacerbate Jeffrey's predictable withdrawal through overwork and emotional distance. In turn, the distance created cycles back to Jessie's feelings of loneliness and rejection. This results in Jessie increasing her demands for attention and intimate contact.

Family Case Conceptualization

Even though Jessie and Jeffrey Lehman have no children, they are a family unit because they have been influenced by family system dynamics from their own families of origin. Further inquiry will reveal how their relational interaction pattern has been influenced by family of origin dynamics. In terms of family interaction patterns, the Lehman family reflects a midrange mixed family pattern (Beavers & Hampson, 1990, 2019). The value of a family case conceptualization for couples, even those without children, is that it can provide an explanation for not only their relational interaction but also particular issues they have or will likely face based on previous generations of their families of origin. Characteristics of midrange mixed families is their attempt to control by authority whether by using demands, blame, or anger expressed overtly or covertly. Unfortunately, such control is not particularly effective in producing consistent results. It is not surprising that neither Jessie nor Jeffrey feel satisfied with their relationship nor do they feel that either has much control. Both feel the brunt of power and control struggles. Lately, they spend little quality time together, and satisfaction is sought outside the family. Furthermore, if one partner is diagnosed with a psychiatric disorder it is most likely to be an externalizing or acting out disorder or condition. Thus, it is not surprising that Jessie exhibits externalization with both her bipolar disorder and histrionic personality style.

Treatment Plan

The plan for this couple includes Jessie continuing individual therapy and beginning couples therapy with both clients. The focus of the couple's therapy would be to educate on and rebalance the interactional pattern. Given Jeffrey's solid patterns of avoidance and emotional distancing, this process might require individual therapy for him to modify and replace that pattern.

Treatment strategies for working effectively with midrange mixed families have been articulated in Beavers and Hampson (1990, 2019).

Concluding Note

Three different forms of case conceptualization have been described in this chapter: individual, couple, and family. Because most clinicians have been and are trained to practice individual therapy, it is not unreasonable to expect them to develop and implement individual case conceptualizations. This is the current standard of care. Hopefully, this chapter has increased the reader's understanding and appreciation of the clinical value of both couple and family case conceptualizations. The prospect of adding information from one or both of these forms of case conceptualization, or just the relational interaction or family interaction patterns, can greatly optimize treatment outcome.

CHAPTER 5 QUESTIONS

1. Discuss the benefits of including a couple and family approach to identifying patterns in individual case conceptualizations.
2. Compare the 11 personality styles presented and discuss the various patterns and movement of these individuals from a case conceptualization framework.
3. Explain how identifying the five relational patterns discussed in this chapter strengthens case conceptualization and how this relates to treatment goals and outcomes.
4. Of the nine family types identified, discuss the six that warrant intervention and what approaches should be incorporated into a treatment plan for a case conceptualization for each.
5. Discuss some examples when it would be most beneficial to incorporate the three case conceptualizations presented in this chapter: individual, couple, and family case conceptualizations.

References

Beavers, W. R. (1981), A systems model of family for family therapists. *Journal of Marital and Family Therapy*, *7*(4), 299–307.

Beavers, W. R., & Hampson, R. B. (1990). *Successful families: Assessment and intervention*. New York, NY: Norton.

Carlson, J., Sperry, L., & Lewis, J. A. (2005). *Family therapy techniques: Integrating and tailoring treatment*. New York, NY: Routledge.

Christensen, A., & Shenk, J. (1991). Communication, conflict, and psychological distance in nondistressed, clinic, and divorcing couples. *Journal of Consulting and Clinical Psychology*, *59*(3), 458–463.

Froude, C., & Tambling, R. (2014). Couples' conceptualizations of problems in couple therapy. *The Qualitative Report*, *19*(13), 1–19.

Fruzzetti, A. (2006). *The high-conflict couple: A dialectical behavior therapy guide to finding peace, intimacy, and validation*. Oakland, CA: New Harbinger Publications.

Fruzzetti, A., & Payne, L. (2015). Couple therapy and borderline personality disorder. In A. Gurman, J. Lebow & D. Snyder (Eds.), *Clinical handbook of couple therapy* (5th ed., pp. 606–434). New York, NY: Guilford.

Gehart, D. (2010). *Mastering competencies in family therapy*. Belmont, CA: Brooks/Cole.

Gehart, D. (2017). Clinical case conceptualization with couples and families. In J. Carlson & S. Dermer (Eds.), *The SAGE encyclopedia of marriage, family, and couples counseling* (pp. 256–260). Thousand Oaks, CA: Sage Publications.

Gottman, J. (2014). *Principia amoris: The new science of love*. New York, NY: Routledge.

Hampson, R. B., & Beavers, W. R. (2012). Observational assessment. In L. Sperry (Ed.), *Family assessment: Contemporary and cutting-edge strategies* (pp. 83–114). New York, NY: Routledge.

Hampson, R. B., & Beavers, W. R. (2019). Observational assessment. In L. Sperry (Ed.), *Family assessment: Contemporary and cutting-edge strategies, Second edition*. 99–132. New York, NY: Routledge.

Holley, S.R., Haase, C.M., Chui, I., & Bloch, L. (2018). Depression, emotion regulation, and the demand/withdraw pattern during intimate relationship conflict. *Journal of Social and Personal Relationships*, *35*(1), 1–23.

Johnson, S. (2008). *Hold me tight: Seven conversations for a lifetime of love*. New York, NY: Little, Brown.

Knobloch-Fedders, L.M., Critchfield, K.L., Boisson, T., Woods, N., Bitman, R., & Durbin, C.E. (2014). Depression, relationship quality, and couples' demand/withdraw and demand/submit sequential interactions. *Journal of Counseling Psychology*, *61*(2), 264–279.

Reiter, M.D. (2013). *Case conceptualization in family therapy*. Upper Saddle River, NJ: Pearson.

Sperry, L. (2004). Family therapy with a historic-obsessive couple. In M. Macfarlane (Ed.), *Family treatment of personality disorders: Advances in clinical practice* (pp. 149–172). Binghamton, NY: Haworth.

Sperry, L. (2005). Case conceptualizations: The missing link between theory and practice. *The Family Journal*, *13*(1), 71–76.

Sperry, L. (2016). Teaching the competency of family case conceptualizations. *The Family Journal*, *24*(3), 279–282.

Part II

In Chapters 6 through 10, the emphasis shifts to the application of theory to practice, and the learning of case conceptualization competencies. In these chapters, the reader is introduced to five methods of case conceptualization. Each chapter provides five examples of full-scale case conceptualization that reflects this model. In each of these chapters, the same five cases are analyzed and written case conceptualizations are provided. Chapter 6 focuses on the Biopsychosocial case conceptualizations. Chapter 7 describes and illustrates Cognitive Behavioral case conceptualizations. Chapter 8 focuses on Time-Limited Dynamic case conceptualizations. Chapter 9 addresses Adlerian case conceptualizations, while Chapter 10 focuses on Acceptance and Commitment Therapy case conceptualizations. The Appendix includes additional tables, figures, and forms.

These chapters present the reader with an integrative model for developing case conceptualizations that is broad enough to incorporate specific therapeutic orientations.

The reader will note that each chapter contains full-scale case conceptualizations for five cases. Each includes a table that summarizes information on 17 elements and a case conceptualization statement that is a narrative version of the information in that table. Emphasized in each chapter is the "predisposition," "treatment strategy," and "treatment interventions" because these are the signature features of the five structured methods.

Many of the remaining elements in the case conceptualization tables and statements are the same or similar for all the cases, as these represent the common structure of a case conceptualization. From a teaching and learning perspective, we have found that this repetition of the non-changing elements of the case conceptualization is useful and necessary in the process of learning and mastering this formidable competency. It is an essential part of the learning strategy we have employed in our courses and workshops. Questions at the end of each chapter add another learning dimension for either group discussion or self-study.

The question may arise: must all 17 elements be included in every case conceptualization? The answer is "no." Some will decide that for certain case conceptualizations, it is sufficient to include fewer elements in the treatment formulation section of their written case conceptualization. Others who work primarily with a non-diverse clientele may decide that a cultural formulation is unnecessary and exclude it. The point is that you need not include all 17 elements. Perhaps, you'll decide that 12 or 13 elements – including presentation, precipitant, pattern, treatment pattern, treatment goals, and treatment interventions – are sufficient. Just recognize that the more elements excluded can lower the explanatory power and/ or predictive power of the case conceptualization.

Readers may wonder why the Time-Limited Dynamic psychotherapy approach was chosen for the Dynamic psychotherapy chapter. There are several reasons. Chief among these is that this approach is among the most commonly practiced and commonly taught versions of psychodynamic therapy today. It is also a research and evidenced-based approach, and is competency based (Binder, 2004; Binder & Betan, 2013). Among the psychodynamics approaches, it is probably the easiest to learn and use. Of particular importance for this book, this approach has a clearly defined and straightforward protocol for developing a case conceptualization.

Finally, each of the chapters in Part II provides the reader with the opportunity to increase their competence in constructing case conceptualizations. Instructions are provided toward the end of each chapter, and suggested answers to the exercises appear in the Appendix of each of these chapters.

References

Binder, J.L. (2004). *Key competencies in brief dynamic psychotherapy: Clinical practice beyond the manual*. New York, NY: Guilford.

Binder, J.L., & Betan, E.J. (2013). *Core competencies in brief dynamic psychotherapy: Becoming a highly effective and competent brief dynamic psychotherapist*. New York, NY: Guilford.

6 Biopsychosocial Case Conceptualizations

This chapter describes and illustrates an atheoretical and broadly based method of case conceptualization. Unlike most case conceptualization methods which are based on one of the many psychodynamic theories, Cognitive Behavior theories, or interpersonal theories, the Biopsychosocial method is largely atheoretical. Also, in contrast to most, if not all, theory-based approaches which are more narrowly focused, the Biopsychosocial method is more broadly based and encompasses the interplay of three domains of human experience: the biological, psychological, and sociocultural. Because of its recognition of the biological domain, the Biopsychosocial method is unique among psychotherapeutic approaches.

Because of its biological basis, this method has considerable appeal to psychiatrists, psychologists, and nurses with prescription privileges, and a growing number of non-prescribing practitioners sensitive to the influence of the biological domain on personal functioning and well-being. Since it encompasses two more domains than approaches that emphasize the psychological domain, this method also has appeal to those with an eclectic view of treatment. This is not to say that all its adherents are eclectic, but rather that the method lends itself to incorporating interventions from all the therapeutic approaches. The implication is that some who are guided by this method will develop narrowly focused conceptualizations that emphasize diagnosis, symptoms reduction, and medication, while others – because of training, experience, and inclination – will incorporate a broad range of treatment interventions based on their more comprehensive diagnostic and clinical formulations. Still others, in their quest to "tailor" treatment to a particular client's needs and preferences, will consider if the signature elements from other case conceptualization methods can improve the "fit" with their client's circumstances and then construct one that looks decidedly similar to a Cognitive-Behavioral (or Dynamic or Adlerian, etc.) case conceptualization.

The chapter begins with a description and the basic premises of the Biopsychosocial perspective. Next, it describes the factors involved in Biopsychosocial assessment and provides some guidelines for summarizing this type of assessment. Then, it describes the process of developing and writing a Biopsychosocial case conceptualization. This process is then applied to the five cases introduced in Chapter 1.

Biopsychosocial Perspective

The Biopsychosocial perspective was proposed by George Engel in 1977 as a more integrative and comprehensive way of thinking about and treating medical and psychological conditions (Engel, 1977). Since then, it has increasingly influenced the fields of psychiatry, psychology, social work, and more recently, counseling. Some consider that this perspective is best understood in terms of systems theory while most do not. In actual practice, the Biopsychosocial method of case conceptualization is utilized as if it were an atheoretical method. The reader should note that this method of case conceptualization is sometimes referred to as the clinical method (Sperry, Gudeman, Blackwell, & Faulkner, 1992).

This perspective emphasizes three sets of vulnerabilities and resources: the biological, the psychological, and the sociocultural domains. Vulnerability means the susceptibility to develop a condition or express symptoms or impairment. In this perspective, stressors, client vulnerabilities and resources, and levels of functioning or impairments are central factors. Four basic premises underlie this perspective (Sperry et al., 1992):

1. A client's problems are best understood in terms of multi-causation involving biological, psychological, and social (BPS) factors rather than a single etiology.
2. A client's problems are best understood in terms of a client's biological, psychological, and social vulnerabilities.
3. A client's problems are best understood as manifestations of the client's attempts to cope with stressors (biological, intrapsychic, interpersonal, environmental) given his or her vulnerabilities and resources.
4. A client's condition is best treated with a multimodal approach that is flexible and tailored to the client's needs and expectations rather than with a single treatment modality.

In short, stressors activate the individual's vulnerabilities and resources, and symptoms are understood as the manifestation of the individual's attempt to cope with stressors given their vulnerabilities and resources. Accordingly, treatment is directed to ameliorating symptoms and increasing the individual's levels of life functioning often with a tailored, multimodal approach.

Biopsychosocial Assessment

Assessment consistent with the Biopsychosocial perspective includes the identification of relevant biological, psychological, and social factors, i.e., vulnerabilities and resources or protective factors. A factor is relevant to the extent to which it offers an explanation for the client's behavior, symptoms, and impaired functioning. The description of biological factors emphasizes the client's health status and familial health and includes health history, medication and medical treatment, exposure to environmental toxins, and substance use: alcohol, illicit drugs, nicotine, and caffeine. The description of psychological factors emphasizes personality style and coping capacities and includes adaptive and maladaptive beliefs, emotions and emotional regulation, behavioral excesses and deficits, skill deficits, as well as resilience and coping capacity. The description of social factors emphasizes family dynamics and social support and includes the influence of friends and peers, school or work demands, environmental and community risks.

Four guidelines for assessing relevant Biopsychosocial factors that could impact a particular client are:

1. Identify and assess relevant biological factors particularly the client's health status and familial health. While being mindful of the client's health history and health behaviors, the presenting problem, that is, the acuity and severity of the symptoms, mental status assessment, and family psychiatric history, consider the likelihood that biological factors such as heredity, medical conditions, prescription or over-the-counter medication and vitamins, substance use including alcohol, drugs, caffeine, nicotine, and so on, may be causing or exacerbating the client's symptoms. Then, write a sentence summarizing these biological factors.

2. Identify and assess relevant psychological factors particularly personality style and coping capacities. While being mindful of the client's presenting problem, past psychiatric and/or alcohol and drug abuse (AODA) history, developmental history, and the results of a personality assessment or other psychological inventories, such as the Beck Depression Inventory, consider the client's personality, coping style, and internal and external stressors, and hypothesize what and how various psychological factors such as intrapsychic conflicts, distorted object relations, maladaptive behaviors, maladaptive beliefs and schemas, and so on, are impacting the client in terms of symptoms and functional impairment. Then, write a sentence summarizing these psychological factors.

3. Identify and assess relevant sociocultural factors, particularly family dynamics and social support. While mindful of the client's social history, consider the client's social context and external stressors, and hypothesize how various social factors such as family dynamics, social support network, ethnicity, marginalization, alienation, poverty, prejudices, boundary violations, power and domination, intimacy conflicts, friendship and relational skills deficits, and so on, are impacting the client in terms of symptoms and functional impairment. Then, write a sentence summarizing these social, family, and cultural factors.

4. Incorporate the above biological, psychological, and sociocultural factors into a Biopsychosocial assessment statement. Specify the various biological, psychological, and sociocultural vulnerabilities that are reflected in the client's symptoms, functional impairment, or conflicts. Look for interactions among these factors. Then, write a composite assessment statement integrating these vulnerabilities. This statement will inform the "predisposition" element of the clinical formulation as well as elements of the treatment formulation.

Biopsychosocial Case Conceptualization Method

The Biopsychosocial method of case conceptualization as presented here is similar to the other four theoretical methods described in this book in that it shares several common elements. Yet, it also differs from the other four methods because of its signature elements. These include predisposition, treatment goals, treatment focus, treatment strategy, and treatment interventions.

Table 6.1 identifies and describes these five signature elements.

Biopsychosocial Case Conceptualization: Five Cases

The process of constructing a Biopsychosocial case conceptualization is illustrated for five different cases. Following background information on each case, there is an assessment paragraph that identifies key information germane to this

Table 6.1 Signature Elements of the Biopsychosocial Case Conceptualization

Predisposition	biological vulnerabilities: esp. health and familial health; psychological vulnerabilities: esp. personality style and coping capacity; sociocultural vulnerabilities: esp. family, social history, and support
Treatment goals	symptom reduction; return to baseline or improve functioning
Treatment focus	troublesome situations triggered or exacerbated by biological, psychological, or sociocultural vulnerabilities
Treatment strategies	***basic treatment strategy***: target all three domains: biological, psychological, and sociocultural, when indicated ***common strategies***: support; replacement; psychoeducation; medication
Treatment interventions	medication evaluation and monitoring; attend to readiness and treatment compliance issues; supportive therapy techniques such as encouragement; Cognitive-Behavioral interventions, e.g., replace maladaptive thoughts and behaviors with more adaptive ones; relaxation; role playing; behavioral activation support groups and/or psychoeducation groups; involve significant other, family, work supervisors, etc.

method. Then, a table summarizes the nine elements from the diagnostic, clinical, and cultural formulations (discussed in Chapters 2 and 3) and the eight elements of the treatment formulation (discussed in Chapter 4) for that specific case. Finally, a narrative integrating this information is provided in a case conceptualization statement. The first paragraph reports the diagnostic and clinical formulation, the second paragraph reports the cultural formulation, while the third paragraph reports the treatment formulation.

Case of Geri

Geri R. is a 36-year-old, African American female who works as an administrative assistant. She is single, lives alone, and was referred by her company's human resources director for evaluation and treatment following three weeks of depression and social isolation. Her absence from work prompted the referral. Her symptoms began soon after her supervisor told Geri that she was being considered for a promotion. As a child she reports isolating and avoiding others when she was criticized and teased by family members and peers.

Biopsychosocial Assessment

Her family history suggests a biological vulnerability to depression. Geri recalls her parents talking about her maternal aunt being prescribed antidepressants. Besides moderate obesity, she reports reasonably good health. She denies the use of medication, alcohol, or recreational drugs. Her developmental and social history reveals demanding, critical, and emotionally distant parents who reportedly provided her with little emotional support and favored her younger brother. In addition, she was regularly teased and criticized by her peers in the neighborhood and at school. There is a lifelong history of social isolation, rejection sensitivity, and avoidance of others instead of fighting back or neutralizing the criticism and teasing of others. She reports no best friends as a child and only one coworker with whom she feels comfortable being around. Besides a paternal aunt, she has limited contact with her family. It is noteworthy that despite the experience of being a college graduate and working for several years in an office setting, she continues to have significant skill deficit in assertive communications, friendship skills, and problem-solving skills. Furthermore, she lacks confidence in being around others whom she cannot fully trust. She meets the criteria for Major Depressive Disorder, Single Episode and for Avoidant Personality Disorder (Table 6.2).

Table 6.2 Case Conceptualization Elements

Presentation	increased social isolation and depressive symptoms
Precipitant	news that she was being considered for a job promotion and a new supervisor (***current precipitant***); demands of close relationships and the expectation that she will be criticized, rejected, and feel unsafe (***continuing precipitant***)
Pattern-maladaptive	avoids and disconnects from others when feeling unsafe
Predisposition	***biological***: family history of depression
	psychological: shy, avoidant, non-assertive; rejection sensitive
	social: *current*: avoids critical and demanding people; *past*: demanding, critical, emotionally unavailable parents; teasing, taunting, critical peers
Perpetuants	maintained by her shyness, living alone, and generalized social isolation
Protective factors & strengths	close, trusting friend and confidante; stable meaningful job; eligible for job accommodation
Cultural identity	middle-class African American with limited ethnic ties
Cultural stress & acculturation	highly acculturated; no obvious acculturative stress but family gender roles reinforce the notion that she is inadequate
Cultural explanation	sadness results from job stress and chemical imbalance in her brain
Culture and/or personality	personality dynamics are significantly operative
Treatment pattern	connect with others while feeling safer
Treatment goals	(1°) reduce depressive symptoms; increase socialization; return to work
	(2°) increase her capacity to connect to others and effectively work with others
Treatment focus	troublesome situations triggered or exacerbated by BPS vulnerabilities
Treatment strategy	medication; support; replacement; skill training
Treatment interventions	medication evaluation/monitoring; supportive therapy; replace maladaptive thoughts and behaviors; psychoeducation group; collaborate with work supervisor
Treatment obstacles	"test" practitioners; likely to resist group therapy; over dependence on practitioners; difficulty with termination
Treatment-cultural	gender may be an issue so assign supportive female practitioners
Treatment prognosis	good, if increased social connections, skills, and returns to work

Case Conceptualization Statement

Geri's increased social isolation and depressive symptoms (*presentation*) seem to be her reaction to the news that she was being considered for a job promotion and a new supervisor (*current precipitant*) as well as demands from close relationships and the expectation that she will be criticized, rejected, and feel unsafe (*continuing precipitants*). Throughout her life, she found it safer to avoid others when possible and conditionally relate to them at other times; as a result, she lacks key social skills and has a limited social network (*pattern*).

_____

_____

_____

_____

_____

_____

(*predisposition*). This pattern is maintained by her shyness, the fact that she lives alone, her limited social skills, and that she finds it safer to socially isolate (*perpetuants*). Geri has a secure attachment with her close work friend and also brings commitment to her workplace through her many years of employment. She also benefits from legislative structures through which she can seek accommodations for her job, such as the Americans with Disabilities Act (*protective factors/strengths*).

She identifies herself as a middle-class African American, but has little interest and no involvement with the African American community (*cultural identity*). She is highly acculturated, as are her parents, but her family system placed a higher value on men. This positive bias toward men appears to reinforce the notion that she is unwanted and inadequate (*cultural stress & acculturation*). She believes that her depression is the result of stress at work and a "chemical imbalance" in her brain (*cultural explanation*). No significant cultural factors are operative. It appears that Geri's personality dynamics are significantly operative in her current clinical presentation, but gender roles should be examined (*culture and/or personality*).

The challenge for Geri is to function more effectively and feel safer in relating to others (*treatment pattern*). First-order goals (1°) are to reduce her depressive symptoms, increase her interpersonal and friendship skills, help her return to work, and increase her social network. Second-order goals (2°) should work to increase her capacity to connect to others and effectively work with others (*treatment goals*). Treatment that is focused on troublesome situations triggered or exacerbated by BPS vulnerabilities will keep the treatment goals in the forefront of therapy (*treatment focus*). The basic strategy for treatment is to target her vulnerabilities while fostering a more adaptive pattern and functioning. Specific treatment strategies include medication, support, replacement, and skill training (*treatment strategy*). Initially, reducing her depressive symptoms will be addressed with medication, support, and behavioral activation in an effort to sufficiently energize her to accomplish daily routines and responsibilities. Next, cognitive and behavior replacement interventions will target her rejection sensitivity and isolation from others. Then, social skills training in a group therapy setting will emphasize assertive communication, trust, and friendship skills. Finally, collaboration with Geri's work supervisor and the human resources director will be arranged in an effort to accommodate Geri's return to a more tolerable work environment. Treatment will be sequenced with medication management by her physician (in consultation with the clinic's psychiatrist) and cognitive and behavioral replacement will begin immediately in an individual treatment format which will prepare her to transition into a group treatment mode (***treatment interventions***). Some obstacles and challenges to treatment can be anticipated. Given her avoidant personality structure, ambivalent resistance is likely. It can be anticipated that she will have difficulty discussing personal matters with practitioners, and that she will "test" and provoke practitioners into criticizing her for changing or canceling appointments at the last minute or being late, and that she might procrastinate, avoid feelings, and otherwise "test" the practitioner's trustability. Once trust in the practitioner is achieved, she is likely to cling to the practitioner and treatment and thus termination may be difficult unless her social support system outside therapy is increased. Furthermore, her pattern of avoidance is likely to make entry into and continuation with group work difficult. Therefore, individual sessions can serve as a transition into group work, including having some contact with the group practitioner who will presumably be accepting and nonjudgmental. This should increase Geri's feeling safe and making self-disclosure in a group setting less difficult. Transference enactment is another consideration. Given the extent of parental and peer criticism and teasing, it is anticipated that any perceived impatience and verbal or non-verbal indications of criticalness by the practitioner will activate this transference. Finally, because of her tendency to cling to others she trusts, increasing her capacity to feel more confident in functioning with greater independence and increasing the time between the last four or five sessions can reduce her ambivalence about termination (***treatment obstacles***).

Given Geri's personality dynamics, treatment progress does not appear to be highly influenced by cultural stress. However, gender dynamics could impact the therapeutic relationship given the gender roles in her family, her strained relationship with her father, and her limited involvement with men ever since. Accordingly, female practitioners for both individual and group therapy appear to be indicated in the initial phase of treatment (***treatment-cultural***). Assuming that Geri increases her self-confidence, relational skills, and social contacts in and outside therapy, as well as returns to work, her prognosis is adjudged to be good; if not it is guarded (***treatment prognosis***).

Case of Antwone

Antwone is an African American Navy seaman in his mid 20s who has lashed out at others with limited provocation. Recently, his commander ordered him to undergo compulsory counseling. From infancy until the time he enlisted in the Navy, he lived in foster placements, mostly with an abusive African American foster family.

Biopsychosocial Assessment

Antwone reports neglect and abuse – emotional, verbal, and physical – by his African American foster family, particularly the mother who used racial slurs to intimidate him, and her older daughter who repeatedly sexually molested him when he was a young boy. At age 15, he reported that he refused to submit to the abuse, and he confronted his foster mother which effectively stopped the abuse. It also led to him being expelled from her home. Afterwards, he became selectively vengeful, aggressive, and defensive and became even more rejection sensitive. Enlisting in the Navy provided stability and a chance to grow and learn. He reported that while he tried to be a good sailor, he was regularly taunted by his peers, and was unfairly treated by white peers and officers. Besides the neglect and abuse of his foster family, he reported that he had one emotionally supportive male friend and confidante. However, he was unexpectedly killed just prior to Antwone's enlistment in the Navy. While he is desirous of having a close, intimate relationship with a female, he is inexperienced and leery of intimacy. No obvious biological predisposing factors are noted (Table 6.3).

Case Conceptualization Statement

Antwone's verbal and physical lashing out at others and his confusion about others' intentions (***presentation***) appear to be his response to the taunting and provocation of his peers that resulted in a physical fight (***current precipitant***) as well as the perceived injustice of peers and authority figures (***continuing precipitants***). Throughout his life, Antwone has sought to be accepted and make sense of being neglected, abused, and abandoned, and to protect himself by aggressively striking back and conditionally relating to others in the face of a perceived threat or injustice (***pattern***).

_____

_____

_____

_____

_____

_____

(***predisposition***). His limited capacity for emotional regulation along with deficits in conflict resolution skills serve to maintain this pattern (***perpetuants***). Antwone brings several protective factors and strengths to therapy, including his childhood

Table 6.3 Case Conceptualization Elements

Presentation	verbal and/or physical retaliation; confusion
Precipitant	conflicts that resulted in a physical fight with other sailors (*current precipitant*); perceived injustice of peers and authority figures (*continuing precipitants*)
Pattern-maladaptive	strikes back and conditionally relates
Predisposition	*biological*: non-contributory
	psychological: aggressive; impulsive; suspicious; defensive; rejection sensitive
	social: *current*: taunting/abuse by peers; arbitrary actions of authority figures; *past*: neglected/abused by foster family; loss of supportive friend and confidante
Perpetuant	suspiciousness; emotional regulation and conflict resolution deficits
Protective factors & strengths	best friend was a secure attachment figure; intelligent, avid reader with wide interests; creative; committed to duty and service
Cultural identity	African American; ambivalent about ethnic involvement
Cultural stress & acculturation	highly acculturated with considerable cultural stress
Cultural explanation	racial degradation; racial provocations of white peers and superiors
Culture and/or personality	personality *and* cultural factors are operative
Treatment pattern	connect and relate to others while being careful
Treatment goals	(1°) anger and impulse control; increase positive coping skills; find family of origin
	(2°) increase his capacity to relate to others safely
Treatment focus	troublesome situations triggered or exacerbated by BPS vulnerabilities
Treatment strategy	target psychological and social vulnerabilities; foster adaptive functioning; support; replacement; skill training and psychoeducation; cognitive restructuring
Treatment interventions	replace maladaptive thoughts and behaviors; group for impulse, emotional regulation skill training; affirm him; encourage finding biological family
Treatment obstacles	transference–countertransference enactments with male practitioner; aggressive acting out; depending on and idealizing the practitioner
Treatment-cultural	therapeutically frame and process his foster family's prejudice and abuse
Treatment prognosis	good to very good

best friend who served as his only secure attachment figure. He is intelligent, he is a reader with wide interests, and he has received regular promotions in rank, at least until recently. He also writes poetry and has learned two foreign languages. Additionally, he benefits from a caring military command and organizational structure that has encouraged counseling and treatment in lieu of punitive measures for past aggressive behaviors (***protective factors/strengths***).

Antwone identifies as African American and maintains some ethnic ties (***cultural identity***). Although he is highly acculturated, he continues to experience considerable racial discrimination which seems to be exacerbated by his cultural beliefs (***cultural stress & acculturation***). He believes that his problems result from the racial degradation and abuse from his African American foster family, as well as from racial provocations by his white peers and Navy superiors (***cultural explanation***). It appears that both personality and cultural factors are operative (***culture and/or personality***).

The challenge for Antwone to function more effectively is to relate to others while being careful in getting to know and trust them (***treatment pattern***).

_____

_____

_____

_____

_____

_____

(***treatment goals***). Treatment that is focused on troublesome situations triggered or exacerbated by Biopsychosocial vulnerabilities will keep the treatment goals in the forefront of therapy (***treatment focus***). Compatible treatment strategies include therapeutic support, replacement, and psychoeducation (***treatment strategy***).

_____

_____

_____

_____

_____

_____

(***treatment interventions***). Specific treatment obstacles and challenges can be anticipated. These include the likelihood that Antwone will quickly identify with a caring practitioner as the positive father figure and role model that he has never had. It is also likely that this will engender a predictable transference–countertransference enactment which may result in him aggressively acting out (***treatment obstacles***). In addition to addressing personality and interpersonal treatment targets, effective treatment outcomes will require addressing the cultural dimension of prejudice, not only prejudice from white peers and superiors, but also his experience of black-on-black prejudice. It may be useful to therapeutically frame his foster family's prejudice and abuse toward him in terms of self-loathing that was passed down from their ancestors to him; then, it can be therapeutically processed. Because he is an avid reader, bibliotherapy, i.e., books and articles that analyze and explain this type of prejudice, could be a useful therapeutic adjunct (***treatment-cultural***). Antwone brings several strengths and resources to therapy including intelligence, a reader with wide interests, regular promotions in rank, at least until recently, poetry writing, and learning two foreign languages. These resources plus his motivation to change suggest a good to very good prognosis (***treatment prognosis***).

Case of Maria

Maria is a 17-year-old, first-generation Mexican American female who was referred for counseling because of mood swings. She is conflicted about her decision to go off to college instead of staying home to care for her terminally ill mother. Her family expects her to stay home. She is angry at her older sister who left home at 17 after her parents insisted that her culture "requires" her to take care of her parents when they get old or become ill. Her Anglo friends encourage her to go to college and pursue her dreams.

Biopsychosocial Assessment

At her parent's insistence, Maria comes to counseling because of a single episode of experimentation with alcohol. There is no family history of substance abuse or other mental disorders and Maria was "turned off by the booze." "It didn't do anything for me except make me sick." She reports no health problems, uses no medication, and, except for the single experimentation with alcohol, has never used recreational drugs. There is no family history of psychological or substance use problems nor treatment for these. In terms of personality style, Maria exhibits a need to please, dependence on others, difficulty expressing her disagreement, and low assertiveness. Her parents are reportedly quite strict and demanding and insist on the "old ways" where the adult daughter relinquishes her life to care for aging or sick parents. While her Anglo friends encourage her to emancipate from her family, her parents insist that she is as rebellious as her older sister. The family emigrated to the United States from Mexico when Maria was four years old. It is noteworthy that her parents rely on her to be their translator (Table 6.4).

Case Conceptualization Statement

Maria's depressive symptoms, confusion, and recent experimentation with alcohol use (***presentation***) seem to be her reaction to pressures and conflict over going away to college or staying to care for her parents (***current precipitant***) as well as expectations of self-reliance, being alone, or need to meet others' needs at the

Table 6.4 Case Conceptualization Elements

Presentation	moodiness; confusion; experimentation with alcohol use
Precipitant	pressures and conflict over going away to college or staying to care for her parents (***current precipitant***); expectations of self-reliance, being alone, or need to meet others' needs at the expense of her own (***continuing precipitants***)
Predisposition	***biological***: none besides a single episode of experimentation
	psychological: need to please; difficulty expressing disagreement with others; dependent; low assertiveness skills
	social: *current*: strict, demanding parents; friends expect her to emancipate; parents call her rebellious; *past*: emigrated as child; translator for parents
Pattern-maladaptive	meet others' needs but not her own
Perpetuant	dependent and pleasing style; low assertiveness; cultural expectation
Protective factors & strengths	strong family, social, and religious values; successful student; tight-knit and safe cultural community
Cultural identity	working-class Mexican American
Cultural stress & acculturation	low to moderate level of acculturation; stress from ambivalence about parental and cultural expectations
Cultural explanation	problems caused by "lack of faith"
Culture and/or personality	personality *and* cultural factors operative
Treatment pattern	meet her needs and the needs of others
Treatment goals	(1°) increase self-efficacy, assertiveness, decision-making; decrease moodiness
	(2°) help her to find a balance between meeting her own needs and her family's needs
Treatment focus	troublesome situations triggered or exacerbated by BPS vulnerabilities
Treatment strategy	target family/interpersonal vulnerabilities; foster adaptive functioning; support; replacement; skill training
Treatment interventions	supportive techniques; Cognitive Behavior replacement; role playing to increase empowerment and assertiveness skills
Treatment obstacles	may capitulate to parents and cultural expectations; pleasing the practitioner; practitioner may unwittingly advocate autonomy
Treatment-cultural	process cultural expectations about caregiver role and need to please; family sessions addressing parents' cultural expectations
Treatment prognosis	fair to good

expense of her own (*continuing precipitants*). Throughout her life, Maria has attempted to be a good daughter and friend, and has become increasingly "stuck" in meeting the needs of others at the expense of her own needs (*pattern*).

_____

_____

_____

_____

_____

_____

(*predisposition*). Her low level of assertiveness and unwillingness to disappoint her parents serve to maintain this pattern (*perpetuant*). Maria brings several protective factors to therapy including strong family, social, and religious values that may motivate her to establish vital life directions. Some of her strengths include her intelligence and past success in school. She also benefits from a tight-knit family and cultural community in which she can feel safe and supported (*protective factors/strengths*).

Maria identifies herself as a working-class Mexican American with a moderate level of involvement in that heritage (*cultural identity*). Her level of acculturation is in the low to moderate range while her parents' level is in the low range. Since her older sister refused to follow the cultural mandate that the oldest daughter would meet her parents needs rather than her own, that responsibility is now on Maria. Maria's ambivalence about whether to follow cultural norms and expectations or her own aspirations is quite distressing for her (*cultural stress & acculturation*). Her explanatory model is that her problems are due to a "lack of faith," a belief that is consistent with a lower level of acculturation. Although she and her family experienced some discrimination upon arrival here, it ended when they moved to a "safer" Mexican American neighborhood (*cultural explanation*). It appears that both personality and cultural factors are operative. Specifically, cultural dynamics that foster dependency, i.e., good daughters care for their parents without question, serve to reinforce her dependent personality dynamics (*culture and/or personality*).

The challenge for Maria to function more effectively is to meet both her own needs in addition to the needs of others (*treatment pattern*).

_____

_____

_____

_____

_____

(*treatment goals*). Treatment that is focused on troublesome situations triggered or exacerbated by Biopsychosocial vulnerabilities will keep the treatment goals in the forefront of therapy (*treatment focus*). Treatment strategies compatible with these treatment goals and treatment focus include therapeutic support, skill training, replacement, and psychoeducation (*treatment strategies*).

_____

_____

_____

_____

_____

_____

(*treatment interventions*). In terms of likely treatment obstacles and challenges, it is likely that Maria will attempt to please the practitioner by readily agreeing to the practitioner's suggestions and between-session assignments, but afterward become conflicted and then fail to follow up. It is also likely that the client will capitulate to her parents' expectations. Accordingly, the practitioner might, early in treatment, make the predictive interpretation that this might occur, but that it does not indicate failure, and that it can be therapeutically processed. Finally, practitioners working with dependent clients need to anticipate how their own needs and values may become treatment obstacles. This can occur when they unwittingly advocate for and expect clients to embrace independence and autonomy before the client is sufficiently ready (*treatment obstacles*). Effective treatment outcomes will also address relevant cultural dynamics. Specifically, this may involve therapeutically processing her explanatory model that lack of faith is the source of her problem. Depending on the saliency and strength of this belief, education and cognitive disputation may be indicated. The cultural expectation about caring for her parents in light of her need to please would also be processed. In addition, family sessions may be indicated wherein her parents can review and revise their cultural expectations of her (*treatment-cultural*). Besides the impact of personality and culture, the resources that Maria brings to therapy influence her prognosis. She is bright, successful in school, and has already identified her needs and career aspirations. At this point, however, given her lower level of acculturation and dependent personality dynamics, her prognosis is in the fair to good range (*treatment prognosis*).

Case of Richard

Richard is a 41-year-old, Caucasian male who is being evaluated for anxiety, sadness, and anger following his recent divorce. He currently lives on his own, is employed as a machine operator, and frequents night clubs where he "is on the lookout for the perfect woman." He has held four jobs over the past six years and was fired from his last job because he smashed his fist through a wall after being confronted by a female coworker. He is an only child of alcoholic parents whom he describes as "fighting all the time."

Biopsychosocial Assessment

Moodiness, impulsivity, and anger are traits common to both Richard and his father. Unlike his father's alcohol abuse, Richard denies any alcohol or drug use, saying "I can't stand the thought of being like him." In terms of personality style, Richard manifests a number of narcissistic traits including entitlement, a lack of empathy, arrogance, haughty attitudes, and superficiality. In addition, difficulty controlling his anger and impulses is prominent. He describes considerable difficulty in relating in a cooperative and cordial manner. He appears to be unwilling to meet the interpersonal demands of others and views women as objects to be used; he also exhibits limited communication skills. His developmental history is positive for being frightened by fights between his angry, abusive, alcoholic father and his alcoholic and emotionally detached mother. He admits that his only friend while growing up was his maternal grandmother. He only felt safe and accepted by her. She died about three years ago, at which time his problems seemed to have intensified (Table 6.5).

Case Conceptualization Statement

Richard's angry outbursts, sadness, and anxiety (***presentation***) seem to be a reaction to his recent divorce and also being fired from his last job for smashing his fist through a wall (***current precipitant***) as well as self-evaluation, being alone, or others' perception of not being special (***continuing precipitants***). From adolescence, he has elevated himself and belittled and abused others in an aggressive way, making it difficult to sustain safe and satisfying relationships (***pattern***).

_____

_____

_____

_____

_____

(***predisposition***). This pattern is maintained by his inability to empathize, impulsivity, and lack of relational skills (***perpetuants***). Richard's secure attachment with his grandmother serves as a protective factor and evidence that he has the capacity to care for others. The most prominent strength Richard brings to therapy is resilience. He is also charismatic and engaging (***protective factors/ strengths***).

Table 6.5 Case Conceptualization Elements

Presentation	angry outbursts, sadness, and anxiety
Precipitant	recent divorce and also being fired from his last job for smashing his fist through a wall (***current precipitant***); evaluation of self, being alone, or others' perception of not being special (***continuing precipitants***)
Predisposition	***biological***: appears to be non-contributory ***psychological***: entitled; superficial; lack of impulse control; lacks empathy; arrogant, haughty attitudes ***social***: *current*: difficulty meeting interpersonal demands and controlling anger; sees women as objects; limited communication skills; *past*: frightened by fights between his abusive, alcoholic father and his mother; felt safe and accepted by maternal grandmother
Pattern-maladaptive	elevates self while belittling and using others
Perpetuant	impulsivity; limited relationship skills; inability to empathize
Protective factors & strengths	secure attachment with his grandmother; resilient, charismatic, and engaging
Cultural identity	middle-class Caucasian male
Cultural stress & acculturation	highly acculturated; no obvious cultural stress, but privilege should be examined in the therapeutic process
Cultural explanation	anxiety, anger, sadness caused by abusive, non-loving parents
Culture and/or personality	personality dynamics operative, but privilege should be examined
Treatment pattern	self-confident and respectful of others
Treatment goals	(1°) anger and impulse control; reduce sadness and anxiety (2°) increase his capacity to connect to others, reduce narcissistic style
Treatment focus	troublesome situations triggered or exacerbated by biological, psychological, and/or sociocultural vulnerability
Treatment strategy	target psychological vulnerabilities and foster adaptive functioning; support; skills training; replacement
Treatment interventions	supportive techniques; Cognitive Behavior replacement; anger and impulse control skill building; role playing to foster restraint and respectfulness
Treatment obstacles	minimization of his own problematic behaviors; idealization or devaluation of practitioner; arrogant attitude
Treatment-cultural	no cultural focus to treatment indicated but address privilege dynamics
Treatment prognosis	fair

Richard identifies as a middle-class Caucasian male (***cultural identity***). He appears to be highly acculturated and there is no obvious indications of acculturative stress (***cultural stress & acculturation***). He believes that his current problems of anger, sadness, and anxiety result from the bad example he received from his abusive and non-loving parents who fought constantly when they drank (***cultural explanation***). Finally, personality dynamics are predominant and adequately explain his presenting problem and pattern, but examining his sense of entitlement and his own experience of privilege would be useful to address in therapy (***culture and/or personality***).

The challenge for Richard to function more effectively is to remain self-confident while endeavoring to be more respectful of others (***treatment pattern***).

_____

_____

_____

_____

_____

_____

(***treatment goals***). Treatment that is focused primarily on troublesome situations triggered or exacerbated by biological, psychological, and/or sociocultural vulnerability will be highlighted (***treatment focus***). Treatment strategies compatible with these treatment goals and focus include therapeutic support, skills training, and replacement (***treatment strategies***).

_____

_____

_____

_____

_____

(***treatment interventions***). With regard to likely treatment obstacles and challenges, it is likely that Richard will minimize his own problematic behaviors by blaming circumstances or others. It can be expected that he will alternate between idealization or devaluation of the practitioner, at least in the beginning phase of therapy. His entitled and arrogant attitude could activate practitioner countertransference. Furthermore, since it is not uncommon for clients with a narcissistic style to discontinue treatment when their symptoms, immediate conflicts, or stressors are sufficiently reduced, the practitioner who believes the client can profit from continued therapy needs to point out – at the beginning of therapy and thereafter – that until the client's underlying maladaptive pattern is sufficiently changed, similar issues and concerns will inevitably arise in the future (***treatment obstacles***). Since the primary influence is personality dynamics, no cultural focus to treatment is indicated besides examining his entitlement and sense of privilege (***treatment-cultural***). Finally, because of the client's conditional manner of relating, multiple job firings, and impulsivity, at this point, his prognosis is considered fair (***treatment prognosis***).

Case of Katrina

Katrina is a 13-year-old female of mixed ethnicity. She was referred for counseling by her guidance counselor due to recent depressive symptoms, poor academic performance, and oppositional behavior and fighting with other students at school. Her aggressive behavior and academic challenges have increased over the past six months since Katrina overheard a conversation between her mother and aunt in which she found out that her father had an affair for eight years. She was shocked to learn that this resulted in two births. Other difficulties include several fights with other students in the classroom, frequent conflict with her mother, skipping 15 days of school over the past six months, and diminished interest in her academic work. While she had previously excelled academically, she now displayed a marked loss of interest in activities that used to give her pleasure, such as drawing and reading. Katrina's father is currently living in Puerto Rico and has no contact with the family. Katrina lives in a small apartment with her mother and younger brother near her school. She reported being frustrated with the lack of space, since they had to downsize from the single-family home they lived in before her father left the family one year ago.

Because Katrina was a minor, it was necessary for the school counselor to speak with Katrina and her mother together during the initial session. Katrina's mother, Julia, stated that she believes that Katrina will not talk to most people about her problems because she does not trust anyone. During the first meeting, Katrina reported that she does not trust anyone and that she is not interested in attending counseling sessions if the practitioner is going to tell her what to do. Self-disclosure was very difficult for Katrina during the initial interview and Julia answered the majority of the questions that were asked, in some cases speaking for Katrina when she made efforts to speak.

Biopsychosocial Assessment

Katrina's mother disclosed a family history of depression and anger issues on Katrina's paternal side of her family. Katrina denied any medication, alcohol, or drug use and also stated, "I don't really have a dad, since real fathers are supposed to take care of their families." She said she was tired of her teachers and her mother always forcing her to do things that she doesn't want to do. As a response to others controlling and not supporting her, she has developed some paranoid and untrusting views of others. Her interpersonal style is often paranoid and aggressive when initially meeting peers. An assessment of her developmental and social history reveals Katrina having an unavailable, controlling, and critical father, few friends, and frequent physical altercations at school with her peers since age seven. Table 6.6 describes the results of the diagnostic and Biopsychosocial assessment summarized for the key elements of a full-scale case conceptualization.

Case Conceptualization Statement

Katrina's increased social isolation, aggressive and oppositional behavior, and depressive symptoms (***presentation***) appear to be Katrina's reaction to the recent news of her father's infidelity and resulting children (***current precipitant***). Katrina has a tendency to retaliate when she perceives that she is being violated or controlled by others (***continuing precipitant***). Given Katrina's lack of connection with her father and lack of trust in both parents, she moves against authority figures and her peers to protect herself from further harm and rejection (***pattern***). In short, her pattern can be understood in light of her lack of trust with her father based on his infidelity; in addition, her perception of being rejected by her father appears to have influenced her core beliefs including mistrust, and paranoia about others' intentions.

_____

_____

_____

_____

_____

_____

(***predisposition***). This pattern is maintained by Katrina's unwillingness to ask for help, her low level of motivation to engage in therapy, her social isolation and lack of support system, her mother and teachers rigidly forcing compliance, her low frustration tolerance, and lack of assertive communication skills (***perpetuants***). Despite some of her current challenges, Katrina reported being very close with her aunt and little brother. Besides her close relationships in her family, Katrina reported that she feels responsible for her brother and does everything she can to protect him from harm. Lastly, her strengths include her being a good artist, determined, intelligent, empathic, and creative (***protective factors/strengths***).

Katrina identifies herself as heterosexual and of mixed ethnicity. She identified as Hispanic and African American but reported having little connection to ethnic and cultural traditions from either identity. She stated that she wants to be more like her friends and doesn't want to feel different or weird by speaking Spanish to her mother in front of friends (***cultural identity***). She is moderately acculturated and prefers not to speak Spanish outside of the home, though her mother

Table 6.6 Biopsychosocial Case Conceptualization Elements

Presentation	depressive symptoms, aggressive behavior, and social isolation
Precipitant	learning of her father's infidelity and resulting children (***current precipitant***); retaliates in situations of perceived violation or control by others (***continuing precipitants***)
Pattern-maladaptive	moves against authority figures and peers to protect herself from potential harm and rejection
Predisposition	***biological***: family history of depression and anger issues ***social***: critical father and controlling mother; few friends and frequent conflict and fighting at school ***psychological***: paranoid; untrusting; avoids being controlled
Perpetuant	social isolation and lack of support system; mother and teachers rigidly forcing compliance; low frustration tolerance; lack of assertive communication skills
Protective factors & strengths	has a close relationship to her aunt and little brother; intelligent, creative, and resilient
Cultural identity	Hispanic and African American; lower income
Cultural stress & acculturation	low to moderate level of acculturation and cultural stress
Cultural explanation	denies depression; believes she would feel better if her teachers and mother were less controlling
Culture and/or personality	personality dynamics and cultural dynamics are operative
Treatment pattern	increase safety and ability to connect with others
Treatment goals	(1°) reduce depressive symptoms and aggressive behavior (2°) increase safety and reduce paranoid style
Treatment focus	troublesome situations triggered or exacerbated by biological, psychological, and/or sociocultural vulnerability
Treatment strategies	skills training; motivational interviewing; anger management; support; family therapy
Treatment interventions	decisional balance; readiness to change scaling question; progressive muscle relaxation; strengths assessment; use of metaphors; and replacing maladaptive thoughts and behaviors
Treatment obstacles	likely to resist individual and group therapy; expected outbursts at mother during family sessions; difficulty with self-disclosure
Treatment-cultural	assign a female practitioner; culturally sensitive therapy and family therapy
Treatment prognosis	fair to good if protective factors are incorporated into treatment

requires her to speak Spanish while at home. Katrina's mother presents with a low level of acculturation as evidenced by having challenges with speaking English, having very few English-speaking friends, being first-generation Puerto-Rican American and also African American, and reporting that she is unhappy living in the United States and plans to move back to Puerto Rico once Katrina graduates from high school (*cultural stress & acculturation*). Katrina does not believe she is depressed but feels that she would be less annoyed with people if they would be less controlling and "less bossy" (*cultural explanation*). There appears to be a moderate level of cultural factors and a moderate level of personality dynamics that influence the presenting issues (*culture and/or personality*).

The challenge for Katrina to function more effectively is to increase her ability to trust others, feel safer, and to better connect with (move toward) others (***treatment pattern***).

_____

_____

_____

_____

_____

_____

(***treatment goals***). Treatment that is focused primarily on troublesome situations triggered or exacerbated by biological, psychological, and/or sociocultural vulnerabilities will be highlighted (***treatment focus***). The basic treatment strategies will be through support, anger management skills training, motivational interviewing, psychoeducation, and referral to group counseling and family therapy (***treatment strategy***).

_____

_____

_____

_____

_____

_____

(***treatment interventions***). Some obstacles and challenges to treatment are anticipated given Katrina's low motivation to engage in therapy and her paranoid traits that are associated with her oppositional behaviors. It can be anticipated that she will have difficulty discussing personal matters with practitioners due to her inability to trust and that she will often engage in testing behaviors toward the practitioner (***treatment obstacles***). Treatment will require some culturally sensitive elements given Katrina's age and her mother's level of acculturation. Culturally sensitive interventions and family therapy will be used to address cultural factors presented by considering Katrina's mixed ethnicity and her personal experience of both cultures. Additionally, gender dynamics may be an issue so it may be useful to assign her a female therapist (***treatment-cultural***). Assuming that Katrina is able to engage more in the therapeutic process as well as utilize her strengths and seek support from her aunt, her prognosis is adjudged to be fair to good (***treatment prognosis***).

Skill Building Exercises: Biopsychosocial Conceptualizations

Our experience is that both trainees and practitioners can increase their competence and confidence in developing case conceptualizations utilizing this and similar skill building exercises. Here is how it works. Besides the complete report of the case of Geri, there are four other cases in this chapter which are incomplete. *You will note that certain elements of the case conceptualization statements contain open lines. These lines provide you with an opportunity to further develop your conceptualization skills with specific prompts.*

To simulate the process of constructing a full case conceptualization, we suggest that you begin with the case of Antwone. Read the background information on the case as well as the Biopsychosocial assessment section. It should provide sufficient information to develop a "predisposition" statement, i.e., an explanation for Antwone's behavior. If you need some help, review the "predisposition" section of Table 6.2. Then, write a sentence or so that translates the key points of Table 6.2 into the open space for "predisposition" in the case conceptualization statement. Write it in such a way that it provides a compelling explanation for Antwone's pattern and presentation.

Then, go to the open space of "Treatment Interventions" in the case conceptualization statement. Draft such a statement and use the key points on "Treatment Interventions" in Table 6.2 if needed. The Appendix to this chapter contains our responses to the open spaces. We don't expect that your responses will be exactly the same, but rather that they are thematically similar.

When you are finished with the case of Antwone, proceed on to the cases of Maria, Richard, and Katrina. Following these same instructions will provide you with additional experience in constructing Biopsychosocial case conceptualizations.

Concluding Note

This chapter emphasized the Biopsychosocial method of case conceptualization. The basic premises of the Biopsychosocial perspective were discussed, and the factors involved in a Biopsychosocial assessment and the signature elements of this method were described. Then, this case conceptualization method was applied to five cases. While one might assume that this method is less commonly used than the Cognitive-Behavioral, Dynamic, Acceptance and Commitment Therapy, Adlerian, and other theory-based methods of case conceptualization, our experience is that many trainees and practitioners prefer this method because it is relatively easy to learn and use. Others prefer it because it easily lends itself to an eclectic approach to clinical practice. Chapter 7 describes and illustrates the Cognitive-Behavioral method of case conceptualization.

CHAPTER 6 QUESTIONS

1. Explain why the three main domains of the Biopsychosocial case conceptualization approach would appeal to both the medical and counseling communities.
2. Discuss the various domains that are incorporated into the Biopsychosocial approach. What are the advantages of taking this perspective?
3. Compare biological, social, and psychological factors and describe at least three domains within each that are part of the Biopsychosocial case conceptualization.
4. Describe some of the components of the four guidelines for assessing relevant Biopsychosocial factors presented in the Biopsychosocial assessment section.
5. Discuss the signature elements of the Biopsychosocial assessment and the distinction and importance these play in an overall assessment and case conceptualization.

Appendix: Case of Antwone

Predisposition

His reaction can be understood as his aggressive and impulsive means of protecting himself against the hurt, arbitrary judgments, rejection, and losses that he has experienced since early life, starting with his mother who abandoned him, his foster family who both neglected and abused him, and the loss of his only supportive friend and confidante. He believes no-one wants him and is leery of getting close to others, although he craves intimacy.

Treatment Goal

Treatment goals that will facilitate this more adaptive pattern include emotional self-regulation, particularly increasing control over his anger and impulsivity, and improving assertive communication and conflict regulations skill. A third goal is to find his biological family and attempt to understand and come to terms with their lack of involvement in his early life which resulted in his foster care placement.

Treatment Interventions

Supportive techniques will be used to affirm him, encourage him to relate more effectively with others, and to seek out and connect with his extended family.

Cognitive-Behavioral interventions will be used to replace maladaptive thoughts and behaviors with more adaptive ones. He will also be involved in a skills training group to increase impulse control, emotional regulation, and conflict resolution.

Case of Maria

Predisposition

Her reaction is understandable in light of her personality dynamics which include her need to please others and her difficulty expressing disagreement with others. Along with these dependent features is a deficit non-assertive communication. While she seems to be clear on the issues and alternatives, she does not want to disappoint others, but finds it difficult to speak her mind. Complicating matters is that her parents are strict and demanding and espouse cultural expectations that differ from her peers. Maria is preoccupied with the worry that if she cares for her family, she will have wasted her potential and her life will be a failure. Also, her single episode of experimentation with alcohol did not provide the self-medication she thought it would and she ceased its use. However, it was of sufficient concern to her parents that they sought counseling for her.

Treatment Goal

First-order goals (1°) are to increase her self-efficacy, assertiveness, and decision-making, and decrease her moodiness. Second-order goals (2°) should work to help her to find a balance between meeting her own needs and those of her family.

Treatment Interventions

Supportive techniques will affirm her and encourage her to balance the expectations of others with her own aspirations, and unproductive thoughts and behaviors associated with these expectations will be processed with a Cognitive Behavior replacement strategy. Increasing self-efficacy, empowerment, and assertiveness skills will be facilitated with role playing. In such enactments, Marie can practice assertive communication while assuming both her role and then switching to the role of her father.

Case of Richard

Predisposition

His reaction can be understood in terms of his entitlement, superficial manner, arrogant and haughty attitudes, and lack of empathy. Along with this narcissistic style is his propensity to act out which further reinforces his impulsiveness and relational skill deficits. He has also exhibited difficulty as well as an unwillingness to meet interpersonal demands for social decorum and anger control. He sees women as objects and demonstrates limited communication skills. His role model of masculinity and relationships was his angry, abusive, alcoholic father who regularly physically and verbally assaulted his alcoholic, emotionally detached mother. Although observing his father frightened him, Richard appears to have internalized this relational behavior. It is noteworthy that he only felt safe, secure, and accepted by his maternal grandmother.

Treatment Goal

First-order goals (1°) are to reduce his anger, sadness, and anxiety and increase his ability to manage his impulses. Second-order goals (2°) should work to increase his capacity to connect to others and also reduce his narcissistic style.

Treatment Interventions

Supportive techniques will be used to affirm him and encourage him to increase relational skills. Skills such as anger and impulse control can be fostered and developed in individual and group sessions. Replacement intervention will be used to replace maladaptive thoughts and behaviors, especially those involving anger and sadness, with more adaptive ones. Role playing will be used in fostering restraint and respectfulness in relating to others.

Case of Katrina

Predisposition

Biologically, her mother reports a family history of depression and anger issues on Katrina's paternal side of her family. Her social isolation and aggressive behavior can be understood as efforts to protect herself from harm by avoiding criticism and abandonment. Her small support system and frequent peer conflicts are understandable in light of her father being historically critical and not trustworthy and also viewing her mother as controlling and secretive.

Treatment Goal

First-order goals (1°) include reducing depressive symptoms, anger management, increasing assertiveness and friendship skills, while second-order goals (2°) include reducing her oppositional behaviors, increase safety in relationships, and reducing her paranoid style.

Treatment Interventions

Once she has been engaged in the therapeutic process through rapport building and motivational interviewing, she will practice various anger management skills, use art therapy to discuss her feelings, and complete thought logs to assist her in managing her depressive symptoms and anger. School counselors will support

Katrina with strengths-based Cognitive-Behavioral Therapy strategies that will build on her identified strengths and also use metaphors generated by Katrina to manage her anger. Family therapy will be used to address the power struggle between Katrina and Julia and also to help them to better communicate their needs and feelings.

References

Engel, G.L. (1977). The need for a new medical model: A challenge for biomedicine. *Science*, *196*(4286), 129–136.

Sperry, L., Gudeman, J., Blackwell, B., & Faulkner, L. (1992). *Psychiatric case formulations*. Washington, DC: American Psychiatric Press.

7 Cognitive-Behavioral Case Conceptualizations

While Chapter 6 described a generic, non-theory-based method of case conceptualization, this chapter describes and illustrates the first of four theory-based methods, one that is based on Cognitive Behavior Therapy (CBT). Cognitive Behavior Therapy is one of the most commonly practiced psychotherapeutic approaches throughout the world today. Currently, there are several variations of it, with some emphasizing the cognitive side and others emphasizing the behavioral side of the approach. Nevertheless, the Cognitive-Behavioral case conceptualization method described here is sufficiently broad to be compatible with most Cognitive-Behavioral Therapy approaches. Two specific Cognitive-Behavioral approaches to case conceptualization are addressed in this book. Both are Third-Wave Cognitive-Behavioral approaches. One of these, Acceptance Commitment Therapy (ACT), is described in Chapter 10. The other, Dialectic Behavior Therapy (DBT) case conceptualization, is described in this chapter.

Cognitive-Behavioral Perspective

Cognitive Behavior Therapy represents a merging of the cognitive therapy perspective with the behavioral therapy perspective (Wright, Basco, & Thase, 2006). While the various Cognitive-Behavioral approaches differ in emphasis, clinicians typically combine cognitive interventions and behavioral interventions in their work with clients. In addition, Cognitive Behavior Therapy has been adapted to nearly all diagnostic conditions and is the most commonly utilized therapeutic approach with culturally diverse clients. Cognitive-Behavioral Therapy is a here-and-now approach that is problem focused. It also seeks to modify or correct maladaptive cognitions and behaviors using a variety of cognitive and behavioral methods to change rigid thinking, mood, and behavior. Since behavior is learned, negative behavior can be unlearned while new and more effective behaviors can be learned. The therapeutic relationship is collaborative in that the client shares responsibility for setting the agenda for the session and doing between-session homework (Sperry & Sperry, 2018).

While cognitions and behaviors are the central focus of assessment and intervention, they are also central to case conceptualization. Cognitions are identified at one of three levels: automatic thoughts, intermediate beliefs, and schemas.

Automatic thoughts are immediate thoughts or running commentary going through an individual's mind at a given point in time.

Intermediate beliefs are the "if-then" rules or conditional assumptions that individuals implicitly follow. This level of belief influences an individual's automatic thoughts. Schemas are core beliefs that individuals have about self, the world, and the future. This level of belief influences an individual's intermediate beliefs. For example, individuals with a schema of abandonment such as "Everybody I really care about always leaves me" are likely to have an intermediate belief such as "Others will leave me if I am not really important to them."

At least three types of problematic or maladaptive behaviors are recognized. These include behavioral excesses, e.g., uncontrollable rage; behavioral deficits, e.g., social withdrawal; and inappropriate behavior, e.g., laughing when another is injured. An additional type of behavior that is potentially problematic is social skill deficits, e.g., lack of assertiveness, undeveloped friendship skills, and limited self-regulation skills. These maladaptive behaviors along with maladaptive cognitions are incorporated into a Cognitive-Behavioral case conceptualization.

The mark of successful Cognitive-Behavioral treatment is healthier and more effective ways of thinking and behaving to achieve desired outcomes. Newman (2012) identified a view of psychological wellness from a Cognitive-Behavioral perspective:

> From a CBT perspective, psychological wellness is comprised of a number of characteristics and capabilities, including a person possessing: (1) a broad behavioral repertoire that can be used effectively to solve problems, to relate well to others, and to respond in differential ways that will be positively reinforced across many different situations; (2) cognitive flexibility, objectivity, astute observational skills, and hopefulness, along with a sense of self-efficacy; and (3) good emotional self-regulation, while still possessing an appropriate range of affect and a capacity for joy.
>
> (p. 31)

The following sections describe Cognitive-Behavioral assessment and Cognitive-Behavioral case conceptualization.

Cognitive-Behavioral Assessment

A Cognitive-Behavioral assessment emphasizes the relevant cognitive and behavioral factors that provide additional information to the diagnostic assessment and facilitate the development of cognitive-behaviorally focused clinical and treatment formulations. The primary goal of a Cognitive-Behavioral assessment is "to agree on a formulation and treatment plan with the client" (Kirk, 1989, p. 15).

A common strategy for doing this type of assessment is to begin with behaviors and then address cognitions. Start by identifying and analyzing problematic behaviors and affects. Behaviors are categorized as behavioral excesses (e.g., uncontrollable rage), behavioral deficits (e.g., social withdrawal), or inappropriateness (e.g., laughing when another is injured). Problematic behaviors and affect can be identified by analyzing a specific situation looking for antecedents, specific behaviors, and consequences, and if there is an ongoing pattern of impaired functioning. A situational analysis is useful in identifying a client's behavioral and cognitive contributions to the distress experienced (McCullough, 2000; McCullough, Schramm, & Penberthy, 2014). It can also evaluate the extent to which clients' maladaptive pattern of behaviors and cognitions diverts them from achieving their desired outcomes. Helpful questions to ask include:

"Describe the situation that was so stressful for you." (elicit the beginning, middle, and end of the problematic situation)

"What were your behaviors in the situation?" (elicit specific behaviors: gestures, eye contact, tone of voice, "What did you say?" "How did you say it?" etc.)

"What did you want out of the situation?" "Did you get what you wanted?"

"What was going on in your life before your symptoms began?" (elicits antecedents)

"What is the effect of these symptoms (behaviors, decreased functioning, etc.)?" (elicits consequences)

"What sort of things are you not doing right now because of this problem?"

"What do you do to try to make your situation more manageable?" (elicits severity and client's efforts to "solve" the problem)

"In what other situations have you experienced these symptoms (conflicts, difficulties etc.)?" Following up on this question helps identify a client's ongoing pattern beyond the current problematic situation.

Next, elicit the client's beliefs and interpretation of the problematic situation. Some useful questions include: "What was your interpretation of the situation?" and "What did it mean to you?" can be useful in eliciting the client's automatic thinking and intermediate beliefs. This inquiry is essential because it "begins to tap into automatic thoughts and deeper, more long-standing core beliefs" (Ledley, Marx, & Heimber, 2005, p. 42). This process helps the client examine their problematic cognitions such as all-or-none thinking, catastrophizing, and disqualifying the positive. In addition, probing the client's earlier experiences can be useful in identifying core maladaptive beliefs and schemas. The three main "levels" of clients' thinking to assess and modify are (in "descending" order) automatic thoughts, intermediate beliefs, and schemas. Schemas are core beliefs that clients have about self, other people, and the world.

Cognitive-Behavioral Case Conceptualization

A Cognitive-Behavioral case conceptualization includes clinical, cultural, and treatment formulations that emphasize the unique characteristics of the Cognitive-Behavioral perspective (Sperry & Sperry, 2016). The clinical formulation provides an explanation of the client's presenting problems and ongoing pattern in terms of maladaptive beliefs and maladaptive behaviors (Young, Klosko, &

Weishaar, 2003). The cultural formulation identifies the client's cultural identification, acculturation, and the explanation or reason believed to be the cause of the presenting problem. Assuming that cultural dynamics influence the client's presenting problem, it identifies the operative mix of cultural dynamics and personality dynamics. The treatment formulation provides a Cognitive-Behavioral framework for setting treatment goals, specifying a treatment focus and treatment strategies and interventions for achieving treatment goals. This formulation emphasizes the modification of both behavior patterns and cognitions using various cognitive and behavioral methods. Preparing the client for termination and relapse prevention strategies is integrated into the therapeutic process at the outset of treatment to foster the client's ability to cope and respond to digressed behavior patterns and cognitions. If indicated, culturally sensitive treatments are also incorporated into the treatment process. Among all the current psychotherapies, the Cognitive-Behavioral approach is the most culturally sensitive as it has been adapted to several ethnicities (Craske, 2010), including African American and Latino (Miranda et al., 2003) and Asian (Hwang, 2006).

Cognitive-Behavioral Case Conceptualization Method

The Cognitive-Behavioral method of case conceptualization is similar to the other four theoretical models described in this book in that it shares several common elements. Yet, it also differs from the other four methods because of its signature elements. These include: predisposition, treatment goals, treatment focus, treatment strategy, and treatment interventions.

Table 7.1 identifies and describes these five signature elements.

Table 7.1 Signature Elements of the Cognitive-Behavioral Case Conceptualization

Predisposition	maladaptive behaviors maladaptive beliefs
Treatment goals	reduce maladaptive beliefs and behaviors develop more adaptive beliefs and behaviors
Treatment focus	troublesome situations triggered or exacerbated by maladaptive beliefs and/or behaviors
Treatment strategies	*basic treatment strategy*: identify and modify specific maladaptive beliefs and behaviors *common strategies*: support; cognitive restructuring; replacement; exposure; skill training/psychoeducation
Treatment interventions	Socratic questioning; examining the evidence; cognitive restructuring, including disputation; self-monitoring and Automatic Thought Record; cognitive and behavioral replacement; thought stopping; behavioral activation; exposure; eye movement desensitization and reprocessing (EMDR); skills training (assertiveness, problem-solving, etc.); behavioral rehearsal and enactment; stress reduction and relaxation

Dialectical Behavior Therapy (DBT). Dialectical Behavior Therapy is one of the best known of the Third-Wave Cognitive-Behavioral Therapy approaches. While it is relatively new on the therapy scene, there have been several developments (Manning, 2018). Among the developments in the DBT case conceptualization literature is a straightforward approach that is form based. The form involves the identification of three elements: "vulnerabilities," "problems with their triggers," and a "hypothesis" statement, that is, a brief narrative that ties together the vulnerabilities, problems, and triggers. Treatment is then planned around each problem trigger that was identified. This form can be downloaded free from Therapist Aid (https://www.therapistaid.com/worksheets/case-form ulation.pdf).

In terms of our Integrative Model, it means plugging the Vulnerabilities and Problems with their Triggers into the Precipitant and Predisposition sections, and the specific Treatment Targets in the Treatment Goals section. Of course, the treatment methods unique to DBT as they relate to the case are added to the Treatment Interventions section.

Biopsychosocial Case Conceptualization: Five Cases

The process of constructing a Cognitive-Behavioral case conceptualization is illustrated for five different cases. Following background information on each case, there is an assessment paragraph that identifies key information germane to this model. Then, a table summarizes the nine elements from the diagnostic, clinical, and cultural formulations (discussed in Chapters 2 and 3) and the eight elements of the treatment formulation (discussed in Chapter 4) for that specific case. Finally, a narrative integrating this information is provided in a case conceptualization statement. The first paragraph reports the diagnostic and clinical formulations, the second paragraph reports the cultural formulation, while the third paragraph reports the treatment formulation.

Case of Geri

Geri R. is a 35-year-old, African American female who works as an administrative assistant. She is single, lives alone, and was referred by her company's human resources director for evaluation and treatment following three weeks of depression and social isolation. Her absence from work prompted the referral. Her symptoms began soon after her supervisor told Geri that she was being considered for a promotion. As a child she reports isolating and avoiding others when she was criticized and teased by family members and peers.

Cognitive-Behavioral Assessment

Besides diagnostic assessment information, the Cognitive-Behavioral assessment added the following: Geri mentioned that her family was demanding, critical, and emotionally distant throughout her childhood. She stated that her parents provided her with very little emotional support as a child and she rarely speaks with them today. Her younger brother reportedly would laugh and call her fat and ugly. Neighborhood kids and classmates at school would also tease her and make fun of her, and she adds that all she can remember about teachers is that they criticized her. Since childhood she has been very shy in most interpersonal relationships and she avoids talking to others when possible. An assessment of maladaptive behaviors and cognitions identified the following: among behavioral deficits was social withdrawal. Also noted were prominent social skill deficits in relational skills and friendship skills. Regarding maladaptive cognitions, she made the following statements: "It's safer not to trust anyone"; "If people got to know me better, they wouldn't like me"; and "Getting close to others isn't worth the risk." She also stated that "I'd rather be safe and alone than get a promotion and a raise." Table 7.2 describes the results of the diagnostic and Cognitive-Behavioral assessment summarized for the key elements of a full-scale case conceptualization.

Case Conceptualization Statement

Geri's increased social isolation and depressive symptoms (***presentation***) seem to be her reaction to the news that she was being considered for a job promotion and a new supervisor (***current precipitant***) as well as demands from close relationships and the expectation that she will be criticized, rejected, and feel unsafe (***continuing precipitants***). Throughout her life, she found it safer to avoid others when possible and conditionally relate to them at other times; as a result, she lacks key social skills and has a limited social network (***pattern***). Geri's overt problems are understandable when viewed as a consequence of her core beliefs. Her self-view involves core beliefs about being inadequate and vulnerable to negative evaluations of others. Her world view involves core beliefs about life being unfair and unpredictable, and others being critical, rejecting, and demanding. These are reflected in maladaptive schemas that include defectiveness and social isolation. Her maladaptive behaviors consist of shyness and avoidance in situations which she perceives as unsafe and prefers social isolation to engagement with others. In the past, Geri preferred to avoid social situations because it protected her from the possibility of making mistakes and being rejected. Her beliefs are consistent with an avoidant personality pattern in which she tends to perceive situations as threatening and unsafe and subsequently withdraws from others to feel safe. Behaviorally, this pattern of avoidance manifests itself in shyness, distrust, and social isolation, and since early life has resulted in skill deficits including assertive communications, negotiation, conflict resolution, and friendship skills. In short, her pattern can be understood in light of demanding, critical, and emotionally unavailable parents, the teasing and criticism of peers, and her response of withdrawal and avoidance behavior which limited the learning of adaptive relational skills (***predisposition***). This pattern is maintained by her shyness, the fact that she lives alone, her limited social skills, and that she finds it safer to socially isolate (***perpetuants***). Geri brings to treatment a demonstrated strength of commitment to her workplace through her many years of employment. She also benefits from

Table 7.2 Cognitive-Behavioral Case Conceptualization Elements

Presentation	increased social isolation and depressive symptoms
Precipitant	news that she was being considered for a job promotion and a new supervisor (***current precipitant***); demands of close relationships and the expectation that she will be criticized, rejected, and feel unsafe (***continuing precipitant***)
Pattern-maladaptive	avoid and disconnect or withdraw when feeling unsafe
Predisposition	***maladaptive cognitions***: views herself as inadequate and frightened of rejection, and views the world as rejecting and critical but wants safe relationships; maladaptive schemas: defectiveness and social isolation
	maladaptive behaviors: history of being teased, criticized, rejected; social isolation and avoidance behavior which limited learning relational and friendship skills
Perpetuant	maintained by her shyness, living alone, and generalized social isolation
Protective factors & strengths	close, trusting friend and confidante; stable meaningful job; eligible for job accommodation
Cultural identity	middle-class African American; limited ethnic ties
Cultural stress & acculturation	highly acculturated; no obvious acculturative stress but family gender roles reinforce the notion that she is inadequate
Cultural explanation	sadness results from job stress and chemical imbalance in her brain
Culture and/or personality	personality dynamics are significantly operative
Treatment pattern	connects while feeling safer
Treatment goals	reduce maladaptive beliefs and behaviors; develop more adaptive beliefs and behaviors
Treatment focus	troublesome situations triggered or exacerbated by maladaptive beliefs and/or behaviors
Treatment strategy	identify and modify specific maladaptive beliefs and behaviors; cognitive restructuring; replacement; exposure; skill training/psychoeducation; medication
Treatment interventions	Socratic questioning; examining the evidence; cognitive restructuring, including disputation; self-monitoring and Automatic Thought Record; cognitive and behavioral replacement; thought stopping; behavioral activation; exposure; skills training
Treatment obstacles	"test" practitioners; likely to resist group therapy; over dependence on practitioners; difficulty with termination
Treatment-cultural	gender may be an issue so assign supportive female practitioners
Treatment prognosis	good, if increased social connections, skills, and returns to work

having a friend whom she can trust and legislative structures through which she can seek accommodations for her job, such as the Americans with Disabilities Act (***protective factors/strengths***).

She identifies herself as a middle-class African American but has little interest and no involvement with the African American community (***cultural identity***). She is highly acculturated, as are her parents, but her family system placed higher value on men. This positive bias toward men appears to reinforce the notion that she is unwanted and inadequate (***cultural stress & acculturation***). She believes that her depression is the result of stress at work and a "chemical imbalance" in her brain (***cultural explanation***). There are no significant cultural factors that are operative. It appears that Geri's personality dynamics are significantly operative in her current clinical presentation, but gender roles should be examined (***culture and/or personality***).

The challenge for Geri is to function more effectively and feel safer in relating to others (***treatment pattern***). Treatment goals include reducing depressive symptoms, increasing interpersonal and friendship skills, and returning to work and establishing a supportive social network there (***treatment goals***). The treatment focus is to analyze troublesome situations triggered or exacerbated by her maladaptive beliefs and behaviors (***treatment focus***). The basic treatment strategy will be to identify and modify specific maladaptive beliefs and behaviors and utilize support, cognitive restructuring, replacement, exposure, and skills training as primary strategies (***treatment strategy***). Initially, behavioral activation will be used in conjunction with medication to reduce her clinical depression and energize her sufficiently to be able to participate in therapy and be ready to return to work, and she will be referred for medication evaluation along with medication monitoring, if indicated. Increasing relational and friendship skills is best accomplished in a psychoeducation group and individual therapy will be useful in transitioning her to such a group. Her maladaptive beliefs will be processed with guided discovery, and she will be taught to self-monitor thoughts, behaviors, and feelings and to challenge them with the Automatic Thought Record (***treatment intervention***). Some obstacles and challenges to treatment can be anticipated. Given her avoidant personality structure, ambivalent resistance is likely. It can be anticipated that she will have difficulty discussing personal matters with practitioners, and that she will "test" and provoke practitioners into criticizing her for changing or canceling appointments at the last minute or being late, and that she might procrastinate, avoid feelings, and otherwise "test" the practitioner's trustability. Once trust in the practitioner is achieved, she is likely to cling to the practitioner and treatment and thus termination may be difficult unless her social support system outside therapy is increased. Furthermore, her pattern of avoidance is likely to make entry into and continuation with group work difficult. Therefore, individual sessions can serve as a transition into group work, including having some contact with the group practitioner who will presumably be accepting and non-judgmental. This should increase Geri's feeling of safety and make self-disclosure in a group setting less difficult. Transference enactment is another consideration. Given the extent of parental and peer criticism and teasing, it is anticipated that any perceived impatience and verbal or non-verbal indications of criticalness by the practitioner will activate this transference. Finally, because of her tendency to cling to others she trusts, increasing her capacity to feel more confident in functioning with greater independence and increasing the time between the last four or five sessions can reduce her ambivalence about termination (***treatment obstacles***). Given Geri's personality dynamics, treatment progress does not appear to be highly influenced by cultural stress. However, gender dynamics could impact the therapeutic relationship given the gender roles in her family, her strained relationship with her father, and her limited involvement with men ever since. Accordingly, female practitioners for both individual and group therapy appear to be indicated in the initial phase of treatment (***treatment-cultural***). Assuming that Geri increases her self-confidence, relational skills, and social contacts in and outside therapy, as well as returns to work, her prognosis is adjudged to be good; if not, it is guarded (***treatment prognosis***).

Case of Antwone

Antwone is an African American Navy seaman in his mid 20s who has lashed out at others with limited provocation. Recently, his commander ordered him to undergo compulsory counseling. From infancy until the time he enlisted in the Navy, he lived in foster placements, mostly with an abusive African American foster family.

Cognitive-Behavioral Assessment

Besides diagnostic assessment information, the Cognitive-Behavioral assessment added the following: He stated that he is aggressive with others because he is trying to protect himself against the hurt, arbitrary judgments, rejection, and loss that he has experienced since early life. This all started with his mother who abandoned him, and then his foster family who both neglected and abused him. He is wary and defensive around others, although he desires caring relationships. An assessment of maladaptive behaviors and cognitions identified the following: He presented with problems with assertive communications, negotiation, conflict resolution, and very few friendship skills. He identified that he gets into physical altercations almost every week and constantly feels angry and confused. One of his automatic thoughts is: "I don't get close to others since they always harm or leave me." Table 7.3 describes the results of the diagnostic and Cognitive-Behavioral assessment summarized for the key elements of a full-scale case conceptualization.

Case Conceptualization Statement

Antwone's verbal and physical lashing out at others and his confusion about others' intentions (***presentation***) appear to be his response to the taunting and provocation of his peers that resulted in a physical fight (***current precipitant***) as well as the perceived injustice of peers and authority figures (***continuing precipitants***).

Table 7.3 Case Conceptualization Elements

Presentation	verbal and/or physical retaliation; confusion
Precipitant	conflicts that resulted in a physical fight with other sailors (***current precipitant***); perceived injustice of peers and authority figures (***continuing precipitants***)
Pattern-maladaptive	strikes back and conditionally relates
Predisposition	***maladaptive cognitions***: views himself not only as defective, but also as industrious and self-protective; views the world as dangerous, unfair, and demanding, and others as hurtful and rejecting; maladaptive schemas: defectiveness, abuse/mistrust, punitiveness ***maladaptive behaviors***: lashes out and becomes defensive at perceived injustices when he anticipates rejection; he is wary and defensive around others; problems with assertive communications, negotiation, conflict resolution, and very few friendship skills
Perpetuant	limited capacity for emotional regulation; lacks conflict resolution skills
Protective factors & strengths	best friend was a secure attachment figure; intelligent, avid reader with wide interests; creativity; committed to duty and service
Cultural identity	African American with some conflict about ethnic ties
Acculturation & cultural stress	highly acculturated with considerable cultural stress
Cultural explanation	racial degradation; racial provocations of white peers and superiors
Culture and/or personality	personality *and* cultural factors are operative
Treatment pattern	connect and relate to others while being careful
Treatment goals	reduce maladaptive beliefs and behaviors; develop more adaptive beliefs and behaviors; increase emotional self-regulation, particularly increasing control over his anger and impulsivity, and improving assertive communication and conflict regulation skills
Treatment focus	troublesome situations triggered or exacerbated by maladaptive beliefs and/or behaviors
Treatment strategy	identify and modify specific maladaptive beliefs and behaviors; cognitive restructuring; replacement; exposure; skill training/psychoeducation
Treatment interventions	Socratic questioning; examining the evidence; cognitive restructuring, including disputation; self-monitoring and Automatic Thought Record; cognitive and behavioral replacement; behavioral activation; exposure; skills training; difficulty with termination
Treatment obstacles	"test" practitioner; aggressive attitude; over dependence on practitioner
Prognosis	good to very good
Cultural treatment	therapeutically frame and process his foster family's prejudice and abuse as self-loathing passed down from their ancestors to him; bibliotherapy

Throughout his life, Antwone has sought to be accepted and make sense of being neglected, abused, and abandoned, and to protect himself by aggressively striking back and conditionally relating to others in the face of a perceived threat or injustice (***pattern***).

_____

_____

_____

_____

_____

(***predisposition***). His limited capacity for emotional regulation, along with deficits in conflict resolution skills, serves to maintain this pattern (***perpetuants***). Antwone brings several protective factors and strengths to therapy, including his childhood best friend who served as his only secure attachment figure. He is intelligent, he is a reader with wide interests, and he has received regular promotions in rank, at least until recently. He also writes poetry and has learned two foreign languages. Additionally, he benefits from a caring military command and organizational structure that has encouraged counseling and treatment in lieu of punitive measures for past aggressive behaviors (***protective factors/strengths***).

Antwone identifies as African American and maintains some ethnic ties (***cultural identity***). Although he is highly acculturated, he continues to experience considerable racial discrimination which seems to be exacerbated by his cultural beliefs (***cultural stress & acculturation***). He believes that his problems result from racial degradation and abuse from his African American foster family, as well as from racial provocations by his white peers and Navy superiors (***cultural explanation***). It appears that both personality and cultural factors are operative (***culture and/or personality***).

The challenge for Antwone is to function more effectively in relating to others while being careful in getting to know and trust them (***treatment pattern***).

_____

_____

_____

_____

_____

(***treatment goals***). These goals would foster a more adaptive pattern in which he can care before more fully connecting with others. The treatment focus is to analyze troublesome situations triggered or exacerbated by maladaptive beliefs and/or behaviors (***treatment focus***). The therapeutic strategy will be to identify and modify specific maladaptive beliefs and behaviors with cognitive restructuring, replacement, exposure, and skill training/psychoeducation (***treatment strategy***).

_____

_____

_____

_____

_____

_____

(***treatment intervention***). Specific treatment obstacles and challenges can be anticipated. These include the likelihood that Antwone will quickly identify with a caring practitioner as the positive father figure and role model that he has never had. It is also likely that this will engender a predictable transference–countertransference enactment which may result in him aggressively acting out (***treatment obstacles***). In addition to addressing personality and interpersonal treatment targets, an effective treatment outcome will require addressing the cultural dimension of prejudice, not only prejudice from white peers and superiors, but also his experience of black-on-black prejudice. It may be useful to therapeutically frame his foster family's prejudice and abuse toward him in terms of self-loathing that was passed down from their ancestors to him; then, it can be therapeutically processed. Because he is an avid reader, bibliotherapy, i.e., books and articles that analyze and explain this type of prejudice, could be a useful therapeutic adjunct (***treatment-cultural***). Antwone brings several strengths and resources to therapy including intelligence, a reader with wide interests, regular promotions in rank, at least until recently, poetry writing, and learning two foreign languages. These resources plus his motivation to change suggest a good to very good prognosis (***treatment prognosis***).

Case of Maria

Maria is a 17-year-old, first-generation Mexican American female who was referred for counseling because of mood swings. She is conflicted about her decision to go off to college instead of staying home to care for her terminally ill mother. Her family expects her to stay home. She is angry at her older sister who left home at 17 after her parents insisted that her culture "requires" her to take care of her parents when they get old or become ill. Her Anglo friends encourage her to go to college and pursue her dreams.

Cognitive-Behavioral Assessment

Besides diagnostic assessment information, the Cognitive-Behavioral assessment added the following: She discussed that her parents, her boyfriend, and her friends regularly tell her what she should be doing with her life. She also believes that she is misunderstood by everyone, her acceptance by others is conditional on her making the "right" decision, and that she will end up being a failure. An assessment of maladaptive behaviors and cognitions identified the following: She identified herself as shy, passive, and "someone who always puts others first." She identified that she tries to avoid conflict as much as possible and she has recently felt "stuck" and started drinking alcohol with friends to relax and forget about everything that is bothering her. Some of her automatic thoughts include "If I go to college my parents will not love me anymore," "Nobody understands me," and "I don't know what to do, I can't handle this situation." Table 7.4 describes the results of the diagnostic and Cognitive-Behavioral assessment summarized for the key elements of a full-scale case conceptualization.

Case Conceptualization Statement

Maria's depressive symptoms, confusion, and recent experimentation with alcohol use (***presentation***) seem to be her reaction to pressures and conflict over going away to college or staying to care for her parents (***current precipitant***) as well as expectations of self-reliance, being alone, or need to meet others' needs at the expense of her own (***continuing precipitants***). Throughout her life, Maria has attempted to be a good daughter and friend and has become increasingly "stuck" in meeting the needs of others at the expense of her own needs (***pattern***).

_____

_____

_____

_____

_____

_____

(***predisposition***). Her low level of assertiveness and unwillingness to disappoint her parents serve to maintain this pattern (***perpetuant***). Maria brings several strengths to therapy including strong family, social, and religious values that may motivate her to establish vital life directions. She is also bright and successful in school, which offers a variety of directions available to her in the future. She also benefits from a tight-knit family and cultural community in which she can feel safe and supported (***protective factors/strengths***).

Maria identifies herself as a working-class Mexican American with a moderate level of involvement in that heritage (***cultural identity***). Her level of acculturation is in the low to moderate range while her parents' level is in the low range. Since her older sister refused to follow the cultural mandate that the oldest daughter would meet her parents needs rather than her own, that responsibility is now on Maria. Maria's ambivalence about whether to follow cultural norms and

Table 7.4 Case Conceptualization Elements

Presentation	moodiness; confusion; experimentation with alcohol use
Precipitant	pressures and conflict over going away to college or staying to care for her parents (***current precipitant***); expectations of self-reliance, being alone, or need to meet others' needs at the expense of her own (***continuing precipitants***)
Pattern-maladaptive	meet others' needs but not her own
Predisposition	***maladaptive cognitions***: views herself as nice yet inadequate and needing to please others; views the world and others as demanding, but insensitive to her needs; maladaptive schemas: self-sacrifice, approval seeking, and defectiveness
	maladaptive behaviors: subservience and pleasing behavior as well as underdeveloped assertive communication skills; alcohol use for coping
Perpetuant	dependent and pleasing style; low assertiveness; cultural expectation
Protective factors & strengths	strong family, social, religious values; successful student; tight-knit and safe cultural community
Cultural identity	working-class Mexican American
Cultural stress & acculturation	low to moderate level of acculturation; stress from ambivalence about parental and cultural expectations
Cultural explanation	problems caused by "lack of faith"
Culture and/or personality	personality *and* cultural factors operative
Treatment pattern	meet her needs and the needs of others
Treatment goals	reduce maladaptive beliefs and behaviors; develop more adaptive beliefs and behaviors
Treatment focus	troublesome situations triggered or exacerbated by maladaptive beliefs and/or behaviors
Treatment strategy	identify and modify specific maladaptive beliefs and behaviors; cognitive restructuring; replacement; exposure; skill training/psychoeducation
Treatment interventions	Socratic questioning; examining the evidence; cognitive restructuring, including disputation; self-monitoring and Automatic Thought Record; cognitive and behavioral replacement; thought stopping; exposure; skills training
Treatment obstacles	may capitulate to parents and cultural expectations; pleasing the practitioner; practitioner may unwittingly advocate autonomy
Treatment-cultural	process cultural expectations about caregiver role and need to please; family sessions addressing parents' cultural expectations
Treatment prognosis	fair to good

expectations or her own aspirations is quite distressing for her (***cultural stress & acculturation***). Her explanatory model is that her problems are due to a "lack of faith," a belief that is consistent with a lower level of acculturation. Although she and her family experienced some discrimination upon arrival here, it ended when they moved to a "safer" Mexican American neighborhood (***cultural explanation***). It appears that both personality and cultural factors are operative. Specifically, cultural dynamics that foster dependency, i.e., good daughters care for their parents without question, serve to reinforce her dependent personality dynamics (***culture and/or personality***).

The challenge for Maria to function more effectively is to meet both her own needs in addition to the needs of others (***treatment pattern***).

_____

_____

_____

_____

_____

_____

(***treatment goals***). The treatment focus is to analyze troublesome situations triggered or exacerbated by maladaptive beliefs and/or behaviors (***treatment focus***). The therapeutic strategy will be to identify and modify specific maladaptive beliefs and behaviors with cognitive restructuring, replacement, exposure, and skill training/psychoeducation (***treatment strategy***).

_____

_____

_____

_____

_____

(***treatment intervention***). In terms of likely treatment obstacles and challenges, it is likely that Maria will attempt to please the practitioner by readily agreeing to the practitioner's suggestions and between-session assignments, but afterwards become conflicted and then fail to follow up. It is also likely that the client will capitulate to her parents' expectations. Accordingly, the practitioner might, early in treatment, make the predictive interpretation that this might occur, but that it does not indicate failure, and that it can be therapeutically processed. Finally, practitioners working with dependent clients need to anticipate how their own needs and values may become treatment obstacles. This can occur when they unwittingly advocate for and expect clients to embrace independence and autonomy before the client is sufficiently ready (***treatment obstacles***). Effective treatment outcomes will also address relevant cultural dynamics. Specifically, this may involve therapeutically processing her explanatory model that a lack of faith is the source of her problem. Depending on the saliency and strength of this belief, education and cognitive disputation may be indicated. The cultural expectation about caring for her parents in light of her need to please would also be processed. In addition, family sessions may be indicated wherein her parents can review and revise their cultural expectations of her (***treatment-cultural***). Besides the impact of personality and culture, the resources that Maria brings to therapy influence her prognosis. She is bright, successful in school, and has already identified her needs and career aspirations. At this point, however, given her lower level of acculturation and dependent personality dynamics, her prognosis is in the fair to good range (***treatment prognosis***).

Case of Richard

Richard is a 41-year-old, Caucasian male who is being evaluated for anxiety, sadness, and anger following his recent divorce. He currently lives on his own, is employed as a machine operator, and frequents nightclubs where he "is on the lookout for the perfect woman." He has held four jobs over the past six years and was fired from his last job because he smashed his fist through a wall after being confronted by a female coworker. He is the only child of alcoholic parents whom he describes as "fighting all the time."

Cognitive-Behavioral Assessment

Besides diagnostic assessment information, the Cognitive-Behavioral assessment added the following: As a child, he observed that adults fight, attack each other, and neglect and terrify their children. Since childhood, he has had challenges with perspective taking, friendship skills, emotional regulation, and anger management. Today, he continues to have tumultuous relationships with a great deal of conflict. During the interview, Richard presented with an arrogant attitude and he even questioned the credentials of the practitioner. An assessment of maladaptive behaviors and cognitions identified the following: He identified problems in controlling his anger and stated that his ex-wife called him impulsive and demanding. He discussed people as being "all good" or "all bad" and reported that he "can't cope with all of these toxic people" in his life. Two of his automatic thoughts are: "If my friends don't call me it means they don't want me around" and "I need women for me to be happy." Table 7.5 describes the results of the diagnostic and Cognitive-Behavioral assessment summarized for the key elements of a full-scale case conceptualization.

Case Conceptualization Statement

Richard's angry outbursts, sadness, and anxiety (***presentation***) seem to be a reaction to his recent divorce and also being fired from his last job for smashing his

Table 7.5 Case Conceptualization Elements

Presentation	angry outbursts, sadness, and anxiety
Precipitant	recent divorce and also being fired from his last job for smashing his fist through a wall (***current precipitant***); evaluation of self, being alone, or others' perception of not being special (***continuing precipitants***)
Pattern-maladaptive	elevates self while belittling and using others
Predisposition	***maladaptive cognitions***: views himself as entitled to special considerations; views the world as his for the taking and that others will be available and responsive to his needs; maladaptive schemas: entitlement, defectiveness, and emotional deprivation
	maladaptive behaviors: angry, short-tempered, impulsive, neglectful, and demanding behaviors
Perpetuant	impulsivity; limited relationship skills; inability to empathize
Protective factors & strengths	resilient, charismatic, and engaging; demonstrated capacity to care for others (i.e., past relationship with grandmother)
Cultural identity	middle-class Caucasian male
Cultural stress & acculturation	highly acculturated; no obvious cultural stress, but privilege should be examined in the therapeutic process
Cultural explanation	anxiety, anger, sadness caused by abusive, non-loving parents
Culture and/or personality	personality are dynamics operative, but privilege should be examined
Treatment pattern	self-confident and respectful of others
Treatment goals	reduce maladaptive beliefs and behaviors; develop more adaptive beliefs and behaviors; reduce angry outbursts, sadness, and anxiety
Treatment focus	troublesome situations triggered or exacerbated by maladaptive beliefs and/or behaviors
Treatment strategy	identify and modify specific maladaptive beliefs and behaviors; cognitive restructuring; replacement; exposure; skill training/psychoeducation
Treatment interventions	Socratic questioning; examining the evidence; cognitive restructuring
Treatment obstacles	"test" practitioners; likely to resist group therapy; over dependence on practitioners; difficulty with termination
Treatment-cultural	gender may be an issue so assign supportive female practitioners
Treatment prognosis	good, if increased social connections, skills, and returns to work

fist through a wall (*current precipitant*), as well as self-evaluation, being alone, or others' perception of not being special (*continuing precipitants*). From adolescence, he has elevated himself and belittled and abused others with an aggressive style, making it difficult to sustain safe and satisfying relationships (*pattern*).

_____

_____

_____

_____

_____

_____

(*predisposition*). This pattern is maintained by his inability to empathize, his impulsivity, and his inability to regulate his emotions (*perpetuant*). Richard's secure attachment with his grandmother serves as a protective factor and evidence that he has the capacity to care for others. The most prominent strength Richard brings to therapy is resilience. He is also charismatic and engaging (*protective factors/strengths*).

Richard identifies as a middle-class Caucasian male (*cultural identity*). He appears to be highly acculturated and there is no obvious indications of acculturative stress (*cultural stress & acculturation*). He believes that his current problems of anger, sadness, and anxiety result from the bad example he received from his abusive and non-loving parents who fought constantly when they drank (*cultural explanation*). Finally, personality dynamics are predominant and adequately explain his presenting problem and pattern, but examining his sense of entitlement and his own experience of privilege would be useful to address in therapy (*culture and/or personality*).

The challenge for Richard to function more effectively is to remain self-confident while endeavoring to be more respectful of others (*treatment pattern*). Treatment goals include increasing his anger and impulse control and reducing his sadness and anxiety. Additionally, treatment will seek to reduce his maladaptive beliefs and behaviors as well as to develop more adaptive beliefs and behaviors.

_____

_____

_____

_____

_____

_____

(*treatment goals*). The treatment focus is to analyze troublesome situations triggered or exacerbated by maladaptive beliefs and/or behaviors (*treatment focus*). The basic treatment strategy will be to identify and modify Richard's maladaptive beliefs and behaviors. Treatment strategies compatible with the treatment goals and focus include cognitive restructuring, replacement, exposure, and skill training (*treatment strategy*).

(*treatment intervention*). With regard to likely treatment obstacles and challenges, it is likely that Richard will minimize his own problematic behaviors by blaming circumstances or others. It can be expected that he will alternate between idealization or devaluation of the practitioner, at least in the beginning phase of therapy. His entitled and arrogant attitude could activate practitioner countertransference. Furthermore, since it is not uncommon for clients with a narcissistic style to discontinue treatment when their symptoms, immediate conflicts, or stressors are sufficiently reduced, the practitioner who believes the client can profit from continued therapy needs to point out – at the beginning of therapy and thereafter – that until the client's underlying maladaptive pattern is sufficiently changed, similar issues and concerns will inevitably arise in the future (*treatment obstacles*). Since the primary influence is personality dynamics, no cultural focus to treatment is indicated besides examining his entitlement and sense of privilege (*treatment-cultural*). Finally, because of the client's conditional manner of relating, multiple job firings, and impulsivity, at this point, his prognosis is considered fair (*treatment prognosis*).

Case of Katrina

Katrina is a 13-year-old female of mixed ethnicity. She was referred for counseling by her guidance counselor due to recent depressive symptoms, poor academic performance, and oppositional behavior and fighting with other students at school. Her aggressive behavior and academic challenges have increased over the past six months since Katrina overheard a conversation between her mother and aunt in which she found out that her father had an affair for eight years. She was shocked to learn that this resulted in two births. Other difficulties include several fights with other students in the classroom, frequent conflict with her mother, skipping 15 days of school over the past six months, and diminished interest in her academic work. While she had previously excelled academically, she now displayed a marked loss of interest in activities that used to give her pleasure, such as drawing and reading. Katrina's father is currently living in Puerto Rico and has no contact with the family. Katrina lives in a small apartment with her mother and younger brother near her school. She reported being frustrated with the lack of space, since they had to downsize from the single-family home they lived in before her father left the family one year ago.

Because Katrina was a minor, it was necessary for the school counselor to speak with Katrina and her mother together during the initial session. Katrina's mother, Julia, stated that she believes that Katrina will not talk to most people about her problems because she does not trust anyone. During the first meeting, Katrina reported that she does not trust anyone and that she is not interested in attending counseling sessions if the practitioner is going to tell her what to do. Self-disclosure was very difficult for Katrina during the initial interview and Julia answered the majority of the questions that were asked, in some cases speaking for Katrina when she made efforts to speak. Julia reported that Katrina's father was highly critical and also emotionally withdrawn throughout Katrina's childhood.

Cognitive-Behavioral Assessment

Katrina stated, "I don't really have a dad, since real fathers are supposed to take care of their families." She said she was tired of her teachers and her mother always forcing her to do things that she doesn't want to do. An assessment of maladaptive behaviors and cognitions included: skill deficits in assertive communication, intermediate beliefs involving "showing weakness means that people will take advantage of you," beliefs about authority figures being controlling and not trustworthy, and schemas that include unworthiness, mistrust, and being unlovable. Table 7.6 describes the results of the diagnostic and Cognitive-Behavioral assessment summarized for the key elements of a full-scale case conceptualization.

Case Conceptualization Statement

Katrina's increased social isolation, aggressive and oppositional behavior, and depressive symptoms (*presentation*) appear to be Katrina's reaction to recent news of her father's infidelity and resulting children (*current precipitant*). Katrina has a tendency to retaliate when she perceives that she is being violated or controlled by others (*continuing precipitant*). Given Katrina's lack of connection with her father and lack of trust in both parents, she moves against authority figures and her peers to protect herself from further harm and rejection (*pattern*).

Table 7.6 Cognitive-Behavioral Case Conceptualization Elements

Presentation	depressive symptoms, aggressive behavior, and social isolation
Precipitant	learning of her father's infidelity and resulting children (***current precipitant***); retaliates in situations of perceived violation or control by others (***continuing precipitants***)
Pattern-maladaptive	moves against to protect herself from potential harm and rejection
Predisposition	**skill deficits:** friendship skills, assertiveness, and anger management **self–other schemas:** (self-view) unworthy, inadequate; (other-view) not trustworthy and controlling
Perpetuant	social isolation and lack of support system, mother and teachers rigidly forcing compliance; low frustration tolerance; lack of assertive communication skills
Protective factors & strengths	has a close relationship to her aunt and little brother; intelligent, creative, and resilient
Cultural identity	Hispanic and African American; lower income
Cultural stress & acculturation	low to moderate level of acculturation and cultural stress
Cultural explanation	denies depression; believes she would feel better of her teachers and mother were less controlling
Culture and/or personality	personality dynamics and cultural dynamics are operative
Treatment pattern	increase safety and ability to connect with others
Treatment goals	reduce maladaptive beliefs and behaviors; develop more adaptive beliefs and behaviors; reduce depressive symptoms and aggressive behavior
Treatment focus	troublesome situations triggered or exacerbated by maladaptive beliefs/behaviors
Treatment strategy	skills training; motivational interviewing; anger management; cognitive restructuring and replacement; strengths-based CBT
Treatment interventions	motivational interviewing; family therapy; thought stopping; CBT-art therapy; mindfulness; building on strengths; replacing maladaptive thoughts and behaviors
Treatment obstacles	likely to resist individual and group therapy; expected outbursts at mother during family sessions; difficulty with self-disclosure
Treatment-cultural	assign a female practitioner; Culturally Focused Cognitive Behavior Therapy and family therapy
Treatment prognosis	fair to good if protective factors are incorporated in treatment

In short, her pattern can be understood in light of her lack of trust with her father based on his infidelity. In addition, her perception of being rejected by her father appears to have influenced her core beliefs about mistrust, paranoia about others' intentions, and a lack of safety with others.

_____

_____

_____

_____

_____

_____

(*predisposition*). This pattern is maintained by Katrina's unwillingness to ask for help, her low level of motivation to engage in therapy, her social isolation and lack of support system, her mother and teachers rigidly forcing compliance, her low frustration tolerance, and lack of assertive communication skills (*perpetuants*). Despite some of her current challenges, Katrina reported being very close with her aunt and little brother. Besides her close relationships in her family, Katrina reported that she feels responsible for her brother and does everything she can to protect him from harm. Lastly, her strengths include her being a good artist, determined, intelligent, empathic, and creative (*protective factors/strengths*).

Katrina identifies herself as being heterosexual and of mixed ethnicity. She identified as Hispanic and African American but reported having little connection to ethnic and cultural traditions from either identity. She stated that she wants to be more like her friends and doesn't want to feel different or weird by speaking Spanish to her mother in front of friends (*cultural identity*). She is moderately acculturated and prefers not to speak Spanish outside of the home, though her mother requires her to speak Spanish while at home. Katrina's mother presents with a low level of acculturation as evidenced by having challenges with speaking English, having very few English-speaking friends, being first-generation Puerto-Rican American and also African American, and reporting that she is unhappy living in the United States and plans to move back to Puerto Rico once Katrina graduates from high school (*cultural stress & acculturation*). Katrina does not believe she is depressed, but feels that she would be less annoyed with people if they would be less controlling and "less bossy" (*cultural explanation*). There appears to be a moderate level of cultural factors and a moderate level of personality dynamics that influence the presenting issues (*culture and/or personality*).

The challenge for Katrina to function more effectively is to increase her ability to trust others, feel safer, and to better connect with others (***treatment pattern***).

_____

_____

_____

_____

_____

_____

(***treatment goals***). The treatment focus is to examine and modify her maladaptive beliefs about others being unsafe and controlling, and to help her modify her behavioral deficits which have been problematic at home and in the school setting (***treatment focus***). The basic treatment strategies will be to identify and modify specific maladaptive beliefs and behaviors and address them through skills training, motivational interviewing, restructuring, psychoeducation, referral to group counseling therapy in her school, and family therapy (***treatment strategy***).

_____

_____

_____

_____

_____

_____

(***treatment intervention***). Some obstacles and challenges to treatment are anticipated given Katrina's low motivation to engage in therapy and her paranoid traits that are associated with her oppositional behaviors. It can be anticipated that she will have difficulty discussing personal matters with practitioners due to her inability to trust and that she will often engage in testing behaviors toward the practitioner (***treatment obstacles***). Treatment will require some culturally sensitive elements given Katrina and her mother's level of acculturation. Culturally Focused Cognitive Behavior Therapy and family therapy will be used to address cultural factors that are present by considering Katrina's mixed ethnicity and her personal experience of both cultures. Additionally, gender dynamics may be an issue so it may be useful to assign her a female therapist (***treatment-cultural***). Assuming that Katrina is able to engage more in the therapeutic process as well as utilize her strengths and seek support from her aunt, her prognosis is adjudged to be fair to good (***treatment prognosis***).

Skill Building Exercises: Cognitive-Behavioral Case Conceptualizations

As mentioned in the Skill Building Exercises in Chapter 6, you will note that *certain elements of the case conceptualization statements contain open lines.*

These lines provide you with an opportunity to further develop your conceptualization skills with specific prompts. Write a short predisposition statement, treatment goals, and a list of corresponding theory-specific treatment interventions for each case.

Concluding Note

The Cognitive-Behavioral model of case conceptualization was described and illustrated. The basic premises of the Cognitive-Behavioral perspective were listed and the factors involved in a Cognitive-Behavioral assessment were discussed. The Cognitive-Behavioral model of case conceptualization was then applied to five cases and illustrated with their clinical, cultural, and treatment formulations. Chapter 8 analyzes and illustrates these same five cases with the Time-Limited Dynamic model of case conceptualization.

CHAPTER 7 QUESTIONS

1. Describe the various emerging aspects of a client's maladaptive behavior to identify using the Cognitive-Behavioral case conceptualization approach.
2. Discuss the goals, rational, and ideal outcomes for using a Cognitive-Behavioral case conceptualization approach.
3. Explain why the most common approach in Cognitive-Behavioral case conceptualization starts with behaviors and then addresses cognitions. What is the advantage?
4. Compare some of the prompted questions for use in the initial assessment. What components of the case conceptualization do these elicit?
5. Describe the components of clinical, cultural, and treatment formulations from a Cognitive-Behavioral approach.

Appendix: Case of Antwone

Predisposition

His reaction can be understood as his aggressive and impulsive means of protecting himself against the hurt, arbitrary judgments, rejection, and loss that he has experienced from his birth mother and adoptive family. Antwone learned that aggressive behavior is used to communicate and to neutralize or defeat others. Antwone had a history of emotional, verbal, and physical abuse as a child. He also experienced neglect and a history of abandonment. Cognitively, his self-view involves core beliefs about being defective and that others typically harm or abuse him. His world view involves core beliefs about life being dangerous and unfair and that others are harmful and rejecting. These are reflected in maladaptive schema of defectiveness, mistrust/abuse, and punitiveness. Behaviorally, this pattern of striking back and conditionally relating to others since early life has resulted in skill deficits including assertive communications, negotiation, conflict resolution, and friendship skills.

Treatment Goal

Treatment goals include emotional self-regulation, particularly increasing control over his anger and impulsivity, and improving assertive communication and conflict regulation skills.

Treatment Interventions

His maladaptive beliefs will be processed with guided discovery, and he will be taught to self-monitor thoughts, behaviors, and feelings and to challenge them with the Automatic Thought Record. Increasing conflict regulation and relational skills will be accomplished in a psychoeducation group. Behavioral replacement will be implemented in individual therapy to help him find alternative behaviors when he becomes angry or is involved in a conflict. Other interventions will include Socratic questioning, examining the evidence, disputation, and cognitive and behavioral replacement.

Case of Maria

Predisposition

Her reaction is understandable given her upbringing in a traditional Mexican American family, in which family is highly valued. Cognitively, her self-view involves core beliefs about being defective and inadequate. Her world view involves core beliefs about the world and others as demanding, and also insensitive to her needs. She believes that she is a bad daughter if she leaves or will let herself down if she capitulates to her parents' expectations. Her beliefs are consistent with a dependent personality pattern in which she tends to perceive situations as difficult and unfair and subsequently puts others' needs first and neglects her own needs. Her maladaptive schemas include self-sacrifice, approval seeking, and defectiveness. Behaviorally, this pattern of pleasing others manifests itself in shyness, passive communication, and neglecting her own needs, and since early life has resulted in skill deficits including assertive communications, negotiation, and conflict resolution.

Treatment Goal

Treatment goals include increasing her sense of self-efficacy and capacity for assertively making and articulating decisions.

Treatment Interventions

Increasing relational and assertiveness skills will be accomplished in a psychoeducation group and individual therapy will be useful in transitioning her to such a group. Her maladaptive beliefs will be processed with guided discovery, and she will be taught to self-monitor her thoughts, behaviors, and feelings, and to challenge them with the Automatic Thought Record. Role play will be used to help her improve her assertiveness skills while the practitioner can also work with her on disputing some of her irrational beliefs about specific situations. Other interventions will include Socratic questioning, examining the evidence, cognitive and behavioral replacement, thought stopping, and exposure.

Case of Richard

Predisposition

Richard's overt problems are understandable when viewed as a consequence of his core beliefs. Richard views himself as entitled to special considerations. He views the world as his for the taking and that others will be available and responsive to his needs. His maladaptive schemas include entitlement, defectiveness, and emotional deprivation. These beliefs are consistent with a narcissistic personality pattern in which he tends to perceive situations as serving his needs. Maladaptive behaviors consist of anger, emotional dysregulation, impulsivity, and demandingness. Behavior deficits include limited relational skills, including the capacity to respond with empathy.

Treatment Goal

Treatment goals include increasing his anger and impulse control and reducing his sadness and anxiety.

Treatment Interventions

Increasing relational and empathy skills and anger management are best accomplished in a psychoeducation group and individual therapy will be useful in transitioning him to such groups. His maladaptive beliefs will be processed with guided discovery, and he will be taught to self-monitor his thoughts, behaviors, and feelings, and to challenge them with the Automatic Thought Record. Cognitive and behavioral replacement will be utilized to help him improve his mood and to start leaving his home on weekends to play golf and spend time with friends. Other interventions will include Socratic questioning, examining the evidence, disputation, thought stopping, behavioral activation, exposure, and behavioral rehearsal and enactment.

Case of Katrina

Predisposition

Katrina views herself as defective and inadequate and views others as controlling and not being trustworthy. Her maladaptive schema includes unworthiness, mistrust, and being unlovable. Her maladaptive behaviors consist of skill deficits in assertive communication, friendship skills, and anger management. These schemas and behavioral deficits appear to be influenced by Katrina experiencing her father as critical and not trustworthy and also viewing her mother as controlling and secretive.

Treatment Goals

Treatment goals include reducing her depressive symptoms, anger management, increasing her assertiveness and friendship skills, and reducing her oppositional behaviors. Additionally, treatment will seek to reduce her maladaptive beliefs and behaviors as well as to develop more adaptive beliefs and behaviors.

Treatment Interventions

Once she has been engaged in the therapeutic process through rapport building and motivational interviewing, her maladaptive beliefs will be processed with guided discovery and cognitive replacement. She will be taught to self-monitor her thoughts, practice mindfulness, use CBT-art therapy to discuss her feelings, and complete thought logs to assist her in managing her depressive symptoms and anger. School counselors will support Katrina in the school setting with strengths-based CBT strategies that will build on her identified strengths and also use metaphors generated by Katrina to manage her anger. Family therapy will be used to address the power struggle between Katrina and Julia and also to help them to better communicate their needs and feelings.

References

Craske, M.G. (2010). *Cognitive-behavioral therapy*. Washington, DC: American Psychological Association.

Hwang, W. (2006). The psychotherapy adaptation and modification framework: Application to Asian Americans. *The American Psychologist, 61*(7), 702–715.

Kirk, J. (1989). Cognitive-behavioral assessment. In K. Hawton, P.M. Salkovskis, J. Kirk & D.M. Clark (Eds.), *Cognitive behaviour therapy for psychiatric problems: A practical guide* (pp. 13–51). New York, NY: Oxford University Press.

Ledley, D.R., Marx, B.P., & Heimberg, R.G. (2005). *Making cognitive-behavioral therapy work: Clinical process for new practitioners*. New York, NY: The Guilford Press.

Manning, S. (2018). Case formulation in DBT: Developing a behavioural formulation. In M. Swales (Ed.), *The Oxford handbook of dialectical behaviour therapy* (pp. 237–258). Oxford, UK: Oxford University Press.

McCullough, J. (2000). *Treatment for chronic depression: Cognitive behavioral analysis system of psychotherapy*. New York, NY: Guilford.

McCullough, J., Schramm, E., & Penberthy, K. (2014). *CBASP as a distinctive treatment for persistent depressive disorder: Distinctive features*. New York, NY: Routledge.

Miranda, J., Nakamura, R., & Bernal, G. (2003). Including ethnic minorities in mental health intervention research: A practical approach to a long-standing problem. *Culture, Medicine, and Psychiatry, 27*(4), 467–486.

Newman, C. (2012). *Core competencies in cognitive behavior therapy*. New York, NY: Routledge.

Sperry, L., & Sperry, J. (2016). *Cognitive behavioral therapy of DSM-5 personality disorders: Assessment, case conceptualization, and treatment* (3rd ed.). New York, NY: Routledge.

Sperry, J., & Sperry, L. (2018). *Cognitive behavior therapy in counseling practice*. New York, NY: Routledge.

Wright, J., Basco, M., & Thase, M. (2006). *Learning cognitive-behavior therapy: An illustrated guide*. Washington, DC: American Psychiatric Press.

Young, J.E., Klosko, J.S., & Weishaar, M.E. (2003). *Schema Therapy: A practitioner's guide*. New York, NY: The Guilford Press.

8 Time-Limited Dynamic Psychotherapy Case Conceptualizations

Of the several psychodynamic approaches, the interpersonal dynamics psychotherapies are currently in vogue. Among these, Time-Limited Dynamic Psychotherapy (TLDP; Strupp & Binder, 1984; Binder, 2004; Binder & Betan, 2013; Levenson, 1995, 2017) is a commonly used and research-based approach and is the focus of this chapter. The goals of Time-Limited Dynamic psychotherapy treatment are to foster client insight and facilitate corrective emotional experiences (Levenson, 2017). This chapter begins with a description of the Time-Limited Dynamic perspective and its basic premises. Next, it describes the factors involved in Biopsychosocial assessment and provides some guidelines for summarizing this type of assessment. Then, it describes the process of developing and writing a Time-Limited Dynamic case conceptualization. This process is then applied to the five cases introduced in Chapter 1.

Time-Limited Dynamic Perspective

This perspective is based on the observation that early in life clients develop a cyclic maladaptive pattern of relating to others and this pattern influences all aspects of their life functioning in the present. Levenson (1995, 2010) identified its major goals as providing new experiences for the client within oneself and relationally with others and assisting the client in finding new understandings or insights into themselves and their relationships. This perspective assumes that a client's maladaptive interpersonal patterns are reenacted in therapy, and the practitioner will be influenced by the client's enactments. Levenson (2017) identified that this orientation uses techniques from attachment theory, interpersonal neurobiology, affective-experiential learning, and systems theory to help clients with disruptive relational patterns. The practitioner's role is that of participant and observer, while also relating to the client in a caring and supportive as well as a directive and active manner. Psychopathology is understood to be rooted in faulty relationship patterns with early caregivers, and these maladaptive patterns are nearly always reflected in presenting symptoms and interpersonal distress and dissatisfaction.

Among all the perspectives described in this book, this one is unique in its emphasis on in-session enactments that foster insight and corrective interpersonal experiences. It also utilizes the practitioner's own objective or interactive countertransferential reaction to the client, objective in the sense that the practitioner's reactions would be similar to most other practitioners who have contact with the client. This contrasts with the more "subjective countertransference" that reflects the practitioner's own unfinished business.

A maladaptive pattern that is cyclic in nature reflects a client's repetitive and maladaptive interactions, particularly inflexible, self-perpetuating behaviors, self-defeating expectations, and negative self-appraisals that lead to dysfunctional interactions with others (Butler & Binder, 1987; Butler, Strupp, & Binder, 1993). Deriving a cyclic maladaptive pattern allows the practitioner to understand the client's current and historical relational pattern and to process it in a brief psychodynamic fashion. Four aspects of the client's maladaptive pattern are specified (Levenson, 2010, 2017):

1. **Acts of Self:** includes thoughts, feelings, motives, perceptions, and behaviors of the client (interpersonally)
2. **Expectations of Others:** pertains to how the client imagines others will react to them in response to their behavior (Acts of Self)
3. **Acts of Others toward the Self:** consists of the actual behaviors of others, as observed or perceived (or assumed) by the client
4. **Acts of the Self toward the Self (introject):** involves all of the client's behaviors or attitudes toward themselves

In short, this approach

> assumes that a client has unwittingly developed over time a self-perpetuating, maladaptive pattern of relating to others, and that this pattern underlies the client's presenting issues. The practitioner's job is to use the clinical relationship to facilitate for the client a new experience of relating, allowing the client to break the old pattern and thereby resolve the presenting issues.
>
> (Levenson & Strupp, 2007, p. 76)

The next two sections describe the Time-Limited Dynamic assessment and the Time-Limited Dynamic case conceptualization method.

Time-Limited Dynamic Assessment

A Time-Limited Dynamic assessment emphasizes factors that add additional information to the diagnostic assessment and facilitate the development of theory-based clinical and treatment formulations. Assessment focuses on both the current situations and predisposing factors, i.e., cyclic maladaptive patterns. This analysis includes steps identified by Levenson (2010):

1. Let the client tell their story.
2. Conduct an "anchored history" in which they identified what precipitated particular actions, feelings, and attributions. They start where the client is and get a deeper understanding of the client's dynamics.

3. Attend to the emotional flavor of the client's narrative. Pay attention to verbal and non-verbal communication.
4. Explore the emotional context of the presenting symptoms or problems: When did the problems start? What interpersonal dynamics were going on in the client's life at that time? Where is the client's pain? What did the client have to disown, tone down, or distort in themselves to be more acceptable to others?
5. Listen, observe, and probe for relevant information to derive the client's maladaptive relational pattern. As they endeavor to understand the client's cyclic pattern, practitioners should ask themselves the following questions (Binder, 2004):

   Acts of Self: What are the client's wishes and intentions regarding the other person? How does the client behave toward the other person?

   Expectations of Others: What does the client assume or expect are the other person's intentions? What are the client's reactions?

   Acts of Others toward the Self: How does the client perceive and interpret the actions and intentions of the other person? What are the client's reactions?

   Acts of the Self toward the Self (introject): How does the client treat himself or herself? How does the client's experience of the interactions and relationship with the other influence the manner in which the client views and treats himself or herself?

   Interactive countertransference: What is my objective reaction to the client: Do I experience being unaffected, drawn toward, pushed back, or repelled by the client, or both drawn toward and pushed back?

Time-Limited Dynamic Case Conceptualization Method

A Time-Limited Dynamic case conceptualization is based on the client's cyclic maladaptive pattern of relating to others and how this pattern influences all aspects of a client's life functioning. Information and inferences derived from the Time-Limited Dynamic assessment are formulated into a full-scale case conceptualization, which can be shared and discussed with the client. Essentially, the diagnostic and clinical formulations components outline the client's patterns of relating to others, the manner in which they treat themselves, and how they view themselves, i.e., introjects. The cultural formulation component provides an explanation of cultural dynamics and interaction with personality dynamics, if operative. Finally, the treatment formulation component provides a map for shifting to a more adaptive relational pattern. The Time-Limited Dynamic model of case conceptualization as presented here is similar to the other four theoretical models described in this book in that it shares several common elements. Yet, it also differs from the other four models because of its signature elements. These include: predisposition, treatment goals, treatment focus, treatment strategy, and treatment interventions.

Table 8.1 identifies and describes these five signature elements.

Table 8.1 Signature Elements of the Time-Limited Dynamic Case Conceptualization

Predisposition	cyclic maladaptive pattern (Acts of the Self, Acts of Others toward the Self, Expectations of Others, Acts of the Self toward the Self)
Treatment goals	insight (new understandings)
	corrective relational experiences (new experiences)
Treatment focus	troublesome interpersonal relationships triggered by their cyclic maladaptive pattern
Treatment strategies	***basic treatment strategy***: use of the therapeutic relationship to foster experiential interpersonal learning and revise and refine the cyclic pattern
	common strategies: support; interpretation; corrective emotional experience
Treatment interventions	revision/refinement of the cyclic maladaptive pattern; dynamics interpretations; transference analysis; clarification and confrontation, working through incisive questioning, coaching, and practice (intentional pragmatism: selective use of other approaches' interventions)

Time-Limited Dynamic Case Conceptualization: Five Cases

The process of constructing a Time-Limited Dynamic case conceptualization is illustrated for five different cases. Following background information on each case, there is an assessment paragraph that identifies key information germane to this model. Then, a table summarizes the nine elements from the diagnostic, clinical, and cultural formulations (discussed in Chapters 2 and 3) and the eight elements of the treatment formulation (discussed in Chapter 4) for that specific case. Finally, a narrative integrating this information is provided in a case conceptualization statement. The first paragraph reports the diagnostic and clinical formulations, the second paragraph reports the cultural formulation, while the third paragraph reports the treatment formulation.

Case of Geri

Geri is a 35-year-old, African American female who works as an administrative assistant. She is single, lives alone, and was referred by her company's human resources director for evaluation and treatment following three weeks of depression and social isolation. Her absence from work prompted the referral. Geri's symptoms began soon after her supervisor told her that she was being considered for a promotion. As a child she reports isolating and avoiding others when she was criticized and teased by family members and peers. She is highly acculturated and believes that her depression is a result of work stress and a "chemical imbalance" in her brain.

Time-Limited Dynamic Assessment

Besides diagnostic assessment information, the dynamic assessment added the following: Geri had difficulty relating to her peers both in early life as well as currently. Then, she was criticized, teased, and made fun of by peers. Now she avoids being criticized and teased by isolating herself from others. She did not have a best friend growing up, but currently has one coworker whom she trusts. She views herself as inadequate and defective and is very self-critical. She described feeling disgusted with herself several times during the interview and cried when she spoke about how she expected others to be critical of her. She also mentioned that others, starting with her father, are demanding and judgmental. She recalled being called "fat" and "stupid" by her peers and family. She reported that for years she has had little or no contact with her parents or her brother and has never been in a long-term relationship. Finally, it is interesting to note the practitioner's own interactive countertransference to Geri. The practitioner initially experienced being drawn toward her and then pushed away.

Table 8.2 describes the results of the diagnostic and Time-Limited Dynamic assessment which are summarized for the key elements of a full-scale case conceptualization.

Case Conceptualization Statement

Geri's increased social isolation and depressive symptoms (***presentation***) seem to be her reaction to news that she was being considered for a job promotion and a new supervisor (***current precipitant***) as well as demands from close relationships and the expectation that she will be criticized, rejected, and feel unsafe (***continuing precipitants***). Throughout her life, she found it safer to avoid others when possible and conditionally relate to them at other times; as a result, she lacks key social skills and has a limited social network (***pattern***). Her reaction and pattern can be understood in light of her history of avoidance and critical figures in her life. She avoids most relationships and has a history of social isolation throughout her life. While this serves to reduce the likelihood of being criticized and to increase her feeling of safety, she feels alone and secretly wishes for more friends and an intimate relationship. Family members and coworkers are critical of her, and she perceives some to be overly demanding. She had no best friend growing up, but has one coworker whom she trusts. She assumes that if she takes the promotion that she was recently offered, her new supervisor will be both overly demanding and critical of her work performance. She views herself as inadequate and is very self-critical, and she expects others to be demanding and critical (***predisposition***). This cyclic pattern is maintained by her shyness, the fact that she lives alone, her limited social skills, and the safety of avoidance and social isolation (***perpetuants***). Geri brings to treatment a demonstrated strength of commitment to her workplace through her many years of employment. She also benefits from having a friend whom she can trust and legislative structures through which she can seek accommodations for her job, such as the Americans with Disabilities Act (***protective factors/strengths***).

She identifies herself as a middle-class African American, but has little interest and no involvement with the African American community (***cultural identity***). She is highly acculturated, as are her parents, but her family system placed higher

Table 8.2 Case Conceptualization Elements

Presentation	increased social isolation and depressive symptoms
Precipitant	news that she was being considered for a job promotion and a new supervisor (***current precipitant***); demands of close relationships and the expectation that she will be criticized, rejected, and feel unsafe (***continuing precipitant***)
Pattern-maladaptive	disconnects (withdraws) when feeling unsafe
Predisposition	*Acts of the Self*: depressed and worried about job promotion
	Acts of Others toward the Self: critical family and peers; one close friend
	Expectations of Others: judgmental, critical, demanding of her
	Acts of the Self toward the Self (introject): inadequate; defective; self-critical
Perpetuant	relational dynamics; shyness; living alone; generalized social isolation
Protective factors & strengths	close, trusted friend and confidante; stable meaningful job; eligible for job accommodation
Cultural identity	middle-class African American; limited ethnic ties
Cultural stress & acculturation	highly acculturated; no obvious acculturative stress but family gender roles reinforce the notion that she is inadequate
Cultural explanation	sadness results from job stress and chemical imbalance of brain
Culture and/or personality	personality dynamics are significantly operative
Treatment pattern	connects while feeling safer
Treatment goals	reduce depressive symptoms; increase socialization; return to work; experience insight and corrective interpersonal experiences
Treatment focus	troublesome interpersonal relationships triggered by her cyclic pattern
Treatment strategy	therapeutic relationship to foster experiential learning and revise cyclic pattern; support; interpretation; corrective emotional experience
Treatment interventions	revise and refine cyclic pattern; dynamic interpretation; transference analysis; coaching on relational skills and practice; role playing
Treatment obstacles	"test" practitioners; likely to resist group therapy; over dependence on practitioners; difficulty with termination
Treatment-cultural	gender may be an issue so assign supportive female practitioners
Treatment prognosis	good, if increased social connections, skills, and returns to work

value on men. This positive bias toward men appears to reinforce the notion that she is unwanted and inadequate (***cultural stress & acculturation***). She believes that her depression is the result of stress at work and a "chemical imbalance" in her brain (***cultural explanation***). No significant cultural factors are operative. It appears that Geri's personality dynamics are significantly operative in her current clinical presentation, but gender roles should be examined (***culture and/or personality***).

The challenge for Geri will be to function more effectively and feel safer in relating to others (***treatment pattern***). The goals are to reduce her depressive symptoms, increase her interpersonal and friendship skills, help her return to work, and increase her social network. From a TLDP perspective, the primary goals of treatment are to decrease depressive symptoms, foster insight, enhance interpersonal problem-solving skills, and encourage corrective emotional and interpersonal experiences (***treatment goals***). Treatment that is focused primarily on addressing Geri's troublesome relational situations that are triggered by her cyclic maladaptive relational pattern will keep the treatment goals in the forefront of therapy (***treatment focus***). The basic treatment strategy is to utilize the therapeutic relationship to facilitate new relational experiences and to understand and revise the maladaptive pattern. Related strategies include support, interpretation, role playing, and medication (***treatment strategy***). Supportive techniques will be used to affirm her and encourage her to be more proactive in seeking out relationships with others. Transference–countertransference enactments will be analyzed and processed as they arise. Role playing specific troubling situations will be used to increase Geri's awareness of her cyclic pattern, and to foster corrective emotional experiences. Other interventions will include dynamic interpretations to foster insight, coaching to develop relational skills, and then practicing these skills. Referral will be made for a medication evaluation and, if indicated, medication monitoring will be arranged (***treatment interventions***). Some obstacles and challenges to treatment can be anticipated. Given her avoidant personality structure, ambivalent resistance is likely. It can be anticipated that she will have difficulty discussing personal matters with practitioners, and that she will "test" and provoke practitioners into criticizing her for changing or canceling appointments at the last minute or being late, and that she might procrastinate, avoid feelings, and otherwise "test" the practitioner's trustability. Once trust in the practitioner is achieved, she is likely to cling to the practitioner and treatment and thus termination may be difficult unless her social support system outside therapy is increased. Furthermore, her pattern of avoidance is likely to make entry into and continuation with group work difficult. Therefore, individual sessions can serve as a transition into group work, including having some contact with the group practitioner who will presumably be accepting and non-judgmental. This should increase Geri's feeling of safety and make self-disclosure in a group setting less difficult. Transference enactment is another consideration. Given the extent of parental and peer criticism and teasing, it is anticipated that any perceived impatience and verbal or non-verbal indications of criticalness by the practitioner will activate this transference. Finally, because of her tendency to cling to others she trusts, increasing her capacity to feel more confident in functioning with greater independence and increasing the time between the last four or five sessions can reduce her ambivalence about termination (***treatment obstacles***). Given Geri's personality dynamics, treatment progress does not appear to be highly influenced by cultural stress. However, gender dynamics could impact the therapeutic relationship given the gender roles in her family, her strained relationship with her father, and her limited involvement with men ever since. Accordingly, female practitioners for both individual and group therapy appear to be indicated in the initial phase of treatment (***treatment-cultural***). Assuming that Geri increases her self-confidence, relational skills, and social contacts in and outside therapy, as well as returns to work, her prognosis is adjudged to be good; if not, it is guarded (***treatment prognosis***).

Case of Antwone

Antwone is an African American Navy seaman in his mid 20s who has lashed out at others with limited provocation. Recently, his commander ordered him to undergo compulsory counseling. He reported being placed in foster care as an infant, and was neglected and abused – emotionally, verbally, and physically – by his African American foster family, particularly the mother who used racial slurs to intimidate him. At age 15, he could no longer endure her abuse and tyranny, and confronted her, resulting in him being thrown out on the street.

Time-Limited Dynamic Assessment

Besides diagnostic assessment information, the dynamic assessment added the following: Antwone had difficulty relating to his peers both in his early life and currently. In the past, he was taunted and teased by his peers. Now, he fights back and identified being extremely sensitive to perceived injustices. He discussed his history of being abused – emotionally, verbally, sexually, and physically – by his African American foster family. He recalled many episodes of corporal punishment based on his behavior not being satisfactory with his adoptive mother. Based on these and related experiences of abuse and neglect, he has come to expect that others will harm him and treat him unfairly. He is often angry with himself and tends to focus on information that makes him angry. He views himself as inadequate and unlovable. During the interview, he shifted from being comfortable with the practitioner to quickly seeming suspicious of the practitioner's intentions and withdrawing from the discussion by using one-word responses and becoming angry with innocuous questions. Finally, the practitioner's own interactive countertransference to Antwone could be noted. The practitioner initially experienced being drawn toward him and then pushed away as Antwone's voice became noticeably strident in describing a past situation.

Table 8.3 describes the results of the diagnostic and Time-Limited Dynamic assessment which are summarized for the key elements of a full-scale case conceptualization.

Table 8.3 Case Conceptualization Elements

Presentation	verbal and/or physical retaliation; confusion
Precipitant	conflicts that resulted in a physical fight with other sailors (*current precipitant*); perceived injustice of peers and authority figures (*continuing precipitants*)
Pattern-maladaptive	strikes back and conditionally relates to others
Predisposition	*Acts of the Self*: angry, enraged outbursts; depressed; isolate
	Acts of Others toward the Self: abuse/neglect from family; taunted by peers
	Expectations of Others: others will harm or treat him unfairly
	Acts of the Self toward the Self: confused/ruminates about losses and rage
Perpetuant	limited capacity for emotional regulation; lacks conflict resolution skills; his cyclic pattern
Protective factors & strengths	best friend was a secure attachment figure; intelligent, avid reader with wide interests; creative; committed to duty and service
Cultural identity	African American with some conflict about ethnic ties
Cultural stress & acculturation	highly acculturated with considerable cultural stress
Cultural explanation	racial degradation; racial provocations of white peers and superiors
Culture and/or personality	personality *and* cultural factors are operative
Treatment pattern	be careful while more fully connecting with others
Treatment goals	anger and impulse control; increase positive coping skills; find family of origin; experience insight and corrective interpersonal experiences
Treatment focus	troublesome interpersonal relationships triggered by his cyclic pattern
Treatment strategy	use therapeutic relationship to foster experiential learning and revise cyclic pattern; support; interpretation; corrective emotional experience
Treatment interventions	revise and refine cyclic pattern; dynamic interpretation; transference analysis; coaching on relational skills and practice; role playing
Treatment obstacles	transference–countertransference enactments with male practitioner; aggressive acting out; depending and idealizing the practitioner
Treatment-cultural	therapeutically frame and process his foster family's prejudice and abuse
Treatment prognosis	good to very good

Case Conceptualization Statement

Antwone's verbal and physical lashing out at others and his subsequent confusion about others' intentions (*presentation*) appear to be his response to the taunting and provocation of his peers that resulted in a physical fight (*current precipitant*) as well as the perceived injustice of peers and authority figures (*continuing precipitants*). Throughout his life, Antwone has sought to be accepted and make sense of being neglected, abused, and abandoned. Over time, he developed a maladaptive pattern of relating to others where he preemptively strikes back and conditionally relates to others in order to protect himself (*pattern*).

(*predisposition*). His limited capacity for emotional regulation, self-justification about striking back, and deficits in conflict resolution skills serve to maintain this cyclic pattern (*perpetuants*). Antwone brings several protective factors and strengths to therapy, including his childhood best friend who served as his only secure attachment figure. He is intelligent, he is a reader with wide interests, and he has received regular promotions in rank, at least until recently. He also writes poetry and has learned two foreign languages. He also benefits from a caring military command and organizational structure that has encouraged counseling and treatment in lieu of punitive measures for past aggressive behaviors (*protective factors/strengths*).

Antwone identifies as African American and maintains some ethnic ties (*cultural identity*). Although he is highly acculturated, he continues to experience considerable racial discrimination which seems to be exacerbated by his cultural beliefs (*cultural stress & acculturation*). He believes that his problems result from racial degradation and abuse from his African American foster family, as well as from racial provocations by his white peers and Navy superiors (*cultural explanation*). It appears that both personality and cultural factors are operative (*culture and/or personality*).

The challenge for Antwone will be to engage more fully with others while at the same time exercising carefulness and discernment. This more adaptive pattern will permit him to experience interpersonal relations that are safe and life giving (*treatment pattern*).

The goals are to help him manage his anger and increase his ability to control his impulsive reactions, increase his positive coping skills, and help him find and reconnect to his family. From a TLDP perspective, the primary goals of treatment are to foster insight, enhance interpersonal problem-solving skills, and encourage corrective emotional and interpersonal experiences.

_____

_____

_____

_____

_____

_____

(***treatment goals***). Treatment that is focused primarily on Antwone's troublesome relationships will keep the treatment goals in the forefront of therapy (***treatment focus***). The basic treatment strategy is to utilize the therapeutic relationship to facilitate new relational experiences and to understand and revise the maladaptive pattern. Supporting treatment strategies include support, dynamic interpretation, and fostering corrective emotional experiences with his Navy peers and superiors (***treatment strategies***).

_____

_____

_____

_____

_____

(***treatment interventions***). Specific treatment obstacles and challenges can be anticipated. These include the likelihood that Antwone will quickly identify with a caring practitioner as the positive father figure and role model that he has never had. It is also likely that this will engender a predictable transference–countertransference enactment which may result in him aggressively acting out (***treatment obstacles***). In addition to addressing personality and interpersonal treatment targets, an effective treatment outcome will require addressing the cultural dimension of prejudice, not only prejudice from white peers and superiors, but also his experience of black-on-black prejudice. It may be useful to therapeutically frame his foster family's prejudice and abuse toward him in terms of self-loathing that was passed down from their ancestors to him; then, it can be therapeutically processed. Because he is an avid reader, bibliotherapy, i.e., books and articles that analyze and explain this type of prejudice, could be a useful therapeutic adjunct (***treatment-cultural***). Antwone brings several strengths and resources to therapy including intelligence, a reader with wide interests, regular promotions in rank, at least until recently, poetry writing, and learning two foreign languages. These resources plus his motivation to change suggest a good to very good prognosis (***treatment prognosis***).

Case of Maria

Maria is a 17-year-old, first-generation Mexican American female who was referred for counseling because of mood swings. She is conflicted about her decision to go off to college instead of staying home to care for her terminally ill mother. Her family expects her to stay home. She is angry at her older sister who left home at 17 after her parents insisted that her culture "requires" her to take care of her parents when they get old or become ill. Her Anglo friends encourage her to go to college and pursue her dreams.

Time-Limited Dynamic Assessment

Besides diagnostic assessment information, the dynamic assessment added the following: Maria began experimenting with alcohol and is currently experiencing guilt and a depressed mood. She is also conflicted, believing that she is a bad daughter if she leaves to go to college or that she will relinquish her career aspirations if she stays home and cares for her parents. She insists that her parents have already made many major decisions for her. She said that she is used to people telling her what to do and even occasionally fears having to make decisions on her own. She admitted to feeling somewhat dependent on her friends and family. She discussed that her culture places a high demand on caring for parents if any assistance is needed. She cried when speaking about her fear that her parents will not love her if she does not stay home and care for them. She views herself as inadequate and also feels stuck. Finally, it is interesting to note the practitioner's own interactive countertransference to Maria. The practitioner initially felt pulled toward Maria and was tempted to tell her to break away from her cultural expectations. Table 8.4 describes the results of the diagnostic and Time-Limited Dynamic assessment which are summarized for the key elements of a full-scale case conceptualization.

Case Conceptualization Statement

Maria's depressive symptoms, confusion, and recent experimentation with alcohol use (***presentation***) seem to be her reaction to pressures and conflict over going away to college or staying to care for her parents (***current precipitant***) as well as expectations of self-reliance, being alone, or need to meet others' needs at the expense of her own (***continuing precipitants***). This is largely because she pleases others, particularly her parents, while neglecting her own needs and dreams (***pattern***).

Table 8.4 Case Conceptualization Elements

Presentation	moodiness; confusion; experimentation with alcohol use
Precipitant	pressures and conflict over going away to college or staying to care for her parents (***current precipitant***); expectations of self-reliance, being alone, or need to meet others' needs at the expense of her own (***continuing precipitants***)
Pattern-maladaptive	meets others' needs but not her own needs and desires and is "stuck"
Predisposition	*Acts of the Self*: symptoms of guilt and depression; drinking alcohol to "relax"
	Acts of Others toward the Self: others tell her what to do with her life
	Expectations of Others: told what to do; lose parents' love if she goes to college
	Acts of the Self toward the Self (*introject*): feels inadequate and stuck
Perpetuant	dependent and pleasing style; low assertiveness; cultural expectations; her cyclic pattern
Protective factors & strengths	strong family, social, and religious values; successful student; tight-knit and safe cultural community
Cultural identity	working-class Mexican American
Cultural stress & acculturation	low to moderate level of acculturation; stress from ambivalence about parental and cultural expectations
Cultural explanation	problems caused by "lack of faith"
Culture and/or personality	personality *and* cultural factors operative
Treatment pattern	meets needs of herself and others
Treatment goals	increase self-efficacy, assertiveness, decision-making; decrease moodiness; experience insight and corrective interpersonal experiences
Treatment focus	troublesome interpersonal relationships triggered by her cyclic pattern
Treatment strategy	use therapeutic relationship to foster experiential learning and revise cyclic pattern; interpretation; corrective emotional experience
Treatment interventions	revise and refine cyclic pattern; dynamic interpretation; transference analysis; support; coaching on relational skills and practice; role playing
Treatment obstacles	may capitulate to parents and cultural expectations; pleasing the practitioner; practitioner may unwittingly advocate autonomy
Treatment-cultural	process cultural expectations about caregiver role and need to please; family sessions addressing parents' cultural expectations
Treatment prognosis	fair to good

(***predisposition***). Her low level of assertiveness and unwillingness to disappoint her parents serve to maintain this pattern (***perpetuant***). Maria brings several protective factors to therapy including strong family, social, and religious values that may motivate her to establish vital life directions. Some of her strengths include her intelligence and past success in school. She also benefits from a tight-knit family and cultural community in which she can feel safe and supported (***protective factors/strengths***).

Maria identifies herself as a working-class Mexican American with a moderate level of involvement in that heritage (***cultural identity***). Her level of acculturation is in the low to moderate range while her parents' level is in the low range. Since her older sister refused to follow the cultural mandate that the oldest daughter would meet her parents needs rather than her own, that responsibility is now on Maria. Maria's ambivalence about whether to follow cultural norms and expectations or her own aspirations is quite distressing for her (***cultural stress & acculturation***). Her explanatory model is that her problems are due to a "lack of faith," a belief that is consistent with a lower level of acculturation. Although she and her family experienced some discrimination upon arrival here, it ended when they moved to a "safer" Mexican American neighborhood (***cultural explanation***). It appears that both personality and cultural factors are operative. Specifically, cultural dynamics that foster dependency, i.e., good daughters care for their parents without question, serve to reinforce her dependent personality dynamics (***culture and/or personality***).

The challenge of growth for Maria will be to achieve a balance between meeting the needs of others and meeting her own needs (***treatment pattern***).

_____

_____

_____

_____

_____

_____

(***treatment goals***). Treatment that is focused primarily on her troublesome interpersonal relationships will keep the treatment goals in the forefront of therapy (***treatment focus***). The basic treatment strategy will be to use the therapeutic relationship to foster experiential learning and modify and refine her cyclic pattern. Treatment strategies compatible with these treatment goals and focus include utilizing the therapeutic relationship to facilitate new relational experiences and understanding and revising the maladaptive pattern (***treatment strategy***).

_____

_____

_____

(*treatment interventions*). In terms of likely treatment obstacles and challenges, it is likely that Maria will attempt to please the practitioner by readily agreeing to the practitioner's suggestions and between-session assignments, but afterwards become conflicted and then fail to follow up. It is also likely that the client will capitulate to her parents' expectations. Accordingly, the practitioner might, early in treatment, make the predictive interpretation that this might occur, but that it does not indicate failure, and that it can be therapeutically processed. Finally, practitioners working with dependent clients need to anticipate how their own needs and values may become treatment obstacles. This can occur when they unwittingly advocate for and expect clients to embrace independence and autonomy before the client is sufficiently ready (*treatment obstacles*). Effective treatment outcomes will also address relevant cultural dynamics. Specifically, this may involve therapeutically processing her explanatory model that a lack of faith is the source of her problem. Depending on the saliency and strength of this belief, education and cognitive disputation may be indicated. The cultural expectation about caring for her parents in light of her need to please would also be processed. In addition, family sessions may be indicated wherein her parents can review and revise their cultural expectations of her (*treatment-cultural*). Besides the impact of personality and culture, the resources that Maria brings to therapy influence her prognosis. She is bright, successful in school, and has already identified her needs and career aspirations. At this point, however, given her lower level of acculturation and dependent personality dynamics, her prognosis is in the fair to good range (*treatment prognosis*).

Case of Richard

Richard is a 41-year-old, Caucasian male who is being evaluated for anxiety, sadness, and anger following his recent divorce. He currently lives on his own, is employed as a machine operator, and frequents nightclubs where he "is on the lookout for the perfect woman." He has held four jobs over the past six years and was fired from his last job because he smashed his fist through a wall after being confronted by a female coworker. He is the only child of alcoholic parents whom he describes as "fighting all the time."

Time-Limited Dynamic Assessment

Besides diagnostic assessment information, the TLDP assessment added the following: Richard presented with sadness, outbursts of anger, and anxiety. Richard has had difficulty relating to his peers both in early life as well as currently. He reported that he has been fired from several jobs due to his anger and even punched his fist into a wall at his former employer's office. He was raised by alcoholic parents whom he describes as "fighting all the time." He identified that his parents were rarely emotionally available to him. He mentioned feeling very lonely and depressed throughout most of his childhood. More recently, his coworkers fear his anger and are often intimidated by him. He typically expects that others will be available and responsive to his needs. He mentioned that he is very determined and will "step on others to get what I need." He doubts his abilities and is often self-critical and angry with himself. Finally, it is interesting to note the practitioner's own interactive countertransference to Richard. The practitioner felt pushed away from Richard and even felt intimidated several times during the interview. Table 8.5 describes the results of the diagnostic and Time-Limited Dynamic assessment which are summarized for the key elements of a full-scale case conceptualization.

Case Conceptualization Statement

Richard's angry outbursts, sadness, and anxiety (***presentation***) seem to be a reaction to his recent divorce and also being fired from his last job for smashing his fist through a wall (***current precipitant***), as well as self-evaluation, being alone, or others' perception of not being special (***continuing precipitants***). Richard views himself as entitled to special considerations. He views the world as his for the taking and that others will be available and responsive to his needs. Throughout his life, he has continued to elevate himself while belittling and using others (***pattern***).

_____

_____

_____

_____

_____

_____

(***predisposition***). This pattern is maintained by his inability to empathize, his impulsivity, and his lack of relational skills (***perpetuants***). Richard's secure attachment with his grandmother serves as a protective factor and evidence that he has the capacity to care for others. The most prominent strength Richard brings to therapy is resilience. He is also charismatic and engaging (***protective factors/ strengths***).

Richard identifies as a middle-class Caucasian male (***cultural identity***). He appears to be highly acculturated and there is no obvious indications of acculturative stress (***cultural stress & acculturation***). He believes that his current problems of anger, sadness, and anxiety result from the bad example he received from his abusive and non-loving parents who fought constantly when they drank (***cultural***

Table 8.5 Case Conceptualization Elements

Presentation	angry outbursts, sadness, and anxiety
Precipitant	recent divorce and also being fired from his last job for smashing his fist through a wall (***current precipitant***); evaluation of self, being alone, or others' perception of not being special (***continuing precipitants***)
Pattern-adaptive	elevates self while belittling and using others
Predisposition	***Acts of the Self***: angry outbursts, sadness, and anxiety
	Acts of Others toward the Self: abusive parent; wife withdrew; fearful coworkers
	Expectations of Others: expects others will be unresponsive to his needs
	Acts of the Self toward the Self (***introject***): doubts his abilities; feels inadequate
Perpetuant	impulsivity; limited relationship skills; inability to empathize; his cyclic pattern
Protective factors & strengths	secure attachment with his grandmother; resilient, charismatic, and engaging
Cultural identity	middle-class Caucasian male
Cultural stress & acculturation	highly acculturated; no obvious cultural stress, but privilege should be examined in the therapeutic process
Cultural explanation	anxiety, anger, sadness caused by abusive, non-loving parents
Culture and/or personality	personality are dynamics operative, but privilege should be examined
Treatment pattern	self-confident and respectful of others
Treatment goals	anger and impulse control; reduce sadness and anxiety; experience insight and corrective interpersonal experiences
Treatment focus	troublesome interpersonal relationships triggered by his cyclic pattern
Treatment strategy	use therapeutic relationship to foster experiential learning and revise cyclic pattern; interpretation; corrective emotional experience
Treatment interventions	revise and refine cyclic pattern; dynamic interpretation; transference analysis; support; coaching on relational skills and practice; role playing
Treatment obstacles	minimization of his own problematic behaviors; idealization or devaluation of the practitioner; arrogant attitude
Treatment-cultural	no cultural focus to treatment indicated
Treatment prognosis	fair

explanation). Finally, personality dynamics are predominant and adequately explain his presenting problem and pattern, but examining his sense of entitlement and his own experience of privilege would be useful to address in therapy (*culture and/or personality*).

The challenge of growth for Richard will be to achieve a more adaptive pattern in which he can feel confident about himself and meeting his needs while being respectful of others (*treatment pattern*).

(*treatment goals*). Treatment that is focused primarily on addressing Richard's troublesome relational situations that are triggered by his cyclic maladaptive relational pattern will keep the treatment goals in the forefront of therapy (*treatment focus*). The basic treatment strategy will be to use the therapeutic relationship to foster experiential learning and revise Richard's cyclic pattern. Treatment strategies supportive of the treatment goals and focus include dynamic interpretations, transference analysis, role playing, and coaching (*treatment strategy*).

(*treatment interventions*). With regard to likely treatment obstacles and challenges, it is likely that Richard will minimize his own problematic behaviors by blaming circumstances or others. It can be expected that he will alternate between idealization or devaluation of the practitioner, at least in the beginning phase of therapy. His entitled and arrogant attitude could activate practitioner countertransference. Furthermore, since it is not uncommon for clients with a narcissistic style to discontinue treatment when their symptoms, immediate conflicts, or stressors are sufficiently reduced, the practitioner who believes the client can profit from continued therapy needs to point out – at the beginning of therapy and thereafter – that until the client's underlying maladaptive pattern is sufficiently changed, similar issues and concerns will inevitably arise in the future (*treatment*

obstacles). Since the primary influence is personality dynamics, no cultural focus to treatment is indicated besides examining his entitlement and sense of privilege (***treatment-cultural***). Finally, because of the client's conditional manner of relating, multiple job firings, and impulsivity, at this point, his prognosis is considered fair (***treatment prognosis***).

Case of Katrina

Katrina is a 13-year-old female of mixed ethnicity. She was referred for counseling by her guidance counselor due to recent depressive symptoms, poor academic performance, and oppositional behavior and fighting with other students at school. Her aggressive behavior and academic challenges have increased over the past six months since Katrina overheard a conversation between her mother and aunt in which she found out that her father had an affair for eight years. She was shocked to learn that this resulted in two births. Other difficulties include several fights with other students in the classroom, frequent conflict with her mother, skipping 15 days of school over the past six months, and diminished interest in her academic work. While she had previously excelled academically, she now displayed a marked loss of interest in activities that used to give her pleasure, such as drawing and reading. Katrina's father is currently living in Puerto Rico and has no contact with the family. Katrina lives in a small apartment with her mother and younger brother near her school. She reported being frustrated with the lack of space, since they had to downsize from the single-family home they lived in before her father left the family one year ago.

Because Katrina was a minor, it was necessary for the school counselor to speak with Katrina and her mother together during the initial session. Katrina's mother, Julia, stated that she believes that Katrina will not talk to most people about her problems because she does not trust anyone. Self-disclosure was very difficult for Katrina during the initial interview and Julia answered the majority of the questions that were asked, in some cases speaking for Katrina when she made efforts to speak.

Brief Dynamic Assessment

Julia reported that Katrina's father was highly critical and also emotionally withdrawn throughout Katrina's childhood. Katrina also stated, "I don't really have a dad, since real fathers are supposed to take care of their families." She said she was tired of her teachers and her mother always forcing her to do things that she doesn't want to do. Katrina struggles to relate to her peers and also presents as angry, oppositional, and defensive when her teachers or her mother enforce rules or expectations. She is often aggressive with her peers when they expect compliance or cooperation. Her teachers describe her as oppositional, irritable, and uncooperative. She had few friends as a younger child, but currently has one close friend whom she trusts. She views herself as inadequate and unlovable and prefers to do most activities alone. Her experience of many of her relationships has included being taken advantage of, neglected, controlled, or lied to. During the first meeting, Katrina reported that she does not trust anyone and that she is not interested in attending counseling sessions if the practitioner is going to tell her what to do. Finally, it is interesting to note the practitioner's own interactive countertransference to Katrina. The practitioner initially experienced feeling pushed away by Katrina's quiet and occasionally defensive demeanor. Table 8.6 describes the results of the diagnostic and Brief Dynamic assessment summarized for the key elements of a full-scale case conceptualization.

Case Conceptualization Statement

Katrina's increased social isolation, aggressive and oppositional behavior, and depressive symptoms (***presentation***) appear to be Katrina's reaction to recent news of her father's infidelity and resulting children (***current precipitant***). Katrina has a tendency to retaliate when she perceives that she is being violated or controlled by others (***continuing precipitant***). Given Katrina's lack of connection with her father and lack of trust in both parents, she moves against authority figures and her peers to protect herself from further harm and rejection (***pattern***).

_____

_____

_____

_____

_____

_____

(***predisposition***). This pattern is maintained by Katrina's unwillingness to ask for help, her low level of motivation to engage in therapy, her social isolation and lack of support system, her mother and teachers rigidly forcing compliance, her low frustration tolerance, and lack of assertive communication skills (***perpetuants***). Despite some of her current challenges, Katrina reported being very close with her aunt and little brother. Besides her close relationships in her family, Katrina reported that she feels responsible for her brother and does everything she can to protect him from harm. Lastly, her strengths include her being a good artist, determined, intelligent, empathic, and creative (***protective factors & strengths***).

Katrina identifies herself as heterosexual and of mixed ethnicity. She identified as Hispanic and African American but reported having little connection to ethnic and cultural traditions from either identity. She stated that she wants to be more like her friends and doesn't want to feel different or weird by speaking Spanish to her mother in front of friends (***cultural identity***). She is moderately acculturated and prefers not to speak Spanish outside of the home, though her mother requires her to speak Spanish while at home. Katrina's mother presents with a low level of acculturation as evidenced by having challenges with speaking English,

Table 8.6 Brief Dynamic Case Conceptualization Elements

Presentation	depressive symptoms, aggressive behavior, and social isolation
Precipitant	learning of her father's infidelity and resulting children (*current precipitant*); retaliates in situations of perceived violation or control by others (*continuing precipitants*)
Pattern-maladaptive	moves against authority figures and peers to protect herself from potential harm and rejection
Predisposition	*Acts of the Self*: aggressive with peers and teachers; sadness; anxiety
	Acts of Others toward the Self: critical and unavailable father; controlling mother; teachers expect compliance and increase punishment
	Expectations of Others: expects others to control, harm, or abandon her
	Acts of the Self toward the Self (*introject*): doubts her abilities; feels inadequate
Protective factors & strengths	has a close relationship to her aunt and little brother; intelligent, creative, and resilient
Perpetuant	social isolation and lack of support system; mother and teachers rigidly forcing compliance; low frustration tolerance; lack of assertive communication skills
Cultural identity	Hispanic and African American; lower income
Cultural stress & acculturation	low to moderate level of acculturation and cultural stress
Cultural explanation	denies depression; believes she would feel better if her teachers and mother were less controlling
Culture and/or personality	personality dynamics and cultural dynamics are operative
Treatment pattern	increase safety and ability to connect with others
Treatment goals	reduce depressive symptoms and aggressive behavior; experience insight and corrective interpersonal experiences
Treatment focus	troublesome interpersonal relationships triggered by her cyclic pattern
Treatment strategy	use therapeutic relationship to foster experiential learning and revise cyclic pattern; interpretation; corrective emotional experience
Treatment interventions	revise and refine cyclic pattern; dynamic interpretation; transference analysis; support; coaching on relational skills and practice; role playing and family therapy to address interpersonal family patterns
Treatment obstacles	likely to resist individual and group therapy; expected outbursts at mother during family sessions; difficulty with self-disclosure
Treatment-cultural	assign a female practitioner; culturally focused cognitive behavior therapy and family therapy
Treatment prognosis	fair to good if protective factors are incorporated in treatment

having very few English-speaking friends, being first-generation Puerto-Rican American and also African American, and reporting that she is unhappy living in the United States and plans to move back to Puerto Rico once Katrina graduates from high school (***cultural stress & acculturation***). Katrina does not believe she is depressed but feels that she would be less annoyed with people if they would be less controlling and "less bossy" (***cultural explanation***). There appear to be a moderate level of cultural factors and a moderate level of personality dynamics that influence the presenting issues (***culture and/or personality***).

The challenge for Katrina to function more effectively is to increase her ability to trust others, feel safer, and to better connect with others (***treatment pattern***).

_____

_____

_____

_____

_____

_____

(***treatment goals***). Treatment that is focused primarily on addressing Katrina's troublesome relational situations that are triggered by her cyclic maladaptive relational pattern will keep the treatment goals in the forefront of therapy (***treatment focus***). The basic treatment strategy is to utilize the therapeutic relationship to facilitate new relational experiences and understand and revise the maladaptive pattern. Related strategies include support, interpretation, and role playing (***treatment strategy***).

_____

_____

_____

_____

_____

(***treatment interventions***). Some obstacles and challenges to treatment are anticipated given Katrina's low motivation to engage in therapy and her paranoid traits that are associated with her oppositional behaviors. It can be anticipated that she will have difficulty discussing personal matters with practitioners due to her inability to trust and that she will often engage in testing behaviors toward the practitioner (***treatment obstacles***). Treatment will require some culturally sensitive elements given Katrina and her mother's level of acculturation. Culturally sensitive treatment and family therapy will be used to address cultural factors present by considering Katrina's mixed ethnicity and her personal experience of both cultures. Additionally, gender dynamics may be an issue so it may be useful to assign her a female therapist (***treatment-cultural***). Assuming that Katrina is able to engage more in the therapeutic process as well as utilize her strengths and seek support from her aunt, her prognosis is adjudged to be fair to good (***treatment prognosis***).

Skill Building Exercises: Time-Limited Dynamic Psychotherapy

As mentioned in the Skill Building Exercises in Chapter 6, you will note that *certain elements of the case conceptualization statements contain open lines. These lines provide you with an opportunity to further develop your conceptualization skills with specific prompts.* Write a short predisposition statement, treatment goals, and a list of corresponding theory-specific treatment interventions for each case.

Concluding Note

The Time-Limited Dynamic model of case conceptualization was described and illustrated. The basic premises of the Time-Limited Dynamic perspective were listed, and the factors involved in a Time-Limited Dynamic assessment were discussed. The Time-Limited Dynamic model of case conceptualization was then applied to five cases and illustrated with their clinical, cultural, and treatment formulations.

CHAPTER 8 QUESTIONS

1. Discuss the key tenets that distinguish Brief Dynamic case conceptualization from the other approaches presented in previous chapters.
2. Describe the explanations of the four aspects of the client's maladaptive patterns as specified (Levenson, 2010): Acts of Self, Expectations of Others, Acts of Others toward the Self, and Acts of the Self toward the Self.
3. Explain how a Brief Dynamic assessment is conducted and how this tries to incorporate, identify, and explain the maladaptive patterns described in Question 2.
4. Compare the questions posed by Binder (2004) to answer the key components of the cyclic maladaptive patterns of this model including interactive countertransference.
5. Describe the signature key elements of the Brief Dynamic case conceptualization model.

Appendix: Case of Antwone

Predisposition

His presentation and pattern can be understood in light of his ongoing experience of the harmful behavior of others beginning with the neglect of his biological mother who abandoned him at birth; several years of physical, emotional, and sexual abuse by his adoptive family; and the taunting by his Navy peers in the present. It is not surprising that he becomes despondent and isolated. He has come to expect that others will attempt to control him, harm him, and treat him unfairly. He is confused about his fate, particularly the recent unexpected loss of his best friend. He spends hours in solitary pursuits and ruminates about the cruelty and injustice he has faced, yet seems convinced that his preemptive striking back is justified and necessary to stay alive.

Treatment Goal

The primary goals of treatment are to foster insight, enhance interpersonal problem-solving skills, and encourage corrective emotional and interpersonal experiences.

Treatment Interventions

Transference–countertransference enactments will be analyzed and processed as they arise. Role playing a specific troubling situation will be used to increase Antwone's awareness of his maladaptive pattern, and to foster corrective emotional experiences. Other interventions will include dynamic interpretations to foster insight, coaching to develop relational skills, and then practicing these skills.

Case of Maria

Predisposition

Maria's presentation can be understood in light of her pattern of being overly sensitive to the conflicting expectations and actions of her parents and of God that she should stay home, and of her friends that she should be independent and go away to college. As a result of these conflicting beliefs and expectations, she acts as if she doesn't care, experiences guilt and depression, and is using alcohol to relax and reduce her discomfort. Her parents, her boyfriend, and her friends regularly tell her what she should be doing with her life. Her parents expect her to stay home and care for them, especially her mother, while her friends keep encouraging her to become more independent and go to college. She believes that her parents will not love her if she does not stay home and care for them. Maria feels inadequate and is also conflicted about believing that she is a bad daughter if she leaves, and that she will let herself down if she capitulates to her parents' expectations.

Treatment Goal

The goals are to increase her self-efficacy, assertiveness, and decision-making, as well as decrease her moodiness. From a TLDP perspective, the primary goals of treatment are to foster insight, enhance interpersonal problem-solving skills, and encourage corrective emotional and interpersonal experiences.

Treatment Interventions

Supportive techniques will be used to affirm her and encourage her to be more proactive in meeting her own needs. A new interpersonal experience could include the practitioner treating Maria in way that empowers her to make her own decisions by avoiding the temptation to tell Maria what to do. Additionally, increasing Maria's awareness of her cyclic pattern by assisting her to achieve awareness and insight into her relational style will help her find a healthier pattern. Transference–countertransference enactments will be analyzed and processed as they arise. The practitioner will use therapeutic enactments to increase Maria's awareness of her cyclic pattern and to foster corrective emotional experiences. The practitioner will facilitate corrective emotional experiences by empowering Maria to meet her own needs and those of others more effectively. Other interventions will include dynamic interpretations to foster insight, coaching to develop relational skills, and then practicing these skills.

Case of Richard

Predisposition

Richard's presentation and pattern can be understood in light of his being abused and then belittling and using others. His pattern is cyclic in that he is rigidly self-focused and expects others to meet his needs for his own personal gain. His parents were described as constantly fighting with each other and emotionally abusive to him. His former wife withdrew from their relationship. His coworkers and friends fear his anger. He expects that others will be unresponsive to his needs so he is overly demanding and he uses others to meet his needs. He views himself as inadequate and doubts his abilities.

Treatment Goal

The goals are to reduce his anger and increase his ability to manage his impulses and also reduce his sadness and anxiety. From a TLDP perspective, the primary goals of treatment are to foster insight, enhance interpersonal problem-solving skills, and encourage corrective emotional and interpersonal experiences.

Treatment Interventions

Supportive techniques will be used to affirm him and encourage him to be more respectful in relating to others. Examining his relational patterns, in-session behavior, and dynamic interpretations to foster insight into his cyclic pattern serves as a prelude to change. The therapeutic relationship will be used to foster corrective emotional experiences with Richard. Coaching and role playing will be utilized to increase his ability to empathize and respond more sensitively to others.

Case of Katrina

Predisposition

Her Acts of the Self include aggressiveness with peers and teachers, feeling sad, and being fearful of others' intentions. Acts of Others toward the Self are her father being critical and unavailable and her mother being busy with work and controlling. Her teachers are very strict with enforcing rules with Katrina because she has a history of aggressive behavior and fighting with her peers. She expects others to control, neglect, abandon, or harm her. Her introject includes self-doubt and inadequacy.

Treatment Goal

Treatment goals include reducing her depressive symptoms, anger management, increasing her assertiveness and friendship skills, and reducing her oppositional behaviors. From a TLDP perspective, the primary goals of treatment are to foster insight, enhance interpersonal problem-solving skills, and encourage corrective emotional and interpersonal experiences.

Treatment Interventions

Supportive techniques will be used to affirm her and encourage her to build safe relationships with others. Transference–countertransference enactments will be analyzed and processed as they arise. Role playing specific troubling situations will be used to increase Katrina's awareness of her cyclic pattern, and to foster corrective emotional experiences. Other interventions will include dynamic interpretations to foster insight, coaching to develop relational skills, and then practicing these skills. Family therapy will be used to address relational patterns between Katrina and Julia and also to help them to better communicate their needs and feelings.

References

Binder, J.L. (2004). *Key competencies in brief dynamic psychotherapy: Clinical practice beyond the manual.* New York, NY: Guilford.

Binder, J.L., & Betan, E.J. (2013). *Core competencies in brief dynamic psychotherapy: Becoming a highly effective and competent brief dynamic psychotherapist.* New York, NY: Guilford.

Butler, S.F., & Binder, J.L. (1987). Cyclical psychodynamics and the triangle of insight. *Psychiatry, 50*(3), 218–231.

Butler, S.F., Strupp, H.H., & Binder, J.L. (1993). Time-limited dynamic psychotherapy. In S. Budman, M. Hoyt & S. Friedman (Eds.), *The first session in brief therapy* (pp. 87–110). New York, NY: Guilford Press.

Levenson, H. (1995). *Time-limited dynamic psychotherapy*. New York: Basic Books.

Levenson, H. (2010). *Brief dynamic therapy*. Washington, DC: American Psychological Association.

Levenson, H. (2017). *Brief dynamic therapy* (2nd ed.). Washington, DC: American Psychological Association.

Levenson, H., & Strupp, H.H. (2007). Cyclical maladaptive patterns: Case formulation in time-limited dynamic psychotherapy. In T.D. Eells (Ed.), *Handbook of psychotherapy case formulation* (pp. 164–197). New York, NY: Guilford.

Strupp, H., & Binder, J. (1984). *Psychotherapy in a new key: A guide to time-limited dynamic psychotherapy*. New York, NY: Basic Books.

9 Adlerian Case Conceptualizations

Adlerian psychotherapy is well suited for clinical practice today because its theory and practice are compatible with a wide range of contemporary approaches (Ansbacher & Ansbacher, 1956). These approaches include the cognitive-behavioral, interpersonally oriented dynamic, systemic, humanistic, and experiential approaches. It is noteworthy that many of the basic principles of Adlerian psychotherapy have influenced and predated these other therapeutic approaches covered in this book (Corey, 2017). This chapter begins with a discussion of the Adlerian perspective. Then, it addresses the Adlerian assessment and identifies the unique factors that are assessed. Next, it describes signature elements of this case conceptualization method. Finally, it illustrates this method by providing Adlerian case conceptualizations for the five clinical cases introduced in Chapter 1.

Adlerian Perspective

Basic Adlerian constructs include lifestyle, belonging, birth order, family constellation, private logic, social interest, lifestyle convictions, and basic mistakes. The Adlerian perspective assumes that the basic human motivation is to belong and develop social interest, i.e., willingness to contribute to the well-being of others. Development is influenced by family constellation, i.e., family dynamics, where individuals find a sense of belonging and self-worth, and birth order, i.e., psychological position in the family. Individuals create their own interpretation of life events derived from their unique subjective private logic which becomes their lifestyle, i.e., the cognitive map which guides their perceptions and actions. Their lifestyle contains personalized convictions about self-view, world view, and conclusions and life strategies which reflect their life narrative. Adler believed that high levels of social interest reflected mental health and well-being (Ansbacher & Ansbacher, 1956). Recent research demonstrates that well-being is a function of social interest (Sperry, 2011). Problems can be understood by an individual not feeling a sense of belonging to a group or community, or that they found unhealthy ways to belong.

Psychopathology is viewed as the way an individual "arranges" symptoms that serve as excuses for failing to meet "life tasks," i.e., one's responsibilities, and for safeguarding self-esteem. Psychopathology reflects discouragement and is manifested in clients' faulty lifestyle convictions, i.e., convictions that run counter to social interest, and are summarized as basic mistakes (Sperry, 2015). In Cognitive Therapy, lifestyle convictions are called schemas.

The Adlerian perspective is optimistic and focuses on assets, strengths, and health rather than on liabilities, deficits, and pathology (Carlson & Englar-Carlson, 2018). The therapeutic relationship is characterized by mutual respect and equality. Client and practitioner are collaborative partners in the therapeutic endeavor wherein clients are expected to assume an active role in the change process. The next two sections describe the Adlerian assessment and the Adlerian method of case conceptualization.

Adlerian Assessment

An Adlerian assessment emphasizes relevant Adlerian factors that add additional information to the diagnostic assessment and facilitate the development of Adlerian-focused clinical and treatment formulations. Assessment focuses on both the current situations and predisposing factors, i.e., lifestyle analysis. This assessment includes gathering information about a client's family constellation and early developmental experiences, including early recollections. This information will assist the practitioner in deriving the individual's unique lifestyle convictions. Adler also posed three life tasks that all individuals strive to achieve: love, friendship, and work (Ansbacher & Ansbacher, 1956). Assessment focuses on the extent that a client has successfully or unsuccessfully attained these life tasks. Understanding clients' lifestyles permits practitioners to help clients better understand how their basic beliefs and perceptions influence their lifestyle and actions.

The following Adlerian constructs are assessed. Inferences are drawn from this data and are formulated into a full-scale case conceptualization. The basic constructs to be assessed are:

Family constellation: The family constellation includes information about a client's relationships with other family members, psychological birth order, family values, and the way the client found a sense of belonging in their family.

Helpful questions to elicit the family constellation are:

- What was it like growing up in your household?
- What was it like being the oldest (youngest, middle, or only) child in your family?
- Describe your relationships with your parents. Which one were you most like? Of your siblings who was your mother's favorite? Father's favorite?
- Describe the relationship between your parents. Who was the breadwinner? Who made the big decisions? How did they solve problems? Conflicts? Did they show affection openly? Who was the disciplinarian? Who did you go to when you got hurt or were frightened?
- What were the family values? What were you expected to do (or be) when you grew up?

- How would you describe your relationships with your siblings? Who got the best grades? Who was the most athletic? Had the most friends? Got into trouble the most? How are they doing now?

Early recollections: Early recollections are a projective technique used to determine a client's self-view, view of others, world view, and his or her overall strategy in dealing with others and life's challenges. Early recollections also reflect the client's level of social interest, their movement toward life tasks, and their lifestyle convictions.

Here is a method for eliciting early recollections:

- "Think back before to your early life – the age of nine – and tell me your first memory. It should be about a single experience that you specifically recall, rather than one that someone told you happened. Not a repeated experience but a single one."
- If the client has difficulty identifying a memory, prompt him or her by asking about a memorable birthday, the first day of school, a specific vacation, etc.
- For each memory, ask how old they were at the time; elicit the sequence of the memory; how it began and ended; who was involved; what each person was doing or saying; the most vivid moment in the sequence; what you felt at that moment; what you were thinking at that moment.

Lifestyle convictions: Lifestyle convictions are conclusions about a client's inner world derived from information about family constellation, birth order, early recollections, and overcompensation. They represent the individual basic pattern.

Here is a formula statement that summarizes these convictions into a pattern:

- I am …. (self-view)
- Life is …. People are …. (world view)
- Therefore …. (life strategy)

The client's "basic mistakes" are derived from this formula/pattern.

Adlerian Case Conceptualization

Like other theory-based and structured case conceptualization methods, the Adlerian case conceptualization method includes clinical, cultural, and treatment formulations that emphasize the client's unique lifestyle and lifestyle conviction. A unique characteristic of the Adlerian method is the view of the clients' situational and longitudinal patterns (Sperry & Binensztok, 2018, 2019). The conceptualization helps clients understand who they are, and how they became who they are. It also helps clients to increase awareness of their faulty logic and unhelpful or socially useless patterns. The cultural formulation provides an explanation in terms of cultural dynamics in relation to the client's personality dynamics. The treatment formulation includes a plan to modify faulty lifestyle convictions and

Table 9.1 Signature Elements of Adlerian Case Conceptualization

Predisposition	*family constellation*: esp. birth order and family environment
	lifestyle convictions: esp. early recollections, self and world view
Treatment goals	increase social interest and constructive action
Treatment focus	situations triggered or exacerbated by mistaken beliefs and/or discouragement
Treatment strategies	*basic treatment strategy*: foster social interest and constructive action
	common strategies: support; cognitive restructuring; interpretation
Treatment interventions	lifestyle assessment; early recollection analysis; encouragement; use of metaphor, stories, humor; acting "as if"; constructive action; paradox

basic mistakes, and to increase social interest. Information from these four components is summarized into a case conceptualization, which is collaboratively discussed with the client.

The Adlerian case conceptualization method is similar to the other four theoretical models described in this book in that it shares several common elements. Yet, it also differs from the other models because of its signature elements. Table 9.1 identifies and describes these five signature elements.

Adlerian Case Conceptualization: Five Cases

The process of constructing an Adlerian case conceptualization is illustrated for five different cases. Following background information on each case, there is an assessment paragraph that identifies key information germane to this model. Then, a table summarizes the nine elements from the diagnostic, clinical, and cultural formulations (discussed in Chapters 2 and 3) and the eight elements of the treatment formulation (discussed in Chapter 4) for that specific case. Finally, a narrative integrating this information is provided in a case conceptualization statement. The first paragraph reports the diagnostic and clinical formulations, the second paragraph reports the cultural formulation, while the third paragraph reports the treatment formulation.

Case of Geri

Geri is a 35-year-old, African American female who works as an administrative assistant. She is single, lives alone, and was referred by her company's human resources director for evaluation and treatment following three weeks of depression and social isolation. Her absence from work prompted the referral. Geri's symptoms began soon after her supervisor told her that she was being considered for a promotion. As a child she reports isolating and avoiding others when she was criticized and teased by family members and peers. She is highly acculturated and believes that her depression is a result of work stress and a "chemical imbalance" in her brain.

Adlerian Assessment

Besides diagnostic assessment information, the Adlerian assessment added the following: Geri had difficulty relating to her peers both in early life as well as currently. Geri is the oldest child and has a brother who is eight years younger than her. She is the psychological "only child." Geri reports that she was her father's favorite until her brother was born. As a child, she had difficulty relating to her peers while in school and was often criticized. She mentioned that her parents have been and continue to be unsupportive, demanding, and critical toward her. Three family values worth noting are "children are to be seen and not heard," "your worth depends on what you achieve in life," and "family secrets do not leave the family." Her earliest recollection involves feeling displaced and no longer wanted by her parents the day her mother brought her newborn brother home. Her father said it was the happiest day of his life and Geri's reaction was to run out of the house and hide in her tree fort feeling angry, alone, sad, and rejected and thinking that nobody wanted her anymore. Another recollection was being told that what she painted in art class was awful, to which she felt sad and hurt. Table 9.2 describes the results of the diagnostic and Adlerian assessment summarized for the key elements of a full-scale case conceptualization.

Case Conceptualization Statement

Geri's increased social isolation and depressive symptoms (***presentation***) seem to be her reaction to the news that she was being considered for a job promotion and a new supervisor (***current precipitant***) as well as demands from close relationships and the expectation that she will be criticized, rejected, and feel unsafe (***continuing precipitants***). She avoids most relationships and has a history of isolating throughout her childhood (***pattern***). Geri's presenting problems are understandable when viewed from the perspective of her lifestyle. Her style of relating with others mirrors the tentative and avoidance manner in which she related to family members. She sought a safe way to connect to family members without being criticized or having unreasonable demands put on her. She views herself as inadequate and defective as a person, and views life and others as demanding, harsh, arbitrary, and critical. Therefore, Geri found her place by avoiding most relationships, socially isolating, and overly investing in those that she deems trustworthy. This allowed her to avoid being criticized and helped her "feel safe." Her strategy of avoiding relationships and withdrawing any time she feels unsafe works, but the price she pays to feel "safe" is high: she is lonely, has limited relational skills and experiences, and desires a close intimate relationship that seems unlikely (***predisposition***). Furthermore, this strategy of shyness, living alone, and social isolation serves to reinforce her maladaptive pattern (***perpetuant***). Geri has

Table 9.2 Case Conceptualization Elements

Presentation	increased social isolation and depressive symptoms
Precipitant	news that she was being considered for a job promotion and a new supervisor (***current precipitant***); demands of close relationships and the expectation that she will be criticized, rejected, and feel unsafe (***continuing precipitant***)
Pattern-maladaptive	avoid and disconnect or withdraw when feeling unsafe
Predisposition	***family constellation***: psychologically an only child; demanding and critical parents; family-valued achievement and secrecy; demanding, critical, and modeled emotional distancing
	lifestyle convictions:
	I am inadequate and defective (self-view)
	life is demanding, harsh, arbitrary, and unsafe (world view)
	therefore, avoid relationships and withdraw when feeling unsafe (life strategy)
Perpetuant	maintained by her shyness, living alone, and generalized social isolation
Protective factors & strengths	close, trusting friend and confidante; stable meaningful job; eligible for job accommodation
Cultural identity	African American conflicted about limited ethnic ties
Cultural stress & acculturation	highly acculturated; no obvious acculturative stress but family gender roles reinforce the notion that she is inadequate
Cultural explanation	sadness results from job stress and chemical imbalance in her brain
Culture and/or personality	personality dynamics are significantly operative
Treatment pattern	connects while feeling safer
Treatment goals	decrease depression and discouragement; increase her social interest and enhance relational skills
Treatment focus	situations triggered/exacerbated by mistaken beliefs or discouragement
Treatment strategy	foster social interest and constructive action; support; interpretation; acting "as if"; medication
Treatment interventions	lifestyle assessment; early recollection analysis; encouragement; acting "as if"
Treatment obstacles	"test" practitioners; likely to resist group therapy; over dependence on practitioners; difficulty with termination
Treatment-cultural	gender may be an issue so assign supportive female practitioners
Treatment prognosis	good, if increased social connections, skills, and returns to work

a secure attachment with her close work friend and also brings commitment to her workplace through her many years of employment. She also benefits from legislative structures through which she can seek accommodations for her job, such as the Americans with Disabilities Act (***protective factors/strengths***).

She identifies herself as a middle-class African American, but has little interest and no involvement with the African American community (***cultural identity***). She is highly acculturated, as are her parents, but her family system placed higher value on men. This positive bias toward men appears to reinforce the notion that she is unwanted and inadequate (***cultural stress & acculturation***). She believes that her depression is the result of stress at work and a "chemical imbalance" in her brain (***cultural explanation***). No significant cultural factors are operative. It appears that Geri's personality dynamics are significantly operative in her current clinical presentation, but gender roles should be examined (***culture and/or personality***).

The challenge for Geri is to function more effectively and feel safer in relating to others (***treatment pattern***). Decreasing discouragement and depressive symptoms, increasing social interest and social relating, and enhancing relational skills are the primary goals of treatment (***treatment goals***). The focus of treatment will be to analyze troublesome situations triggered or exacerbated by her mistaken beliefs (***treatment focus***). The basic treatment strategy is to foster social interest and constructive action. Compatible treatment strategies include medication, support, and interpretation (***treatment strategy***). The practitioner will include support in the form of encouragement to engage and connect with Geri throughout the entire treatment process. Interpretation will be utilized regarding Geri's lifestyle convictions or basic mistakes by analyzing and modifying her faulty convictions regarding her avoidance to feel safe. While Geri says she really wished she could be more comfortable talking with a neighbor, she will be encouraged to act "as if" she was comfortable. A referral will be made for a medication evaluation and, if indicated, medication monitoring will be arranged (***treatment interventions***). Some obstacles and challenges to treatment can be anticipated. Given her avoidant personality pattern, ambivalent resistance is likely. It can anticipated that she will have difficulty discussing personal matters with practitioners, and that she will "test" and provoke practitioners into criticizing her for changing or canceling appointments at the last minute or being late, and that she might procrastinate, avoid feelings, and otherwise "test" the practitioner's trustability. Once trust in the practitioner is achieved, she is likely to cling to the practitioner and treatment and thus termination may be difficult unless her social support system outside therapy is increased. Furthermore, her pattern of avoidance is likely to make entry into and continuation with group work difficult. Therefore, individual sessions can serve as a transition into group work, including having some contact with the group practitioner who will presumably be accepting and non-judgmental. This should increase Geri's feeling of safety and make self-disclosure in a group setting less difficult. Transference enactment is another consideration. Given the extent of parental and peer criticism and teasing, it is anticipated that any perceived impatience and verbal or non-verbal indications of criticalness by the practitioner will activate this transference. Finally, because of her tendency to cling to others she trusts, increasing her capacity to feel more confident in functioning with greater independence and increasing the time between the last four or five sessions can reduce her ambivalence about termination (***treatment obstacles***). Given Geri's personality dynamics, treatment progress does not appear to be highly influenced by cultural stress. However, gender dynamics could impact the therapeutic relationship given the gender roles in her family, her strained relationship with her father, and her limited involvement with men ever since. Accordingly, female practitioners for both individual and group therapy appear to be indicated in the initial phase of treatment (***treatment-cultural***). Assuming that Geri increases her self-confidence, relational skills, and social contacts in and outside therapy, as well as returns to work, her prognosis is adjudged to be good; if not, it is guarded (***treatment prognosis***).

Case of Antwone

Antwone is an African American Navy seaman in his mid 20s who has lashed out at others with limited provocation. Recently, his commander ordered him to undergo compulsory counseling. He reported being placed in foster care as an infant and then neglected and abused – emotionally, verbally, and physically – by his African American foster family, particularly the mother who used racial slurs to intimidate him. At age 15, he could no longer endure her abuse and tyranny and confronted her which resulted in him being thrown out on the street.

Adlerian Assessment

Besides diagnostic assessment information, the Adlerian assessment added the following: in terms of family constellation, Antwone found his place in his family through pleasing and meeting every need of his abusive adoptive mother. He was placed in foster care with an African American family, where he was alternately neglected and then abused emotionally, verbally, and physically by his foster mother and was sexually abused by her adult daughter. Antwone had difficulty relating to his peers both in early life as well as currently. He recalls experiencing very little love and affection from anyone during his childhood. Antwone was the middle of three African American foster boys in the home. As a child, an unspoken value in the household was "do what mama says or get beat." He experienced feeling like a middle child in his adoptive home based on his age in respect of his older sister and two younger brothers. His earliest recollection involves feeling hurt and unfairly treated by a peer in school, then getting into a fight in the playground. An additional early recollection was about him being physically abused and left crying for hours without anyone coming to his aid. Table 9.3 describes the results of the diagnostic and Adlerian assessment summarized for the key elements of a full-scale case conceptualization.

Case Conceptualization Statement

Antwone's verbal and physical lashing out at others and his subsequent confusion about others' intentions (***presentation***) appear to be his response to the taunting

Table 9.3 Case Conceptualization Elements

Presentation	verbal and/or physical retaliation; confusion
Precipitant	conflicts that resulted in a physical fight with other sailors (***current precipitant***); perceived injustice of peers and authority figures (***continuing precipitants***)
Pattern-maladaptive	strikes back and conditionally relates
Predisposition	*family constellation*: middle child in his adoptive home; abused by adoptive mother and her adult daughter; very little love and affection from anyone
	lifestyle convictions:
	I am defective and unlovable but strong (self-view)
	life is unfair and abusive (world view)
	therefore, retaliate against injustice, be wary of others, don't take risks, and avoid close relationships (life strategy)
Perpetuant	limited capacity for emotional regulation; lacks conflict resolution skills
Protective factors & strengths	best friend was a secure attachment figure; intelligent, avid reader with wide interests; creative; committed to duty and service
Cultural identity	lower middle–class African American
Cultural stress & acculturation	highly acculturated with considerable cultural stress
Cultural explanation	racial degradation; racial provocations of white peers and superiors
Culture and/or personality	personality *and* cultural factors are operative
Treatment pattern	connect and relate to others while being careful
Treatment goals	decrease discouragement; increase his social interest; increase capacity to form close relationships; reduce aggressive behaviors; find family
Treatment focus	situations triggered/exacerbated by mistaken beliefs or discouragement
Treatment strategy	foster social interest and constructive action; support; interpretation
Treatment interventions	lifestyle assessment; early recollection analysis; encouragement; acting "as if"
Treatment obstacles	transference–countertransference enactments with male practitioner; aggressive acting out; dependency and idealizing the practitioner
Treatment-cultural	therapeutically frame and process his foster family's prejudice and abuse as self-loathing passed down from their ancestors to him; bibliotherapy
Treatment prognosis	good to very good if protective factors are incorporated in treatment

and provocation of his peers that resulted in a physical fight (***current precipitant***) as well as the perceived injustice of peers and authority figures (***continuing precipitants***). Throughout his life, Antwone has sought to be accepted and make sense of being neglected, abused, and abandoned, and to protect himself by aggressively striking back and conditionally relating to others in the face of a perceived threat or injustice (***pattern***).

_____

_____

_____

_____

_____

_____

(***predisposition***). His limited capacity for emotional regulation along with deficits in conflict resolution skills serve to maintain this pattern (***perpetuants***). Antwone brings several protective factors and strengths to therapy, including his childhood best friend who served as his only secure attachment figure. He is intelligent, he is a reader with wide interests, and he has received regular promotions in rank, at least until recently. Additionally, he writes poetry and has learned two foreign languages. He also benefits from a caring military command and organizational structure that has encouraged counseling and treatment in lieu of punitive measures for past aggressive behaviors (***protective factors/strengths***).

The challenge for Antwone to function more effectively is to relate to others while being careful in getting to know and trust them (***treatment pattern***).

_____

_____

_____

_____

_____

_____

(***treatment goals***). The focus of treatment will be to analyze troublesome situations triggered or exacerbated by his mistaken beliefs (***treatment focus***). The basic treatment strategy is to foster social interest and constructive action. Compatible treatment strategies include medication, support, and interpretation (***treatment strategy***).

_____

_____

(***treatment interventions***). Specific treatment obstacles and challenges can be anticipated. These include the likelihood that Antwone will quickly identify with a caring practitioner as the positive father figure and role model that he has never had. It is also likely that this will engender a predictable transference–countertransference enactment which may result in him aggressively acting out (***treatment obstacles***). In addition to addressing personality and interpersonal treatment targets, an effective treatment outcome will require addressing the cultural dimension of prejudice, not only prejudice from white peers and superiors, but also his experience of black-on-black prejudice. It may be useful to therapeutically frame his foster family's prejudice and abuse toward him in terms of self-loathing that was passed down from their ancestors to him; then, it can be therapeutically processed. Because he is an avid reader, bibliotherapy, i.e., books and articles that analyze and explain this type of prejudice, could be a useful therapeutic adjunct (***treatment-cultural***). Antwone brings several strengths and resources to therapy, including intelligence, a reader with wide interests, regular promotions in rank, at least until recently, poetry writing, and learning two foreign languages. These resources plus his motivation to change suggest a good to very good prognosis (***treatment prognosis***).

Case of Maria

Maria is a 17-year-old, first-generation, Mexican American female who was referred for counseling because of mood swings. She is conflicted about her decision to go off to college instead of staying home to care for her terminally ill mother. Her family expects her to stay home. She is angry at her older sister who left home at 17 after her parents insisted that her culture "requires" her to take care of her parents when they get old or become ill. Her Anglo friends encourage her to go to college and pursue her dreams.

Adlerian Assessment

Besides diagnostic assessment information, the Adlerian assessment added the following: in terms of family constellation, she is the psychological and ordinal last born child (youngest sibling), and plays the roles of the "baby" and "good daughter" of the family. Maria was closest with her father and she was considered his favorite child. A major family value is culturally based, in which children are responsible for caretaking their elderly or needy family members. Maria is expected to be a homemaker and is discouraged from attending college. One of her earliest recollections involves her feeling sad and neglected when she was at the zoo and lost a toy that was very important to her. She acted like she was unaffected about the toy being lost because she did not want to overwhelm her father by asking him to look for it since her older sister was throwing a tantrum at the time.

Table 9.4 describes the results of the diagnostic and Adlerian assessment summarized for the key elements of a full-scale case conceptualization.

Case Conceptualization Statement

Maria's depressive symptoms, confusion, and recent experimentation with alcohol use (***presentation***) seem to be her reaction to pressures and conflict over going away to college or staying to care for her parents (***current precipitant***) as well as expectations of self-reliance, being alone, or need to meet others' needs at the expense of her own (***continuing precipitants***). This is largely because she pleases others, particularly her parents, while neglecting her own needs and desires (***pattern***).

_____

_____

_____

_____

_____

_____

(***predisposition***). This lifestyle has served her well until recently, but the price she pays is a failure to develop her talents and achieve her dreams. Her low level of assertiveness and unwillingness to disappoint her parents serve to maintain this pattern (***perpetuant***). Maria brings several protective factors to therapy including strong family, social, and religious values that may motivate her to establish vital life directions. Some of her strengths include her intelligence and past success in school. She also benefits from a tight-knit family and cultural community in which she can feel safe and supported (***protective factors/strengths***).

Maria identifies herself as a working-class Mexican American with a moderate level of involvement in that heritage (***cultural identity***). Her level of acculturation is in the low to moderate range while her parents' level is in the low range. Since her older sister refused to follow the cultural mandate that the oldest daughter would meet her parents needs rather than her own, that responsibility is now on Maria. Maria's ambivalence about whether to follow cultural norms and expectations or her own aspirations is quite distressing for her (***cultural stress & acculturation***). Her explanatory model is that her problems are due to a "lack of faith," a belief that is consistent with a lower level of acculturation. Although she and her family experienced some discrimination upon arrival here, it ended when they moved to a "safer" Mexican American neighborhood (***cultural explanation***). It

Table 9.4 Case Conceptualization Elements

Presentation	moodiness; confusion; experimentation with alcohol use
Precipitant	pressures and conflict over going away to college or staying to care for her parents (***current precipitant***); expectations of self-reliance, being alone, or need to meet others' needs at the expense of her own (***continuing precipitants***)
Predisposition	*family constellation*: plays roles of "baby" and "good daughter"; father's favorite; family values caring for elderly/needy family members
	lifestyle convictions:
	I am nice but inadequate (self-view)
	life is demanding and unfair (world view)
	therefore, please others and put their needs first at the expense of my own happiness (life strategy)
Pattern-maladaptive	meet others' needs but not hers
Perpetuant	dependent and pleasing style; low assertiveness; cultural expectation
Protective factors & strengths	strong family, social, religious values; successful student; tight-knit and safe cultural community
Cultural identity	working-class Mexican-American
Cultural stress & acculturation	low to moderate level of acculturation; stress from ambivalence about parental and cultural expectations
Cultural explanation	problems caused by "lack of faith"
Culture and/or personality	personality *and* cultural factors operative
Treatment pattern	meet her needs and the needs of others
Treatment goals	decrease moodiness, confusion, and alcohol consumption; decrease discouragement, increase her social interest, and achieve a better balance between her own needs and desires and those of others
Treatment focus	situations triggered or exacerbated by mistaken beliefs and/or discouragement
Treatment strategy	foster social interest and constructive action; support; interpretation
Treatment interventions	lifestyle assessment; early recollection analysis; encouragement, acting "as if"
Treatment obstacles	may capitulate to parents and cultural expectations; pleasing the practitioner; practitioner may unwittingly advocate autonomy
Treatment-cultural	process cultural expectations about caregiver role and need to please; family sessions addressing parents' cultural expectations
Treatment prognosis	fair to good

appears that both personality and cultural factors are operative. Specifically, cultural dynamics that foster dependency, i.e., good daughters care for their parents without question, serve to reinforce her dependent personality dynamics (***culture and/or personality***).

The challenge for Maria to function more effectively is to meet both her own needs in addition to the needs of others (***treatment pattern***).

_____

_____

_____

_____

_____

_____

(***treatment goals***). The focus of treatment will be to analyze troublesome situations triggered or exacerbated by her mistaken beliefs (***treatment focus***). The basic treatment strategy is to foster social interest and constructive action. Compatible treatment strategies include support and interpretation (***treatment strategy***).

_____

_____

_____

_____

_____

(***treatment interventions***). In terms of likely treatment obstacles and challenges, it is likely that Maria will attempt to please the practitioner by readily agreeing to the practitioner's suggestions and between-session assignments, but afterward become conflicted and then fail to follow up. It is also likely that the client will capitulate to her parents' expectations. Accordingly, the practitioner might, early in treatment, make the predictive interpretation that this might occur, but that it does not indicate failure, and that it can be therapeutically processed. Finally, practitioners working with dependent clients need to anticipate how their own needs and values may become treatment obstacles. This can occur when they unwittingly advocate for and expect clients to embrace independence and autonomy before the client is sufficiently ready (***treatment obstacles***). Effective treatment outcomes will also address relevant cultural dynamics. Specifically, this may involve therapeutically processing her explanatory model that a lack of faith is the source of her problem. Depending on the saliency and strength of this belief, education and cognitive disputation may be indicated. The cultural expectation about caring for her parents in light of her need to please would also be processed. In addition, family sessions may be indicated wherein her parents can review and revise their cultural expectations of her (***treatment-cultural***). Besides the impact of personality and culture, the resources that Maria brings to therapy influence her prognosis. She is bright, successful in school, and has already identified her needs and career aspirations. At this point, however, given her lower level of acculturation and dependent personality dynamics, her prognosis is in the fair to good range (***treatment prognosis***).

Case of Richard

Richard is a 41-year-old, Caucasian male who is being evaluated for anxiety, sadness, and anger following his recent divorce. He currently lives on his own, is employed as a machine operator, and frequents night clubs where he "is on the lookout for the perfect woman." He has held four jobs over the past six years and was fired from his last job because he smashed his fist through a wall after being confronted by a female coworker. He is the only child of alcoholic parents whom he describes as "fighting all the time."

Adlerian Assessment

Besides diagnostic assessment information, the Adlerian assessment added the following: in terms of family constellation, Richard is the only child of alcoholic parents whom he describes as "fighting all the time." His parents often involved him in their conflict and often used him to get revenge or to victimize each other. He reported that his parents were rarely emotionally available to him and recalled feeling depressed through much of his childhood. He said he had very few friends but was still very sociable as a child largely because he tried to be like his grand-mother who was kind and loving toward him. Even though she moved away, he indicated that he managed to keep in touch with her a few times a year. She died a year ago and he says he misses her a lot. Relationally, he reports a number of failed romantic relationships starting in high school. One of his early recollections was about receiving an A in second grade on a spelling quiz and being scolded by his teacher for bragging about having the highest grade in the class. He says he felt angry and wanted to throw something at her.

Table 9.5 describes the results of the diagnostic and Adlerian assessment summarized for the key elements of a full-scale case conceptualization.

Case Conceptualization Statement

Richard's angry outbursts and sadness (***presentation***) seem to be a reaction to his recent divorce and also being fired from his last job for smashing his fist through a wall (***current precipitant***) as well as self-evaluation, being alone, or others'

Table 9.5 Case Conceptualization Elements

Presentation	angry outbursts, sadness, and anxiety
Precipitant	recent divorce and also being fired from his last job for smashing his fist through a wall (***current precipitant***); evaluation of self, being alone, or others' perception of not being special (***continuing precipitants***)
Pattern-maladaptive	elevates self while belittling and using others
Predisposition	*family constellation*: only child; emotionally uninvolved alcoholic parents; sociable; felt lonely and depressed throughout childhood
	lifestyle convictions:
	I am entitled, strong, but defective (self-view)
	life is dangerous, but others should meet my needs (world view)
	Therefore, elevate myself, use others for my own gain, and strike back at those who don't give me what I need (life strategy)
Pattern-maladaptive	elevates self while belittling and using others
Perpetuant	impulsivity; limited relationship skills; inability to empathize
Protective factors & strengths	secure attachment with his grandmother; resilient, charismatic, and engaging
Cultural identity	middle-class Caucasian male
Cultural stress & acculturation	highly acculturated; no obvious cultural stress, but privilege should be examined in the therapeutic process
Cultural explanation	anxiety, anger, sadness caused by abusive, non-loving parents
Culture and/or personality	personality are dynamics operative, but privilege should be examined
Treatment pattern	self-confident and respectful of others
Treatment goals	decrease discouragement, increase his social interest, decrease his entitled style, and help him manage his anger
Treatment focus	situations triggered or exacerbated by mistaken beliefs and/or discouragement
Treatment strategy	foster social interest and constructive action; support; interpretation
Treatment interventions	lifestyle assessment; early recollection analysis; encouragement; acting "as if"
Treatment obstacles	minimization of problematic behaviors; idealization or devaluation of practitioner; arrogant attitude
Treatment-cultural	no cultural focus to treatment indicated but address privilege dynamics
Treatment prognosis	fair

perception of not being special (***continuing precipitants***). Throughout his life, he has continued to elevate himself while belittling and using others (***pattern***).

_____

_____

_____

_____

_____

_____

(***predisposition***). This pattern is maintained by his inability to empathize, impulsivity, and lack of relational skills (***perpetuants***). Richard's secure attachment with his grandmother serves as a protective factor and evidence that he has the capacity to care for others. The most prominent strength Richard brings to therapy is resilience. He is also charismatic and engaging (***protective factors/strengths***).

Richard identifies as a middle-class Caucasian male (***cultural identity***). He appears to be highly acculturated and there is no obvious indications of acculturative stress (***cultural stress & acculturation***). He believes that his current problems of anger, sadness, and anxiety result from the bad example he received from his abusive and non-loving parents who fought constantly when they drank (***cultural explanation***). Finally, personality dynamics are predominant and adequately explain his presenting problem and pattern, but examining his sense of entitlement and his own experience of privilege would be useful to address in therapy (***culture and/or personality***).

The challenge for Richard to function more effectively is to remain self-confident while endeavoring to be more respectful of others (***treatment pattern***).

_____

_____

_____

_____

_____

(***treatment goals***). The focus of treatment will be to analyze troublesome situations triggered or exacerbated by his mistaken beliefs (***treatment focus***). The basic treatment strategy is to foster social interest and constructive action. Compatible treatment strategies include support and interpretation (***treatment strategy***).

_____

_____

_____

_____

_____

_____

(***treatment interventions***). With regard to likely treatment obstacles and challenges, it is likely that Richard will minimize his own problematic behaviors by blaming circumstances or others. It can be expected that he will alternate between idealization or devaluation of the practitioner, at least in the beginning phase of therapy. His entitled and arrogant attitude could activate practitioner counter-transference. Furthermore, since it is not uncommon for clients with a narcissistic style to discontinue treatment when their symptoms, immediate conflicts, or stressors are sufficiently reduced, the practitioner who believes the client can profit from continued therapy needs to point out – at the beginning of therapy and thereafter – that until the client's underlying maladaptive pattern is sufficiently changed, similar issues and concerns will inevitably arise in the future (***treatment obstacles***). Since the primary influence is personality dynamics, no cultural focus to treatment is indicated besides examining his entitlement and sense of privilege (***treatment-cultural***). Finally, because of the client's conditional manner of relating, multiple job firings, and impulsivity, at this point, his prognosis is considered fair (***treatment prognosis***).

Case of Katrina

Katrina is a 13-year-old female of mixed ethnicity. She was referred for counseling by her guidance counselor due to recent depressive symptoms, poor academic performance, and oppositional behavior and fighting with other students at school. Her aggressive behavior and academic challenges have increased over the past six months since Katrina overheard a conversation between her mother and aunt in which she found out that her father had an affair for eight years. She was shocked to learn that the affair resulted in two births. Other difficulties include several fights with other students in the classroom, frequent conflict with her mother, skipping 15 days of school over the past six months, and diminished interest in her academic work. While she had previously excelled academically, she now displays a marked loss of interest in activities that used to give her pleasure, such as drawing and reading. Katrina's father is currently living in Puerto Rico and has no contact with the family. Katrina lives in a small apartment with her mother and younger brother near her school. She reported being frustrated with the lack of space, since they had to downsize from the single-family home they lived in before her father left the family one year ago.

Because Katrina was a minor, it was necessary for the school counselor to speak with Katrina and her mother together during the initial session. Katrina's mother, Julia, stated that she believes that Katrina will not talk to most people about her problems because she does not trust anyone. Self-disclosure was very difficult for Katrina during the initial interview and Julia answered the majority of the questions that were asked, in some cases speaking for Katrina when she made efforts to speak. Julia reported that Katrina's father was highly critical and also emotionally withdrawn throughout Katrina's childhood. Katrina also stated, "I don't really have a dad, since real fathers are supposed to take care of their families." She said she was tired of her teachers and her mother always forcing her to do things that she doesn't want to do. Katrina has difficulty relating to her peers and also presents as angry, oppositional, and defensive when her teachers or her mother enforce rules or expectations. She is often aggressive with her peers when they expect compliance or cooperation. Her teachers describe her as oppositional, irritable, and uncooperative. She had few friends as a child, but currently has one close friend whom she trusts.

Adlerian Assessment

Besides diagnostic assessment information, the Adlerian assessment added the following: in terms of family constellation, she is the oldest child and has a younger brother. She reported having few positive emotional encounters with her parents because they both frequently worked and often did not speak to her with warmth or encouragement. When asked about relationships, she stated that everyone tries to control her. She described her mother as controlling, unsupportive, and busy; while she described her father as a liar, controlling, and uninvolved. She described a history of people taking advantage of her, neglecting her, or trying to control her. During the first meeting, Katrina reported that she does not trust anyone and that she is not interested in attending counseling sessions if the practitioner is going to tell her what to do. One of her early recollections included a memory in which her mother was talking to her friend on the phone during dinner and forced Katrina to eat her carrots at the dinner table. She remembers yelling and screaming at her mother and feeling sad and angry. She also said that the memory reminds her that her mother always expected Katrina to comply with her rules. Table 9.6 describes the results of the diagnostic and Adlerian assessment summarized for the key elements of a full-scale case conceptualization.

Case Conceptualization Statement

Katrina's increased social isolation, aggressive and oppositional behavior, and depressive symptoms (***presentation***) appear to be her reaction to the recent news of her father's infidelity and resulting children (***current precipitant***). Katrina has a tendency to retaliate when she perceives that she is being violated or controlled by others (***continuing precipitant***). Given Katrina's lack of connection with her

Table 9.6 Brief Dynamic Case Conceptualization Elements

Presentation	depressive symptoms, aggressive behavior, and social isolation
Precipitant	learning of her father's infidelity and resulting children (***current precipitant***); retaliates in situations of perceived violation or control by others (***continuing precipitants***)
Pattern-maladaptive	moves against to protect herself from potential harm and rejection
Predisposition	*family constellation*: Oldest of two children; neglectful and critical parents; parents force compliance and use corporal punishment
	lifestyle convictions:
	I am inadequate and unlovable (self-view)
	life is unfair and abusive (world view)
	therefore, oppose people who try to control, be wary of others, and avoid close relationships (life strategy)
Protective factors & strengths	has a close relationship to her aunt and little brother; intelligent, creative, and resilient
Perpetuant	social isolation and lack of support system; mother and teachers rigidly forcing compliance; low frustration tolerance; lack of assertive communication skills
Cultural identity	Hispanic and African American; lower income
Cultural stress & acculturation	low to moderate level of acculturation and cultural stress
Cultural explanation	denies depression; believes she would feel better if her teachers and mother were less controlling
Culture and/or personality	personality dynamics and cultural dynamics are operative
Treatment pattern	increase safety and ability to connect with others
Treatment goals	reduce depressive symptoms and aggressive behavior; decrease discouragement and increase her social interest
Treatment focus	situations triggered or exacerbated by mistaken beliefs and/or discouragement
Treatment strategy	foster social interest and constructive action; support; interpretation
Treatment interventions	lifestyle assessment; early recollection analysis; encouragement; acting "as if"
Treatment obstacles	likely to resist individual and group therapy; expected outbursts at mother during family sessions; difficulty with self-disclosure
Treatment-cultural	assign a female practitioner; culturally focused Cognitive Behavior Therapy and family therapy
Treatment prognosis	fair to good if protective factors are incorporated into treatment

father and lack of trust in both parents, she moves against authority figures and her peers to protect herself from further harm and rejection (***pattern***).

_____

_____

_____

_____

_____

_____

(***predisposition***). This pattern is maintained by Katrina's unwillingness to ask for help, her low level of motivation to engage in therapy, her social isolation and lack of support system, her mother and teachers rigidly forcing compliance, her low frustration tolerance, and lack of assertive communication skills (***perpetuants***). Despite some of her current challenges, Katrina reported being very close with her aunt and little brother. Besides her close relationships in her family, Katrina reported that she feels responsible for her brother and does everything she can to protect him from harm. Lastly, her strengths include her being a good artist, determined, intelligent, empathic, and creative (***protective factors/strengths***).

Katrina identifies herself as heterosexual and of mixed ethnicity. She identified as Hispanic and African American but reported having little connection to ethnic and cultural traditions from either identity. She stated that she wants to be more like her friends and doesn't want to feel different or weird by speaking Spanish to her mother in front of friends (***cultural identity***). She is moderately acculturated and prefers not to speak Spanish outside of the home, though her mother requires her to speak Spanish while at home. Katrina's mother presents with a low level of acculturation as evidenced by having challenges with speaking English, having very few English-speaking friends, being first-generation Puerto-Rican American and also African American, and reporting that she is unhappy living in the United States and plans to move back to Puerto Rico once Katrina graduates from high school (***cultural stress & acculturation***). Katrina does not believe she is depressed but feels that she would be less annoyed with people if they would be less controlling and "less bossy" (***cultural explanation***). There appears to be a moderate level of cultural factors and a moderate level of personality dynamics that influence the presenting issues (***culture and/or personality***).

The challenge for Katrina to function more effectively is to increase her ability to trust others, feel safer, and to better connect with others (***treatment pattern***).

_____

_____

_____

_____

_____

_____

(*treatment goals*). Treatment is focused primarily on addressing Katrina's troublesome situations triggered or exacerbated by her mistaken beliefs (*treatment focus*). The basic treatment strategy is to foster social interest and constructive action. Compatible treatment strategies include support and interpretation (*treatment strategy*).

_____

_____

_____

_____

_____

_____

(*treatment interventions*). Some obstacles and challenges to treatment are anticipated given Katrina's low motivation to engage in therapy and her paranoid traits that are associated with her oppositional behaviors. It can be anticipated that she will have difficulty discussing personal matters with practitioners due to her inability to trust and that she will often engage in testing behaviors toward the practitioner (*treatment obstacles*). Treatment will require some culturally sensitive elements given Katrina and her mother's level of acculturation. Culturally sensitive treatment and family therapy will be used to address cultural factors present by considering Katrina's mixed ethnicity and her personal experience of both cultures. Additionally, gender dynamics may be an issue so it may be useful to assign her a female therapist (*treatment-cultural*). Assuming that Katrina is able to engage more in the therapeutic process as well as utilize her strengths and seek support from her aunt, her prognosis is adjudged to be fair to good (*treatment prognosis*).

Skill Building Exercises: Adlerian Psychotherapy

As mentioned in the Skill Building Exercises in Chapter 6, you will note that *certain elements of the case conceptualization statements contain open lines. These lines provide you with an opportunity to further develop your conceptualization skills with specific prompts.* Write a short predisposition statement, treatment goals, and a list of corresponding theory-specific treatment interventions for each case.

Concluding Note

The Adlerian model of case conceptualization was described and illustrated. The basic premises of the Adlerian perspective were listed, and the factors involved in an Adlerian assessment were discussed. The Adlerian model of case conceptualization was then applied to five cases and illustrated with their clinical, cultural, and treatment formulations.

CHAPTER 9 QUESTIONS

1. Discuss the basic constructs and historical influences of the Adlerian approach to case conceptualization.
2. Compare the main tenets of the Adlerian assessment as it relates to case conceptualization and how these are distinguished from the other approaches presented in previous chapters.
3. Explore the questions related to family constellation then discuss how this impacts the formulation of an Adlerian case conceptualization.
4. Explain the importance of early recollections, how these are selected, and in what section of the case conceptualization these should be included.
5. Discuss the signature elements of an Adlerian case conceptualization and how these influence the key elements of the components of a case conceptualization.

Appendix: Case of Antwone

Predisposition

Antwone's presenting problem and reactions can be understood as his aggressive and impulsive means of protecting himself against the hurt, arbitrary judgments, rejection, and loss that he has experienced since early life, including his mother who abandoned him and his foster family who both neglected and abused him. He reported experiencing little love and affection from anyone as a child. He found his place in his foster family, at first with fear and submission and later by fighting back and protecting himself. He views himself as defective and unlovable but strong, and he views others as abusive and unfair. Therefore, he lashes out at any perceived injustice, is wary of others, seldom takes risks, and avoids getting close to others. His early recollections included themes of victimization, others being harmful and unfair, and the world being challenging and dangerous.

Treatment Goal

Treatment goals are to help him manage his anger and increase his ability to control his impulsive reactions, increase positive coping skills, and help him find and reconnect to his family. From an Adlerian perspective, treatment goals also include decreasing discouragement, increasing social interest and social relating, and enhancing relational skills.

Treatment Interventions

Interventions will include helping him engage in constructive behaviors. Encouragement will be utilized to foster a more positive appraisal of situations.

Volunteering will be used as a social interest enhancing intervention to help him experience feeling useful to others and to increase his ability to connect with others while still being careful. Interpretation will be utilized to process his basic mistakes, by particularly retaliating in the face of injustices and avoiding close relationships. Since Antwone indicated he wished he could respond to conflict with a calm attitude, he will be encouraged to act "as if" he was calm during times of conflict.

Case of Maria

Predisposition

Maria's presenting problem and pattern are understandable given her lifestyle. To the extent to which she continues to be pleasing and non-assertive, she reinforces the expectation that others' needs must be met instead of her own needs and desires, and that her life is a failure and she will have wasted her potential. The current situation mirrors her lifelong pattern in which she has played the role of "good daughter," unlike her siblings who have rebelled against family and cultural expectations. Maria found her place in her family through goodness and a desire to please her parents, and so she is nice, agreeable, and pleasing. She is the psychological youngest child and she found a place in her family through goodness and pleasing her parents without question. She views herself as nice but inadequate, and she views others as demanding and dependent upon her. Her early recollections included themes of a negative self-view, others being dependent on her, pleasing others, and approval seeking.

Treatment Goal

Treatment goals are to decrease her moodiness, confusion, and alcohol consumption. From an Adlerian perspective, treatment goals also include decreasing discouragement, increasing social interest and social relating, and enhancing relational skills.

Treatment Interventions

The practitioner will provide support particularly by encouraging her to consider ways in which she could care for her parents and follow her dreams. Collaboratively investigating her lifestyle could increase Maria's self-awareness and help her examine the usefulness of her behaviors. Interpretation will be utilized regarding her basic mistakes by analyzing and modifying her faulty convictions regarding putting others' needs first at the expense of her own happiness. While Maria says she really wished she could be more comfortable in making decisions by herself, she will be encouraged to act "as if" she was comfortable making decisions.

Case of Richard

Predisposition

His reaction and pattern is understandable given his upbringing and lifestyle. He is the only child of alcoholic parents whom he observed fighting constantly and who would sometimes pull him into their conflict. Richard found his place in his family by being aggressive, entitled, but also sociable. He views himself as entitled and strong but somehow defective. The world is viewed as dangerous and unpredictable, and he views others as serving his needs but who can be withholding and manipulative. Therefore, he elevates himself while belittling and using others and strikes back at those who don't give him what he expects. His early recollections included themes of an entitled self-view, others as serving to his needs but also being harmful and unavailable, and situations having negative outcomes.

Treatment Goal

Goals for treatment include increasing his ability to reduce his anger and to manage his impulses and also reduce his sadness and anxiety. From an Adlerian perspective, treatment goals also include decreasing discouragement, increasing social interest and social relating, and enhancing relational skills.

Treatment Interventions

He will be encouraged to experience feeling whole and effective and to relate to others more benignly. Interpretation will be utilized to process his basic mistakes by analyzing and modifying faulty convictions particularly his entitled and defective self-view and his pattern of elevating himself while belittling and using others. Social interest enhancing interventions will be utilized to help Richard experience feeling useful to others and to increase his ability to empathize with others. While Richard says he would like to feel less depressed and go out on weekends, he will be encouraged to act "as if" he was feeling well and to go out on weekends.

Case of Katrina

Predisposition

In short, her pattern can be understood in light of her lack of trust in her father based on his infidelity. In addition, her private logic of being rejected by her father appears to have influenced her lifestyle convictions of mistrust and paranoia about others' intentions. Katrina is the oldest of two children and is described by her mother as "a strong-willed child." Her role in her family system was as a parentified child who took on instrumental parenting roles toward her younger brother. She views herself as inadequate and unlovable and views others as controlling and unsupportive. Her lifestyle convictions are to oppose people who try to control her, be wary of others, and avoid close relationships. Her goal of misbehavior is revenge, in which she retaliates against others when she feels threatened or that others are trying to control her. She presents with a low level of social interest and sense of community feeling as she has few friends or positive relationships in her life.

Treatment Goal

Treatment goals include reducing depressive symptoms, anger management, increasing assertiveness and friendship skills, and reducing her oppositional behaviors. From an Adlerian perspective, treatment goals also include decreasing discouragement, increasing social interest and social relating, and enhancing relational skills.

Treatment Interventions

The practitioner will include support in the form encouragement to engage and connect with Katrina throughout the entire treatment process. Interpretation will be utilized regarding Katrina's lifestyle convictions or basic mistakes by analyzing and modifying her faulty convictions regarding her belief that others are controlling, unsafe, and harmful. Social interest homework will be assigned to engage her in acts of service toward others once she commits to treatment.

References

Ansbacher, H.L., & Ansbacher, R.R. (Eds.). (1956). *The individual psychology of Alfred Adler*. New York, NY: Harper & Row.

Carlson, J., & Englar-Carlson, M. (2018). *Adlerian psychotherapy*. Washington, DC: American Psychological Association.

Corey, G. (2017). *Theory and practice of counseling and psychotherapy* (10th ed.). Boston, MA: Cengage Learning.

Sperry, J. (2011). *The relationship of self-transcendence, social interest, and spirituality to well-being in HIV-AIDS adults*. Retrieved from Dissertations and Theses database. (UMI No. 3320105).

Sperry, L. (2015). Diagnosis, case conceptualization, and treatment. In L. Sperry, J. Carlson, J.D. Sauerheber & J.Sperry (Eds.), *Psychopathology and psychotherapy* (3rd ed., pp. 36–50). New York, NY: Routledge.

Sperry, L., & Binensztok, V. (2018). Adlerian pattern focused therapy: A treatment manual. *The Journal of Individual Psychology*, *74*(3), 309–348.

Sperry, L., & Binensztok, V. (2019). *Learning and practicing Adlerian therapy*. San Diego, CA: Cognella Academic Publishing.

10 Acceptance and Commitment Therapy Case Conceptualizations[*]

Introduction

Acceptance and Commitment Therapy (ACT; pronounced as the word "act") is one of the prominent "Third-Wave" behavior therapies. It is also emerging as one of the most rigorously researched and evidence-based treatments for a multitude of psychological difficulties (American Psychological Association, n.d.). This chapter begins with an overview of the ACT perspective, including theoretical underpinnings, assessment, and theory of psychopathology and wellness. In addition, unique clinical, cultural, and treatment formulations methods are described consistent with this approach. Following this summary, five ACT case conceptualizations for clinical cases are presented.

ACT Perspective

Categorized as a "third-wave" behavioral therapy, ACT began as "Comprehensive Distancing" (Hayes, 1981), alluding to the process of creating "distance" between the individual and their uncomfortable and unwanted private experiences. ACT also has prominent roots in traditional behavioral analysis (Hayes, Strosahl, & Wilson, 2012). Many consider ACT to be more behavioral leaning than other Third-Wave approaches. While some deem it a "radical behavioral" approach, "'Radical Behaviorism' is a poor umbrella term for ACT" (Hayes, 2004, p. 646). A "radical behaviorist" perspective would make strong assertions of an externalist position, whereby the locus of study and the control of human behavior lie in the triggering stimuli for human responses; ACT does not. Both the context and the individual's ability to influence the context are regarded as equally important to understanding human behavior. ACT is an integrative approach; it weaves processes of acceptance, attention to the present moment (i.e., mindfulness), emphasizes the therapeutic relationship, and includes motivation for change (Hayes, Villatte, Levin, & Hildebrandt, 2011).

Based on the philosophical theory of functional contextualism, ACT conceptualizes psychological events as interactions between the organism and contexts which are historically and situationally defined (Biglan & Hayes, 1996; Hayes, Hayes, & Reese, 1988). Functional contextualism focuses on the function of

[*] This chapter was co-authored by Gerardo A. Casteleiro.

behavior in context. It also emphasizes a pragmatic truth criterion and specific scientific goals against which to apply it (Hayes, 2004). Essentially, functional contextualism posits that something is "true" if it works (Hayes et al., 1988), which can serve to ameliorate the "radical" behaviorism misconception.

The ACT perspective also challenges the "disease" and "illness" assumptions about human psychological distress. It conceptualizes human suffering as a challenge to be accepted and experienced, rather than a burden to be avoided. Derived from Relational Frame Theory, a post-Skinnerian approach to language and cognition, ACT addresses the perils of the entanglement between individuals and their thoughts (i.e., fusion), and the instinct to avoid experiential hardships (i.e., avoidance). It views the concept of "normal" as inherently destructive, resulting in distress and perceived defectiveness in individuals due to their interpretations of suffering (i.e., "having pain is 'bad'"). Breaking away from the medical model, with which the second-wave behavior therapies align more closely, symptom reduction (first-order goals) is not presented as a priority. Instead, ACT encourages individuals to make decisions that are in line with valued life directions toward vitality and freedom (Hayes et al., 2012; Wilson & DuFrene, 2009). However, given that individuals largely prefer to feel favorable emotions as opposed to painful ones, it is not an easy sell. Therefore, ACT therapy typically begins with immersion into "Creative Hopelessness," by which clients are guided toward giving up the agenda of emotional or experiential control (Luoma, Hayes, & Walser, 2017).

Relational Frame Theory shines a bright light on the typical, evolutionarily driven, "traps" of human language and cognition. It points toward the risks of avoidance and fusion, unclear values, persistent inaction or disengagement, rigid concepts of self, and attachment to the conceptualized past or future (Villatte, Villatte, & Hayes, 2016). These categorical processes make up the three "pillars" of psychological rigidity (e.g., closed, mindless, and disconnected), which constitute the theory of human suffering from the ACT perspective. Its opposite, psychological flexibility, composed of openness, awareness, and engagement, contains the six processes that form the ACT theory of wellness. These will be defined and discussed below as they are central to assessment and treatment.

ACT Assessment and Treatment

Assessment in ACT involves a systematic exploration of all six act processes, organized into three distinct pillars. Defusion and acceptance processes comprise the "openness" pillar. These two processes assess the individual's ability to turn toward his or her experience, as opposed to turning away from, rejecting, or avoiding it. Cognitive fusion is defined as "a process by which verbal events exert strong stimulus control over responding, to the exclusion of other contextual variables" (Hayes et al., 2012, p. 69). An individual who is suffering, for instance, may think that "I am having the worst day of my life." An assessment of fusion explores the individual's "closeness" with this thought, ranging from perceiving the thought as a thought (defused) to vehemently viewing the thought as the literal truth (fused). Whereas other Cognitive-Behavioral approaches might target the content of the thought through disputation or by examining the evidence, defusion targets the relationship and distance between the thought and the individual. The process of undermining cognitive fusion has been established as a key component of ACT (Hayes et al., 2012). This process provides a tool with which the individual can view thoughts as a product of their mind.

- "How close is this thought to you?" (elicit the distance between the thought and the individual)
- "How useful is this thought?" (probe for the client's ability to gauge workability)
- "Can you notice who is saying that?" (elicit the individual's ability to notice their mind)

Acceptance is the other half that comprises the openness pillar of psychological flexibility. Defined as "taking an open, receptive, nonjudgmental posture with respect to various aspects of experience" (Wilson & DuFrene, 2009, p. 46), acceptance processes rival experiential avoidance. Avoidance is a common culprit in many psychological difficulties. The instinct to vilify and reject human suffering as "maladaptive" kindles the fire of avoidance. In cases such as anxiety, for example, sufferers engage in damning their experience. Nervousness and worry can be perceived as "bad" and avoided through social disengagement, distraction, or numbing through substance use. Avoidance strategies can therefore result in unfavorable outcomes, such as isolation and procrastination. Acceptance is a process that counters avoidance through willingness. Clients are assessed for the "workability" of their avoidance. The inquiry aims to assess whether the client's avoidance behaviors have led to the favorable outcomes, leading the client toward the life they want to live. As the clients endorse the unworkability of their avoidance, they consider or outright collaborate in acceptance processes.

- "Is this a problem that you are willing to have?" (probe the client's willingness)
- "Does it seem to you like you have been running from this? How long have you run?" (assess the client's history of avoidance)

The awareness pillar of psychological flexibility is divided into mindfulness and Self-as-Context processes. These two interventions aim to expand the flexibility with which individuals see themselves in context and remain connected to the present moment. Mindfulness is defined as flexible contact with the present moment (Hayes et al., 2012). Many psychological difficulties are influenced by the individual's attachment to the concept of their past or future. For example, in the case of depression, severe rumination often includes thinking and contemplating past events, failures, and mistakes. Assessment of the individual's ability to remain connected to the present moment is of crucial importance in ACT. Additionally, mindfulness provides individuals with the tools to live through their experiences as an observer. It allows individuals to observe their pain and witness their hardships with equanimity, eliminating judgments about their experience.

- "What is showing up for you right now?" (elicit description of the client's ongoing experience – internal and external)
- "Where do you feel that in your body in this moment?" (elicit bodily sensations in the *here and now*)

Similarly, Self-as-Context (or perspective-taking sense of self) assesses the client's fusion to their conceptualized self (Hayes et al., 2012). Clients who have an unchangeable or a rigid sense of self can be fused with thoughts such as "I am a failure – I have always failed and I know I'm always going to fail." The concept of self as unchangeable can lead to other forms of rigid responding and various forms of psychological difficulties. Flexible and workable concepts of self are conceptualized in three levels. The conceptualized self contains all the data on the individual's story. This is also referred to as "Self-as-Content." The individual's history makes up the story and the "facts" can be perceived as literal and unchangeable. Individuals who are fused with this level perceive themselves as their story. The "Self-as-Process" is one level above, which allows the client to have an outsider's perspective and witness their experience. This ongoing awareness can provide just enough distance for individuals to engage in behavioral experiments. The final level is "Self-as-Context," which is the self that notices the process. This level of awareness allows the individual to notice themselves as the "container" for their experiences. With enough distance from their stories, individuals typically experience increased freedom to engage in broader behavioral repertoires.

- "How would you describe yourself as a person? How well does that description define you?" (assess for fusion with conceptualized self)
- "Is there a particular story about yourself that restricts what you are able to do or how you go about your life?" (elicit life stories and limitations they imposes on the client's behaviors)

Engagement is the final pillar of psychological flexibility. It is composed of committed action and values. Values are "freely chosen, verbally constructed consequences of ongoing, dynamic, evolving patterns of activity, which establish predominant reinforcers for that activity that are intrinsic in engagement in the valued behavioral pattern itself" (Wilson, 2009, p. 66). All ACT processes aim to enhance the individual's ability to move toward the life that they want to live. ACT emphasizes derivation of goals from chosen values. Individuals with unknown or unclear values, with little direction as to where they are going, typically end up where they are headed. Clarifying values in ACT establishes directions for the individual's life as well as for the therapeutic endeavor.

- "What kind of life do you want to live? What kind of person do you want to be?" (elicit life directions listening for what is important to the client)
- "What do you find meaningful in life?" (probe for vitality, vulnerability, choice, and orientations to the present)
- "What gets in the way of establishing a life direction?" (assess for obstacles to freely choosing values)

Committed action is the process of engaging in valued behaviors or activities and returning to those behaviors once the individual notices that the behaviors have drifted from the values (Hayes et al., 2012). Following the concept of flexibility, this means that bumps, obstacles, and failures can – and probably will – occur. Assessment of this process explores the individual's ability to rebound, to assess where they took a misstep, and re-engage in their values-based behaviors. On the other hand, lack of committed action can result in extremes of procrastination and impulsivity. This could signal that the individual is unclear about their values or that their agreed-upon actions were not freely chosen.

- "What steps can we take in the service of living the life you want to live?" (assess for willingness to engage in behavioral experiments)
- "What seems most pressing for us to focus on right now?" (elicit goals and listen for difficulty in current or other ACT processes)

ACT Case Conceptualization

An ACT case conceptualization, as presented here, will include clinical, cultural, and treatment formulations stemming from an ACT perspective. While case conceptualization is a crucial tool with which to choose interventions and plan treatment, the conceptualization itself is seldom shared or discussed with the client. Experiential, rather than didactic, learning is emphasized (Hayes et al., 2012). The clinical formulation aims to explain the client's presenting problems in terms of unworkable beliefs and behaviors. When operative, the cultural formulation explains the interactions of culture and personality. The treatment formulation provides clinical guidance for interventions that can be chosen to facilitate movement toward adaptive patterns (i.e., valued life directions). Experienced and purist ACT therapists and researchers may note that "adaptive" is not an ACT-consistent modifier, as it may denote judgment of the "goodness" of a particular behavior or a collection of behaviors and attitudes. Wherever possible, an ACT-consistent alternative will be provided. As this chapter aims to provide an overview of Acceptance and Commitment Therapy and its potential within the Integrative Case Conceptualization Model, the model is respected and the reader's flexibility is highly encouraged. Finally, the ACT conceptualization differs from other presented models due to its signature elements including: predisposition, treatment goals, treatment focus, treatment strategy, and treatment interventions.

Table 10.1 identifies the five signature elements.

Table 10.1 Signature Elements of the Acceptance and Commitment Therapy Case Conceptualization

Predisposition	psychological rigidity; closed, mindless, and disconnected behavior or responding
Treatment goals	increase psychological flexibility; foster openness, awareness, and engagement
Treatment focus	to decrease persistent avoidance and psychological rigidity by exploring flexibility processes and expanding behavioral repertoire
Treatment strategies	to increase psychological flexibility by addressing entanglement with thoughts, poor contact with present moment, ambiguous values, experiential avoidance, to develop a stable and flexible sense of self, and encourage committed action
Treatment interventions	***defusion***: writing thoughts down; hierarchical framing; Milk Milk Milk
	acceptance: tug-of-war with a monster, uninvited party guest
	mindfulness: Leaves on a Stream, body scan
	perspective-taking (Self-as-Context): deictic framing; temporal framing; Chessboard metaphor
	values: Cycling Jersey, values card-sort
	committed action: Two Trains, Walking the Path

ACT Case Conceptualization: Five Cases

Five cases are presented in order to illustrate the process of constructing ACT case conceptualizations. An assessment paragraph will follow background information on each case, identifying key features of the ACT perspective. A table will summarize nine elements from the diagnostic, clinical, and cultural formulations (discussed in Chapters 2 and 3) and the eight elements of the treatment formulation (discussed in Chapter 4). A narrative integrating the information will be provided in the form of a case conceptualization statement. The first paragraph will report diagnostic and clinical formulations, followed by the cultural formulation in the second paragraph, and the treatment formulation in the third and final paragraph.

Case of Geri

Geri is a 35-year-old, African American female who works as an administrative assistant. She is single, lives alone, and was referred by her company's human resources director for evaluation and treatment following three weeks of depression and social isolation. Her absence from work prompted the referral. Her symptoms began soon after her supervisor told Geri that she was being considered for a promotion. As a child she reported isolating and avoiding others when she was criticized and teased by family members and peers.

ACT Assessment

Beyond diagnostic assessment, the ACT assessment provided the following information: Geri stated that she was extremely worried and nervous about the possibility of failing in the new position. She has been thinking about it nonstop and she cannot seem to "get the thoughts out of her head." Therefore, she began to miss work because she thought that she was likely to fail either way. She stated that throughout her life she had been treated with disdain and disrespect, which made her feel inadequate and "less than." Assessment of avoidance strategies revealed that Geri isolates and disengages from social situations or circumstances that bring about uncertainty. She shows a strong preference for routines and thus has demonstrated success in a stable and unchanging work environment for the past 16 years. When assessed for barriers to changing her work environment and some of the emotional consequences that surfaced as a result, Geri seemed perplexed, stating "I don't know what's going on with me. This is not like me. I just don't want to do anything." When asked what her ideal outcome would be in her work environment, she stated "I want things to go back to what they were" (Table 10.2).

Case Conceptualization Statement

Geri's isolation and emotional difficulties (*presentation*) seem to be her reaction to the news that she was being considered for a job promotion and a new supervisor (*current precipitant*), as well as demands from close relationships and the expectation that she will be criticized, rejected, and feel unsafe (*continuing precipitants*). Throughout her life, she found it safer to avoid others when possible and conditionally relate to them at other times; as a result, she lacks key social skills and has a limited social network (*pattern*). She seems to be fused with thoughts such as "I'm going to fail" or "I'm not going to be able to do this." Therefore, the "damning" of her difficult internal experiences (thoughts/feelings/memories/sensations) seems to be driving avoidance strategies such as staying at home, isolating from others, and potentially "sabotaging" her opportunity to be promoted. Additionally, she demonstrates difficulty understanding her internal experiences. She stated, "I don't know what is going on with me," as she seemingly is taken by her mind into the unknowable future. She also seems to have rigid and limiting beliefs about who she is and what she is capable of. Her isolation and absenteeism, difficulty with assertiveness, and general disengagement seem to be influenced by absent or unclear values (*predisposition*). These indicators of rigid responding are likely perpetuated by isolation and avoidance strategies (*perpetuants*). Geri has a secure attachment with her close work friend and also brings commitment to her workplace through her many years of employment. She also benefits from legislative structures through which she can seek accommodations for her job, such as the Americans with Disabilities Act (*protective factors/strengths*).

She identifies herself as a middle-class African American but has little interest and no involvement with the African American community (*cultural identity*).

Table 10.2 Acceptance and Commitment Therapy Case Conceptualization Elements

Presentation	increased social isolation and depressive symptoms
Precipitant	news that she was being considered for a job promotion and a new supervisor (***current precipitant***); demands of close relationships and the expectation that she will be criticized, rejected, and feel unsafe (***continuing precipitant***)
Pattern-maladaptive	avoid and disconnect from others when feeling unsafe
Predisposition	***fusion***: entangled with thoughts about impending hardship and potential failure
	avoidance: "damning" difficult experiences such as nervousness and anxiety
	rigid attention: demonstrates skills deficits in identifying and assigning language to her emotional hardships; difficulty with maintaining focus on present moment
	attached to conceptualized self: rigid beliefs about how past experiences define and narrow choices and behaviors for her ongoing life
	disconnected action: isolation and absenteeism, potential skills deficits in assertiveness
	unclear values: vague or absent principles that serve as a guide toward chosen life directions
Protective factors/ strengths	close, trusting friend and confidante; stable meaningful job; eligible for job accommodation
Perpetuant	isolation and avoidance strategies; vague or absent values; unaware of internal experiences
Cultural identity	middle-class African American; limited ethnic ties
Cultural stress & acculturation	highly acculturated; no obvious acculturative stress but family gender roles reinforce the notion that she is inadequate
Cultural explanation	sadness results from job stress and chemical imbalance in her brain
Culture and/or personality	personality dynamics are significantly operative
Treatment pattern	connects while feeling safer
Treatment goals	increase acceptance of unwanted private experiences; foster stable sense of self that supports flexible social engagement; develop values-consistent goals related to work
Treatment focus	to decrease persistent avoidance and psychological rigidity by exploring flexibility processes and expanding behavioral repertoire
Treatment strategy	to increase psychological flexibility by addressing entanglement with thoughts, poor contact with present moment, ambiguous values, experiential avoidance, to develop a stable and flexible sense of self, and encourage committed action

(Continued)

Table 10.2 Continued

Treatment interventions	values card-sort, Thanking Your Mind, pop-up blocker metaphor, Chessboard metaphor, tug-of-war with a monster
Treatment obstacles	"test" practitioners; likely to resist group therapy; over dependence on practitioners; difficulty with termination
Treatment cultural	gender may be an issue so assign supportive female practitioner
Treatment prognosis	good prognosis if she is more flexible in responding, and returns to work

She is highly acculturated, as are her parents, but her family system placed higher value on men. This positive bias toward men appears to reinforce the notion that she is unwanted and inadequate (*cultural stress & acculturation*). She believes that her depression is the result of stress at work and a "chemical imbalance" in her brain (*cultural explanation*). No significant cultural factors are operative. It appears that Geri's personality dynamics are significantly operative in her current clinical presentation, but gender roles should be examined (*culture and/or personality*).

The challenge of change for Geri will be to engage with her experience and with others while maintaining intra- and interpersonal safety (*treatment pattern*). General goals for treatment are to reduce her depressive symptoms, increase her interpersonal and friendship skills, help her return to work, and increase her social network. The primary goals of treatment are to increase acceptance of unwanted private experiences, foster a stable sense of self that supports flexible social engagement, and develop values-consistent goals related to work (*treatment goals*). Treatment will be focused on decreasing persistent avoidance and psychological rigidity by exploring flexibility processes and expanding behavioral repertoire (*treatment focus*). The aim will be to increase psychological flexibility by addressing entanglement with thoughts, poor contact with present moment, ambiguous values, and experiential avoidance, and developing a stable and flexible sense of self, and encouraging committed action (*treatment strategy*). Given Geri's assessment, treatment interventions will first endeavor to clarify values. The clinician will collaborate with Geri on a values card-sort in order to reach a more sophisticated understanding of the kind of life she wants to create for herself. Geri's freely chosen values will serve as guide and reinforcement for the following interventions. The clinician will engage with Geri on defusion exercises such "Thanking Your Mind." The clinician will also guide Geri in hierarchical framing, eliciting her to state her thoughts such as "I am having the thought that I will always fail." The "Chessboard" metaphor will be used to foster a more flexible sense of self (*treatment interventions*). Some obstacles and challenges to treatment can be anticipated. Given her avoidant personality structure, ambivalent resistance is likely. It can be anticipated that she will have difficulty discussing personal matters with practitioners, that she will "test" and provoke practitioners into criticizing her for changing or cancelling appointments at the last minute or being late, and that she might procrastinate, avoid feelings, and otherwise test how much the practitioner can be trusted. Once trust in the practitioner is achieved, she is likely to cling to the practitioner and treatment; termination may be difficult unless her social support system outside therapy is increased. Furthermore, her pattern of avoidance is likely to make entry into and continuation with group work difficult. Therefore, individual sessions can serve as a transition into group work, including having some contact with the group practitioner who will presumably be accepting and non-judgmental. This should increase Geri's feeling of safety and make self-disclosure in a group setting less difficult. Stimulus generalization on Geri's part is another consideration. Given the extent of parental and peer criticism and teasing, it is anticipated that any perceived impatience and verbal or non-verbal indications of criticalness by the practitioner will activate unwanted feelings. Finally, because of her tendency to cling to others she trusts, increasing her capacity to feel more confident in functioning with greater independence and increasing the time between the last four or five sessions can reduce her ambivalence about termination (***treatment obstacles***). Given Geri's personality dynamics, treatment progress does not appear to be highly influenced by cultural stress. However, gender dynamics could impact the therapeutic relationship given the gender roles in her family, her strained relationship with her father, and her limited involvement with men ever since. Accordingly, female practitioners for both individual and group therapy appear to be indicated in the initial phase of treatment (***treatment-cultural***). Assuming that Geri develops a flexible and stable sense of self, relational skills, and social contacts outside of therapy, as well as returns to work, her prognosis is adjudged to be good; if not, it is guarded (***treatment prognosis***).

Case of Antwone

Antwone is an African American Navy seaman in his mid 20s who has lashed out at others with limited provocation. Recently, his commander ordered him to undergo compulsory counseling. From infancy until the time he enlisted in the Navy, he lived in foster placements, mostly with an abusive African American foster family.

ACT Assessment

Further assessment provided the following details: due to a significant history of neglect and abuse, Antwone integrated rules of diminished safety and expectations that others would hurt or leave him. His foster mother's berating behavior gave way to further expectations that others cannot be trusted. This likely established a rigid pattern of lashing out at others at the slightest provocation. Antwone endorsed that "This is what I have to do. I'm not going to let other people walk all over me." He also disclosed that he felt weak and emasculated when his foster mom would call him names or hit him. Antwone's emotional control goals were to never again be made to feel less-than. He stated, "I'm never going to let someone punk me or get anything over me," demonstrating a sense of self that is defined by seemingly unchangeable rules. He also seems to have derived rules about his worth from the loss of his parents, the loss of his best friend, and the sexual abuse he suffered in childhood, all of which are worthy of further exploration. Antwone also seems fused with his conceptual past. The neglect and abuse he experienced in the past seem to significantly affect how he responds to current stressors, especially around others. Additionally, he stated, "I don't know what happens to me. I just get angry and the next thing I know, I'm getting consequences." Therefore, he relates to others with overly aggressive or "lashing out" behaviors. He shared that his military career is of the utmost importance to him and he also wishes to pursue a meaningful relationship and start a family (Table 10.3).

Case Conceptualization Statement

Antwone's verbal and physical lashing out at others and his confusion about others' intentions (**presentation**) appear to be his response to the taunting and provocation of his peers that resulted in a physical fight (**current precipitant**) as well as perceived injustice of peers and authority figures (**continuing precipitants**). Throughout his life, Antwone has sought to be accepted and make sense of being neglected, abused, and abandoned, and to protect himself by striking back and conditionally relating to others in the face of perceived threats or injustice (**pattern**).

_____

_____

_____

_____

_____

_____

(**predisposition**). Deficits in conflict resolution, emotional identification, and high suspiciousness are likely perpetuating the pattern (**perpetuants**). Antwone brings several protective factors and strengths to therapy, including his childhood best friend who served as his only secure attachment figure. He is intelligent, he is a reader with wide interests, and he has received regular promotions in rank, at least until recently. Additionally, he writes poetry and has learned two foreign languages. He also benefits from a caring military command and organizational structure that has encouraged counseling and treatment in lieu of punitive measures for past aggressive behaviors (**protective factors/strengths**).

Antwone identifies as African American and maintains some ethnic ties (**cultural identity**). Although he is highly acculturated, he continues to experience considerable racial discrimination which seems to be exacerbated by his cultural

Table 10.3 Acceptance and Commitment Therapy Case Conceptualization Elements

Presentation	verbal and/or physical retaliation, confusion
Precipitant	conflicts that resulted in a physical fight with other sailors (*current precipitant*); perceived injustice of peers and authority figures (*continuing precipitants*)
Pattern-maladaptive	strikes back and conditionally relates
Predisposition	*fusion*: entangled with thoughts and feelings of being abandoned
	avoidance: feelings of sadness, abandonment, memories of childhood
	rigid attention: insufficient skills of emotional identification; fusion with conceptualized past
	attached to conceptualized self: inflexible beliefs of self as "weak" or "unmanly" in situations in which he feels inferior
	disconnected action: lashing out and aggressive behaviors to neutralize threats
	values: known values about military and family life; difficulty establishing behavioral goals that are in adherence to values
Protective factors/ strengths	best friend was a secure attachment figure; intelligent, avid reader with wide interests; creative; committed to duty and service
Perpetuant	suspiciousness; emotional regulation and conflict resolution deficits
Cultural identity	African American; ambivalent about ethnic involvement
Cultural stress & acculturation	highly acculturated; considerable acculturative stress
Cultural explanation	racial degradation; racial provocations of white peers and superiors
Culture and/or personality	personality *and* cultural factors operative
Treatment pattern	connect and relate to others while being careful
Treatment goals	acceptance and mindfulness to develop emotional identification, support resilience, and increase impulse control; foster stable sense of self through processing past trauma and family conflict; clarify values and set values-consistent goals
Treatment focus	to decrease persistent avoidance and psychological rigidity by exploring flexibility processes and expanding behavioral repertoire
Treatment strategy	to increase psychological flexibility by addressing entanglement with thoughts, poor contact with present moment, ambiguous values, experiential avoidance, to develop a stable and flexible sense of self, and encourage committed action

(Continued)

Table 10.3 Continued

Treatment interventions	the "sweet" spot, The Sky and the Weather, Two Trains metaphor, Leaves on a Stream, mindfulness processes to foster emotional identification and impulse control
Treatment obstacles	stimulus generalization with male practitioners; aggressive acting out; dependence and idealizing of practitioner
Treatment cultural	therapeutically frame and process his foster family's prejudice and abuse as self-loathing passed down from their ancestors to him; bibliotherapy
Treatment prognosis	good to very good

beliefs (***cultural stress & acculturation***). He believes that his problems result from racial degradation and abuse from his African American foster family, as well as from racial provocations by his white peers and Navy superiors (***cultural explanation***). It appears that both personality and cultural factors are operative (***culture and/or personality***).

The challenge of change for Antwone to function more effectively is to relate to others while being careful in getting to know and trust them (***treatment pattern***).

_____

_____

_____

_____

_____

_____

(***treatment goals***). Treatment will be focused on decreasing persistent avoidance and psychological rigidity by exploring flexibility processes and expanding behavioral repertoires (***treatment focus***). The aim will be to increase psychological flexibility by addressing entanglement with thoughts, poor contact with present moment, ambiguous values, and experiential avoidance, and developing a stable and flexible sense of self, and encouraging committed action (***treatment strategy***). "Leaves on a Stream" is a mindfulness intervention that will support awareness and defusion with thoughts. It can also support his ability to identify emotions that have been destabilizing, resulting in impulsive decision-making and aggressive responding. Other mindfulness interventions such as the body scan and skills such as focusing on the senses will increase Antwone's skills in staying in the present moment, noticing that he is remembering, as opposed to "reliving," past abuse and trauma. "The Sky and the Weather" is a Self-as-Context and perspective-taking guided imagery exercise that will aid Antwone in understanding that whereas he contains experiences of abandonment feelings, humiliation, and memories of abuse, he is not those memories. This process will promote understanding of self as a container of the experiences and provide distance and freedom to make decisions that are more consistent with goals and values. Finally, values clarification through the "Pain and Values – Two Sides of the Same Coin" exercise will support and increase understanding that those things which cause Antwone to experience internal discomfort typically point to areas of life that are meaningful to him (i.e., being sensitive to feelings of abandonment because he values intimacy and connection) (*treatment interventions*). Specific treatment obstacles and challenges can be anticipated. These include the likelihood that Antwone will quickly identify with a caring practitioner as the positive father figure and role model that he never had. It is also likely that this will engender a predictable stimulus generalization in terms of both the client and the practitioner, which may result in Antwone acting out (*treatment obstacles*). In addition to addressing personality and interpersonal treatment targets, an effective treatment outcome will require addressing the cultural dimension of prejudice, not only prejudice from white peers and superiors, but also his experience of black-on-black prejudice. It may be useful to therapeutically frame not only his foster family's prejudice from white peers and superiors, but also his experience of black-on-black prejudice and abuse toward him in terms of self-loathing that was passed down from their ancestors to him; then, it can be therapeutically processed. Because he is an avid reader, bibliotherapy, i.e., books and articles that analyze and explain this type of prejudice, could be a useful therapeutic adjunct (*treatment-cultural*). These resources plus his motivation to change suggest a good to very good prognosis (*treatment prognosis*).

Case of Maria

Maria is a 17-year-old, first-generation Mexican American female who was referred for counseling because of mood swings. She is conflicted about her decision to go off to college instead of staying home to care for her terminally ill mother. Her family expects her to stay home. She is angry at her older sister, who left home at 17 after her parents insisted that her culture "requires" her to take care of her parents when they get old or become ill. Her Anglo friends encourage her to go to college and pursue her dreams.

ACT Assessment

Although Maria is referred by her parents for the single experimentation episode with alcohol, she affirms that she does not use alcohol or any other drugs. There is no family history of substance use or mental health disorders. Maria stated that she was "turned off" by her experience with alcohol and that it "didn't do anything but make me sick." She denies having any health problems or using any medication. She also denied any other recreational use of drugs in the past. Maria demonstrates a pleasing disposition. She endorsed dependence on others and difficulty dealing with disagreement and confrontation. Her parents are reportedly strict and demanding. They insist that Maria should conform to "old ways" based on cultural expectations that children become caretakers for aging or sick parents.

On the other hand, Maria is conflicted given her Anglo friends' encouragement that she go off to college and pursue her dreams. This has created conflict between Maria and her parents, who do not want her to "end up like her sister." The family emigrated to the United States from Mexico when Maria was four years old. Maria's parents rely on her to serve as a translator (Table 10.4).

Case Conceptualization Statement

Maria's depressive symptoms, confusion, and recent experimentation with alcohol use (*presentation*) seem to be her reaction to pressures and conflict over going away to college or staying to care for her parents (*current precipitant*) as well as expectations of self-reliance, being alone, or need to meet others' needs at the expense of her own (*continuing precipitants*). Throughout her life, Maria has attempted to be a good daughter and friend, and has become increasingly stuck in meeting the needs of others at the expense of her own needs (*pattern*). Maria seems fused with thoughts of being "stuck in the middle" and feeling "down" and "pressured" by both her friends and her parents. Experiential avoidance is also indicated in this case. Although it has not, at this juncture, escalated to a clinical concern, Maria has experimented with alcohol consumption as a means of avoiding feeling confrontation, conflict, or guilt. She also demonstrates rigid attention to a conceptualized future in which she thinks she will invariably disappoint either her friends or her parents. Thus, she sees herself as one of two variants: a "rebellious daughter" akin to her sister, who chose to move away from the family, and a "failure" in terms of someone who cannot decide for herself to chase her dreams, according to her Anglo friends. The chief concerns in Maria's case seem to relate to logical conflict between U.S. societal values and the values of her culture and family of origin. Maria has derived "rules" from this conflict that strictly determine that she will either fail to be a "good daughter" or fail entirely to live a good life (*predisposition*). Maria brings several protective factors to therapy including strong family, social, and religious values that may motivate her to establish vital life directions. Some of her strengths include her intelligence and past success in school. She also benefits from a tight-knit family and cultural community in which she can feel safe and supported (*protective factors/strengths*).

Maria identifies herself as a working-class Mexican American with a moderate level of involvement in that heritage (*cultural identity*). Her level of acculturation is in the low to moderate range while her parents' level is in the low range. Since her older sister refused to follow the cultural mandate that the oldest daughter would meet her parents needs rather than her own, that responsibility is now on Maria. Maria's ambivalence about whether to follow cultural norms and expectations or her own aspirations is quite distressing for her (*cultural stress & acculturation*). Her explanatory model is that her problems are due to a "lack of faith," a belief that is consistent with a lower level of acculturation. Although she and her family experienced some discrimination upon arrival here, it ended when they moved to a "safer" Mexican American neighborhood (*cultural explanation*). It appears that both personality and cultural factors are operative. Specifically, cultural dynamics that foster dependency, i.e., good daughters care for their parents

Table 10.4 Acceptance and Commitment Therapy Case Conceptualization Elements

Presentation	moodiness; confusion; experimentation with alcohol use
Precipitant	pressures and conflict over going away to college or staying to care for her parents (***current precipitant***); expectations of self-reliance, being alone, or need to meet others' needs at the expense of her own (***continuing precipitants***)
Pattern-maladaptive	meets others' needs but not her own
Predisposition	***fusion***: entangled with thoughts of being "stuck in the middle" and feeling "down" and "pressured"
	avoidance: confrontation, conflict, failure
	rigid attention: rigid attention to conceptualized future as "a bad daughter" if she defies her parents, incognizant of emotional responding
	attached to conceptualized self: fused with the concept of self as "rebellious daughter" or "failure" if she moves in the direction her supports want her to take
	disconnected action: attempts to numb or avoid via substance use experimentation
	values: unclear and conflicting cultural and societal values
Protective factors/ strengths	strong family, social, religious values; successful student; tight-knit and safe cultural community
Perpetuant	dependent and pleasing style; low assertiveness; cultural expectation
Cultural identity	working-class Mexican American
Cultural stress & acculturation	low to moderate level of acculturation; stress from ambivalence about parental and cultural expectations
Cultural explanation	problems caused by "lack of faith"
Culture and/or personality	personality *and* cultural factors operative
Treatment pattern	meet her needs and the needs of others
Treatment goals	understand and freely choose personal and cultural values; provide family education and interventions to support holistic acceptance and well-being
Treatment focus	increase awareness of life principles and establish goals that are consistent with individual as well as family and cultural values
Treatment strategy	increase psychological flexibility by decreasing ambiguity of values, addressing entanglement with thoughts, poor contact with present moment and ongoing emotional experience, experiential avoidance of conflict and confrontation, to develop a stable and flexible sense of self, and encourage committed action
Treatment interventions	writing down thoughts; "tombstone" and "eulogy" exercises; family and cultural values; goal clarification; the three selves; assertiveness training – boundary setting; role playing "taking a stand"

(*Continued*)

Table 10.4 Continued

Treatment obstacles	may capitulate to parents and cultural expectations; pleasing the practitioner; practitioner may unwittingly advocate autonomy
Treatment cultural	process cultural expectations about caregiver role and need to please; family sessions addressing parents' cultural expectations; pair with Spanish-speaking therapist or obtain translator
Treatment prognosis	fair to good

without question, serve to reinforce her dependent personality dynamics (***culture and/or personality***).

The challenge of change for Maria is to meet both her own needs in addition to the needs of others (***treatment pattern***).

(***treatment goals***). Treatment will be focused on increasing awareness of life principles and establishing goals that are consistent with individual as well as family and cultural values (***treatment focus***). The aim will be to increase psychological flexibility by decreasing ambiguity of values, addressing entanglement with thoughts, poor contact with present moment and ongoing emotional experience, and experiential avoidance of conflict and confrontation, and developing a stable and flexible sense of self, and encouraging committed action (***treatment strategy***).

(***treatment interventions***). In terms of likely treatment obstacles and challenges, it is likely that Maria will attempt to please the practitioner by readily agreeing to suggestions and between-session assignments, but afterward become conflicted and then fail to follow up. It is also likely that the client will capitulate to her parents' expectations. Accordingly, the practitioner might, early in treatment, make the predictive interpretation that this might occur, but that it does not indicate failure, and that it can be therapeutically processed. Finally, practitioners working with dependent clients need to anticipate how their own needs and values may become treatment obstacles. This can occur when they unwittingly advocate for and expect clients to embrace independence and autonomy before the client is sufficiently ready (***treatment obstacles***). Effective treatment outcomes will also address relevant cultural dynamics. Specifically, this may involve therapeutically processing her explanatory model that lack of faith is the source of her problem. Depending on the saliency and strength of this belief, education and cognitive disputation (i.e., defusion) may be indicated. The cultural expectation about caring for her parents in light of her need to please would also be processed. In addition, family sessions may be indicated wherein her parents can review and revise their cultural expectations of her. Given that Maria regularly serves as her parents' translator, it is crucial to pair Maria with a Spanish-speaking therapist or secure a translator for sessions involving the family (***treatment-cultural***). At this point, however, given her lower level of acculturation and dependent personality dynamics, her prognosis is in the fair to good range (***treatment prognosis***).

Case of Richard

Richard is a 41-year-old, Caucasian male who is being evaluated for anxiety, sadness, and anger following his recent divorce. He currently lives on his own, is employed as a machine operator, and frequents night clubs where he is "on the lookout for the perfect woman." He has held four jobs over the past six years and was fired from his last job because he smashed his fist through a wall after being confronted by a female coworker. He is an only child of alcoholic parents whom he describes as "fighting all the time."

ACT Assessment

From previous counseling, Richard has verbalized some insight into his behavior. "I know that I'm just like my dad. He was always harsh and abusive with my mom and other people." This indicates that Richard seems to be responding in accordance with a narrow and seemingly unchangeable sense of self, informed by the history of his father's aggressive tendencies. He also reported that when he is in conflict with others or he does not achieve favorable outcomes, he gets angry and lashes out to "get even." Aggression appears to function as both an avoidance strategy and a disconnected action. Although he appears to have declarative insight of this pattern, he struggles with the behavioral application of it. Also, rigid attention to the conceptualized past seems operative in maintaining this pattern of responding. Fusion with thoughts of "getting my way" and feelings of inferiority serve to exacerbate situations in which he acts out. In sessions with the practitioner, he demands extra time, ignores or steamrolls the therapy agenda, and blames others for his ongoing difficulties. Many of his ongoing behaviors seem counterproductive to provisional values and goals of being accepted and feeling safe, evidenced by what he has disclosed about his relationship with his grandmother (Table 10.5).

Table 10.5 Acceptance and Commitment Therapy Case Conceptualization Elements

Presentation	angry outbursts, sadness, and anxiety
Precipitant	recent divorce and also being fired from his last job for smashing his fist through a wall (***current precipitant***); evaluation of self, being alone, or others' perception of not being special (***continuing precipitants***)
Pattern-maladaptive	elevates self while belittling and using others
Predisposition	***fusion***: thoughts – "I am going to have it my way one way or another" feelings – frustration, sadness, anxiety
	avoidance: avoids feelings of perceived inferiority
	unaware/rigid attention: attention to conceptualized past
	attached to conceptualized self: sees self as a product of his father and his environment during childhood
	disconnected action: lashing out, fighting, aggressive behavior
	values: non-judgment, acceptance, and interpersonal safety
Protective factors/ strengths	secure attachment with his grandmother; resilient, charismatic, and engaging
Perpetuant	impulsivity; limited relationship skills; inability to empathize
Cultural identity	middle-class Caucasian male
Cultural stress & acculturation	highly acculturated; no obvious cultural stress, but privilege should be examined in the therapeutic process
Cultural explanation	anxiety, anger, sadness caused by abusive, non-loving parents
Culture and/or personality	personality dynamics operative
Treatment pattern	self-confident and respectful to others
Treatment goals	introduce defusion skills and the concept of "workability"; undermine agenda of emotional control; increase clarity of values and life acceptance; process divorce and grief over death of grandmother
Treatment focus	to decrease persistent avoidance and rigid aggressive responding by exploring flexibility processes
Treatment strategy	to target psychological flexibility by addressing entanglement with self-concept and introducing perspective-taking skills; to address poor awareness of values and ongoing private experiences
Treatment interventions	the clipboard exercise; tin can monster mindfulness exercise; attending your own funeral values exercise; and committed action through in-session behavioral experiments of interpersonal process
Treatment obstacles	minimization of his own problematic behaviors; idealization or devaluation of practitioner; arrogant attitude
Treatment-cultural	no cultural focus to treatment indicated but address privilege dynamics
Treatment prognosis	fair

Case Conceptualization Statement

Richard's angry outbursts, sadness, and anxiety (***presentation***) seem to be a reaction to his recent divorce and also being fired from his last job for smashing his fist through a wall (***current precipitant***), as well as self-evaluation, being alone, or others' perception of not being special (***continuing precipitants***). From adolescence, he has elevated himself and belittled and abused others with an aggressive style, making it difficult to sustain safe and satisfying relationships (***pattern***).

_____

_____

_____

_____

_____

_____

(***predisposition***). This pattern is maintained by his inability to empathize, impulsivity, and lack of relational skills (***perpetuants***). Richard's secure attachment with his grandmother serves as a protective factor and evidence that he has the capacity to care for others. The most prominent strength Richard brings to therapy is resilience. He is also charismatic and engaging (***protective factors/strengths***).

Richard identifies as a middle-class Caucasian male (***cultural identity***). He appears to be highly acculturated and there is no obvious indications of acculturative stress (***cultural stress & acculturation***). He believes that his current problems of anger, sadness, and anxiety result from the bad example he received from his abusive and non-loving parents who fought constantly when they drank (***cultural explanation***). Finally, personality dynamics are predominant and adequately explain his presenting problem and pattern, but examining his sense of entitlement and his own experience of privilege would be useful to address in therapy (***culture and/or personality***).

The challenge of change for Richard to function more effectively is to remain self-confident while endeavoring to be more respectful of others (***treatment pattern***).

_____

_____

_____

_____

_____

_____

(***treatment goals***). Treatment will focus primarily on decreasing persistent avoidance and rigid aggressive responding by exploring flexibility processes (***treatment focus***). The treatment strategy is to target psychological flexibility by addressing entanglement with self-concept and introducing perspective-taking skills. Also, strategies to address poor awareness of values and ongoing private experiences will be utilized (***treatment strategy***). The clipboard exercise will be employed to orient Richard to the therapy and develop an experiential understanding of defusion from private experiences. The tin can monster exercise will be used to introduce the client's experience not as one big and overwhelming component, but instead many different parts (i.e., "a thirty foot monster made of individual tin cans connected by a string"), allowing the client to increase his awareness of the parts of his experience: thoughts, feelings, bodily sensations, behaviors, and memories. The client will then be led through a guided imagery exercise of attending his own funeral. This will aim at creating a sense of perspective in which the client can notice his behavior and responding through others' frame of reference. This exercise will facilitate choosing and clarifying values (i.e., "Who will attend your funeral?"; "What might they say?"; "What would you want them to say?"). Once Richard has a firm understanding of the kind of person he wants to be, the kind of life he wants to live, and how he wants to behave toward others, the practitioner will provide a context in which to practice these behaviors: the therapy. Richard will be probed for his willingness to practice committed action in the way he responds to the therapist, allowing for the practice of empathy, acceptance, and humility, in the service of establishing the kinds of relationships that are accepting, caring, non-judgmental, and safe (***treatment interventions***). With regard to treatment obstacles and challenges, it is likely that Richard will minimize his own problematic behaviors by blaming circumstances or others. It can be expected that he will alternate between idealization or devaluation of the practitioner, at least in the beginning phase of therapy. His entitled and arrogant attitude could activate inflexible responding in the practitioner. Furthermore, since it is not uncommon for clients with a narcissistic style to discontinue treatment when their symptoms, immediate conflicts, or stressors are sufficiently reduced, the practitioner who believes the client can profit from continued therapy needs to point out – at the beginning of therapy and thereafter – that until the client's underlying maladaptive (i.e., unworkable) pattern is sufficiently changed, similar issues and concerns will inevitably arise in the future (***treatment obstacles***). Since the primary influence is personality dynamics, no cultural focus to treatment is indicated besides examining his entitlement and sense of privilege. However, because of the client's conditional manner of relating, multiple job firings, and impulsivity, at this point, his prognosis is considered fair (***treatment prognosis***).

Case of Katrina

Katrina is a 13-year-old female of mixed ethnicity. She was referred for counseling by her guidance counselor due to recent depressive symptoms, poor academic performance, and oppositional behavior and fighting with other students at school. Her aggressive behavior and academic challenges have increased over the past six months since Katrina overheard a conversation between her mother and aunt in which she found out that her father had an affair for eight years. She was shocked to learn that this resulted in two births. Other difficulties include several fights with other students in the classroom, frequent conflict with her mother, skipping 15 days of school over the past six months, and diminished interest in her academic work. While she had previously excelled academically, she now displayed a marked loss of interest in activities that used to give her pleasure, such as drawing and reading. Katrina's father is currently living in Puerto Rico and has no contact with the family. Katrina lives in a small apartment with her mother and younger brother near her school. She reported being frustrated with the lack of space, since they had to downsize from the single-family home they lived in before her father left the family one year ago.

ACT Assessment

Because Katrina is a minor, an initial meeting with both Katrina and her mother, Julia, was required for the first session. Julia stated that Katrina essentially does not discuss her problems with anyone because she "doesn't trust anyone." Katrina endorsed this interpretation and further disclosed that she was not interested in attending counseling if it meant that she was going to be told what to do. It became clear that self-disclosure was difficult for Katrina, and Julia often stepped in, speaking for her when she made efforts to speak. Julia described Katrina's father as critical and emotionally withdrawn throughout Katrina's childhood. Katrina also stated, "I don't really have a dad, since real fathers are supposed to take care of their families." She described feeling frustrated that her mother and teachers want to impose their will on her. A functional analysis revealed that Katrina's acting out behavior likely gave her a sense of autonomy and power. She also appears to be fused with thoughts such as "showing weakness means that people will take advantage of you," which is a rule that is likely derived from her father having taken advantage of her mother in the past. This seems to have resulted in other rigid rules about authority and control. Table 10.6 provides a description and results of the diagnostic and ACT assessment, within a summary of key elements of the full-scale case conceptualization.

Case Conceptualization Statement

Katrina's increased social isolation, aggressive and oppositional behavior, and depressive symptoms (***presentation***) appear to be her reaction to recent news of her father's infidelity and resulting children (***current precipitant***). Katrina has a tendency to retaliate when she perceives that she is being violated or controlled by others (***continuing precipitant***). Given Katrina's lack of connection with her father and lack of trust in both parents, she moves against authority figures and her peers to protect herself from further harm and rejection. In short, her pattern

Table 10.6 Acceptance and Commitment Therapy Case Conceptualization Elements

Presentation	social isolation; oppositional and aggressive behavior; depressive symptoms
Precipitant	learning of her father's infidelity and resulting children (***current precipitant***); retaliates in situations of perceived violation or control by others (***continuing precipitants***)
Pattern-maladaptive	moves against authority figures and peers to protect herself from harm/rejection
Predisposition	*fusion*: thoughts – "showing weakness means people will take advantage of you" feelings – loneliness, defectiveness, frustration
	avoidance: avoids feelings of perceived rejection and loss of autonomy
	unaware/rigid attention: attention to conceptualized past; poor insight into feelings
	attached to conceptualized self: sees self as defective and unimportant
	disconnected action: lashing out, oppositional and aggressive behavior; loss of interest in academics
	values: independence, creativity, and strength
Protective factors/ strengths	close relationship to her aunt and little brother; intelligent, creative, and resilient
Perpetuant	unwilling to ask for help; low level of motivation for therapy; social isolation and lack of support system
Cultural identity	Hispanic and African American
Cultural stress & acculturation	moderately acculturated; Katrina's mom – low level of acculturation with some acculturative stress
Cultural explanation	does not believe she is depressed and believes that she would be better off if others were less demanding or controlling
Culture and/or personality	both culture and personality seem to influence the presenting problem
Treatment pattern	increase ability to trust, feel safer, and better connect with others
Treatment goals	introduce defusion skills to better relate to unworkable thoughts, challenge workability of lashing out and aggressive behaviors, and support values-based responding
Treatment focus	to decrease persistent avoidance and rigid aggressive responding by exploring flexibility processes
Treatment strategy	to target psychological flexibility by addressing entanglement with self-concept and introducing perspective-taking skills; to address poor awareness of values and ongoing private experiences

(Continued)

Table 10.6 Continued

Treatment interventions	Passengers on a Bus; the Two Trains metaphor; behavioral rehearsal; creative mindfulness and journaling activities; family sessions
Treatment obstacles	low motivation to engage in therapeutic process; oppositional behavior; low capacity for establishing trust with practitioner; potential for testing behavior
Treatment-cultural	culturally sensitive treatment is indicated given moderate and low levels of acculturation in both Katrina and her mother
Treatment prognosis	fair to good

can be understood in light of her lack of trust in her father based on his infidelity; in addition, her perception of being rejected by her father appears to have influenced her core beliefs about mistrust, paranoia about others' intentions, and a lack of safety with others (***pattern***).

_____

_____

_____

_____

_____

_____

(***predisposition***). Katrina's pattern is maintained by her unwillingness to ask for help, her low level of motivation to engage in therapy, her social isolation and lack of support system, her mother and teachers rigidly forcing compliance, her low frustration tolerance, and lack of assertive communication skills (***perpetuants***). Despite some of her current challenges, Katrina reported being very close with her aunt and little brother. Besides her close relationships in her family, Katrina reported that she feels responsible for her brother and does everything she can to protect him from harm. Lastly, her strengths include her being a good artist, determined, intelligent, empathic, and creative (***protective factors/ strengths***).

Katrina identifies as heterosexual and of mixed ethnicity. She identified as Hispanic and African American but reported having little connection to the ethnic and cultural traditions from either identity. She stated that she wants to be more like her friends and doesn't want to feel different or weird by speaking Spanish to her mother in front of friends (***cultural identity***). She is moderately acculturated and prefers not to speak Spanish outside of the home, though her mother requires her to speak Spanish while at home. Katrina's mother presents with a low level of acculturation as evidenced by having challenges with speaking English, having very few English-speaking friends, being first-generation Puerto-Rican American and also African American, and reporting that she is unhappy living in the United States and plans to move back to Puerto Rico once Katrina graduates from high school (*cultural stress & acculturation*). Katrina does not believe she is depressed but feels that she would be less annoyed with people if they would be less controlling and "less bossy" (*cultural explanation*). There appears to be a moderate level of cultural factors and a moderate level of personality dynamics that influence the presenting issues (*culture and/or personality*).

The challenge for Katrina to function more effectively is to increase her ability to trust others, feel safer, and to better connect with others (*treatment pattern*).

_____

_____

_____

_____

_____

_____

(*treatment goals*). The treatment focus is to decrease persistent avoidance and rigid aggressive responding by exploring flexibility processes (*treatment focus*). The basic treatment strategies will be to target psychological flexibility by addressing entanglement with self-concept and introducing perspective-taking skills. The practitioner will also endeavor to help Katrina foster a better understanding of her values and ongoing private experiences (*treatment strategy*).

_____

_____

_____

_____

_____

_____

(*treatment interventions*). Some obstacles and challenges to treatment are anticipated given Katrina's low motivation to engage in therapy and her paranoid traits that are associated with her oppositional behaviors. It can be anticipated that she will have difficulty discussing personal matters with practitioners due to her inability to trust and that she will often engage in testing behaviors toward the practitioner (*treatment obstacles*). Treatment will require some culturally sensitive elements given Katrina and her mother's level of acculturation. It will be important for the practitioner to remain cognizant that the function of the client's behavior, particularly the mother's, may include significant contextual and cultural influences. Therefore, given her Hispanic background, some caution must be taken not to unwittingly encourage drastic individuality. Additionally, gender dynamics may be an issue so it may be useful to assign Katrina a female therapist (***treatment-cultural***). Assuming that Katrina is able to engage more in the therapeutic process as well as utilize her strengths and seek support from her aunt, her prognosis is adjudged to be fair to good (***treatment prognosis***).

Skill Building Exercises: Acceptance and Commitment Therapy

As mentioned in the Skill Building Exercises in Chapter 6, you will note that *certain elements of the case conceptualization statements contain open lines. These lines provide you with an opportunity to further develop your conceptualization skills with specific prompts.* Write a short predisposition statement, treatment goals, and a list of corresponding theory-specific treatment interventions for each case.

CHAPTER 10 QUESTIONS

1. Discuss how the ACT perspective and current practices differ from the previous case conceptualization models presented in previous chapters.
2. Compare the various ACT pillars presented and discuss how these tenets are infused in an Acceptance and Commitment case conceptualization.
3. Explore some of the prompts provided to elicit components of an Acceptance and Commitment case conceptualization and discuss the goal of obtaining this insight from the client.
4. Discuss the signature elements of an Acceptance and Commitment case conceptualization and how these key elements influence the components of a case conceptualization from this perspective.
5. Contrast the five signature features of ACT (Table 10.1) from the case of Geri with the signature features of Time Limited Dynamic Psychotherapy (Table 8.1).

Appendix: Case of Antwone

Predisposition

Antwone seems fused with rigid rules of aggressive responding in situations he perceives as threatening or when he feels distressed. This likely stems from childhood memories in which he was berated and abused, informing the potential for rigid attention to the conceptualized past. Current circumstances may direct Antwone's attention to past events and incite past responding strategies, such as "lashing out." Antwone employed this strategy in adolescence to cope with being displaced from his foster mother's home due to his unwillingness to endure any further abuse. Rigid attention to the past may also exacerbate a concept of self as "weak" or "unwanted," which can drive aggressive behaviors to neutralize real or perceived threats. Aggressive behaviors may also function to suppress or bypass sadness, perceptions of abandonment, and other unwanted feelings that relate to unfavorable childhood experiences. Although Antwone seems to have strong values and desires to do well in the military and have a family life, he seems to struggle to connect goals and ongoing behaviors to those values.

Treatment Goal

Given that many of Antwone's problems stem from internal confusion and turmoil, the primary goals of treatment are to increase acceptance and mindfulness to develop emotional identification, support resilience, and increase impulse control. Secondly, awareness processes will aim at developing a stable sense of self through processing trauma and family conflict. Finally, values will be clarified, and values-consistent goals will be established.

Case of Maria

Treatment Goal

Noting that Maria's chief concerns stem from values ambiguity, the goals of treatment will seek to facilitate a comprehensive understanding and choosing of personal and cultural values. The family will also be provided with education and intervention to support holistic acceptance and well-being.

Treatment Interventions

At the outset of treatment, defusion will be addressed through writing down thoughts and establishing a separation between self and cognition. This will allow Maria to perceive herself and the contents of her mind as separate. Values exercises will follow, employing techniques such as the "tombstone" exercise, by which Maria will choose her epitaph (e.g., "Here lies Maria, who suffered greatly throughout her life in order to avoid making her parents and friends unhappy"). Subsequently, goals can be clarified and established in order to provide vital and meaningful life directions. Maria will be assisted in skills deficit training such as assertiveness, emotional identification, and boundary setting. Finally, given that Maria has demonstrated difficulty with confrontation and conflict, a behavioral skills-training approach is warranted for her to engage in committed actions such as disclosing or stating values and goals. The therapist and Maria will role play scenarios in which she can practice "taking a stand" against either her friends, her parents, or both, depending on clarified goals and chosen life directions.

Case of Richard

Predisposition

Richard seems fused with thoughts of getting his way and feelings of frustration, sadness, and anxiety. When these feelings surface for him, he seems to have difficulty changing his focus or understanding the experiences as a part of him, instead of over-identifying with them (i.e., Self-as-Content). Thus, he avoids the feelings and thoughts by employing strategies of aggressive and violent behaviors, up to punching walls when confronted. He also appears to have difficulty remaining connected to his ongoing experience in the present moment. When unwanted or unfavorable private experiences surface for him, he responds with past behaviors. This leads him to actions that are disconnected and counterproductive to his goals. From the information gathered about Richard's relationship with his grandmother, values of non-judgment, acceptance, and interpersonal safety can be derived. However, Richard's behaviors do not reflect these values, perhaps because he sees himself as a product of his father and the chronic lack of safety of his environment during childhood.

Treatment Goal

Goals of treatment to support more workable responding will include introduction to defusion skills and the concept of "workability," undermine the agenda of emotional control, and increase clarity of values and life acceptance. Once a strong therapeutic alliance is formed, it may be important for Richard to process his divorce and the death of his grandmother.

Case of Katrina

Predisposition

Katrina demonstrates several fused thoughts such as "showing weakness means people will take advantage of you." Current avoidance patterns point to her wanting to forgo feelings of perceived rejection or loss of autonomy, especially as she continues to claim that others want to control her. There seems to be rigid attention to the conceptualized past, as she seems to be making a connection between learning of her father's betrayal of her mother and his perceived abandonment and how she currently views herself. Katrina's concept of herself is also characterized as defective or unimportant. Her disconnected action has comprised of acting out behaviors, isolation, aggressiveness and opposition, and lack of engagement in academic or school tasks that she previously excelled in. She seems to strongly value independence, creativity, and strength.

Treatment Goal

Treatment goals include introducing cognitive defusion skills so that she can better relate to unworkable thoughts, to challenge the workability of lashing out and aggressive behaviors, and support values-based behavior and engagement in academic and creative goals.

Treatment Interventions

Once sufficient rapport has been established, the practitioner will engage Katrina with experiential exercises such as Passengers on a Bus. Throughout this experience, Katrina will be able to view her thoughts as thoughts (i.e., look *at* her thoughts instead of *from* her thoughts). This will allow her to more flexibly respond to feelings and thoughts about being controlled, being abandoned, and being alone. The therapist will engage with the client on significant behavioral rehearsal such as role playing and reverse role play. Through this process, the client's rigid responding to her mother will also be addressed. The client will be encouraged to engage in behavioral experiments such as completing her assigned work and engaging in activities she previously found pleasurable (i.e., reading, drawing). The Two Trains metaphor will be used to support committed action. A collaborative environment will be encouraged; values-clarification and goal-setting will be utilized throughout to focus the treatment and support empowerment, self-efficacy, and autonomy. Finally, Katrina and Julia will participate in family sessions to increase collaborative and assertive communication.

References

American Psychological Association. (n.d.). Psychological treatments. Retrieved from https://www.div12.org/treatments/.

Biglan, A., & Hayes, S.C. (1996). Should the behavioral sciences become more pragmatic? The case for functional contextualism in research on human behavior. *Applied and Preventive Psychology: Current Scientific Perspectives*, 5(1), 47–57.

Hayes, S.C. (1981). *Comprehensive cognitive distancing procedures* (Unpublished manuscript). Greensboro, NC: University of North Carolina at Greensboro.

Hayes, S.C. (2004). Acceptance and commitment therapy, relational frame theory, and the third wave of behavioral and cognitive therapies. *Behavior Therapy*, 35, 639–665.

Hayes, S.C., Hayes, L.J., & Reese, H.W. (1988). Finding the philosophical core: A review of Stephen C Popper's World Hypotheses. *Journal of Experimental Analysis of Behavior*, 50, 97–111.

Hayes, S.C., Strosahl, K.D., & Wilson, K.G. (2012). *Acceptance and commitment therapy: The process and practice of mindful change* (2nd ed.). New York, NY: The Guilford Press.

Hayes, S.C., Villatte, M., Levin, M., & Hildebrandt, M. (2011). Open, aware, and active: Contextual approaches as an emerging trend in the behavioral and cognitive therapies. *Annual Review of Clinical Psychology*, 7, 141–168.

Luoma, J.B., Hayes, S.C., & Walser, R.D. (2017). *Learning ACT: An acceptance & commitment therapy skills-training manual for therapists* (2nd ed.). Oakland, CA: New Harbinger & Reno, NV: Context Press.

Villatte, M., Villatte, J.L., & Hayes, S.C. (2016). *Mastering the clinical conversation: Language as intervention*. New York, NY: The Guilford Press.

Wilson, K.G., & DuFrene, T. (2009). *Mindfulness for two: An acceptance and commitment therapy approach to mindfulness in psychotherapy*. Oakland, CA: New Harbinger.

Appendix: Forms

1. Clinical Formulation Worksheet
2. Elements of a Case Conceptualization: Descriptions
3. Elements of a Case Conceptualization: Worksheet
4. Case Conceptualization Evaluation Form

Clinical Formulation Worksheet*

Clinical Formulation Worksheet*

_____

_____

_____

_____

Predisposition

↓

Precipitant ----------------------> **Pattern** --------------------------> **Presentation**

_____

_____   _____

_____   _____

↑

Perpetuants

_____

_____

_____

_____

---

* Sperry, L., & Sperry, J. (2020). *Case conceptualization: Mastering this competency with ease and confidence*. Second edition. New York, NY: Routledge.

Elements of a Case Conceptualization: Description*

Presentation	presenting problem and characteristic response to precipitants
Precipitant	triggers that activate the pattern resulting in presenting problem
Pattern-maladaptive	inflexible, ineffective manner of perceiving, thinking, acting
Predisposition	factors fostering adaptive or maladaptive functioning
Protective Factors	factors that decrease the likelihood of developing a clinical condition
Perpetuants	triggers that activate one's pattern resulting in presentation
Cultural identity	sense of belonging to a particular ethnic group
Cultural stress & acculturation	level of adaptation to the dominant culture; stress rooted in acculturation including psychosocial difficulties
Cultural explanation	beliefs regarding cause of distress, condition, or impairment
Culture and/or personality	operative mix of cultural and personality dynamics
Treatment pattern	flexible, effective manner of perceiving, thinking, acting
Treatment goals	stated short- and long-term outcomes of treatment
Treatment focus	central therapeutic emphasis providing directionality treatment that is keyed to the adaptive pattern
Treatment strategy	action plan and vehicle for achieving a more adaptive pattern
Treatment interventions	specific change techniques and tactics related to the treatment strategy for achieving treatment goals and pattern change
Treatment obstacles	predictable challenges in the treatment process anticipated from the maladaptive pattern
Treatment-cultural	incorporation of cultural intervention, culturally sensitive therapy, or interventions when indicated
Treatment prognosis	prediction of the likely course, duration, and outcome of a mental health condition with or without treatment

* Sperry, L., & Sperry, J. (2020). *Case conceptualization: Mastering this competency with ease and confidence*. Second edition. New York, NY: Routledge.

Elements of a Case Conceptualization: Worksheet**

Presentation

Precipitant

Pattern-maladaptive

Predisposition

Protective Factors

Perpetuants

Cultural identity

Cultural stress & acculturation

Cultural explanation

Culture and/or personality

Treatment pattern

Treatment goals

Treatment focus

Treatment strategy

Treatment interventions

Treatment obstacles

Treatment-cultural

Treatment prognosis

** Sperry, L., & Sperry, J. (2020). *Case conceptualization: Mastering this competency with ease and confidence*. Second edition. New York, NY: Routledge.

Case Conceptualization Evaluation Form***

Instructions: Rate the case conceptualization statement using a scale where 1 = very poor and 10 = excellent

1. *Diagnostic Formulation*: Presentation and precipitant are directly linked to the Pattern–maladaptive

   1   2   3   4   5   6   7   8   9   10

2. *Clinical Formulation*: Predisposition is clearly stated and convincingly explains the Pattern and Presentation; *CF* accurately reflects BPS, CB, Dynamic, S-F, or Adlerian (*circle one*)

    1   2   3   4   5   6   7   8   9   10

3. *Cultural Formulation*: Incorporates identity; acculturation level and stress; explanatory model; culture vs. psychological factors; anticipates influence of cultural factors on treatment process

    1   2   3   4   5   6   7   8   9   10

4. *Treatment Formulation*: Tx Goals reflect Presentation and Predisposition; *TF* accurately reflects BPS, CB, Dynamic, S-F, or Adlerian (*circle one*); Tx Focus consistent with method; Tx Strategy and specific Tx Interventions are appropriate and linked to Tx Goals; Tx Obstacles reflect client's personality and cultural dynamics. If indicated, appropriate Tx-Cultural interventions are specified

    1   2   3   4   5   6   7   8   9   10

5. *Explanatory Power*: Overall explanation of pattern, presenting problem, and cultural factors is compelling, as is the rationale for the proposed treatment plan/implementation strategy

    1   2   3   4   5   6   7   8   9   10

6. *Predictive Power*: Realistic and sufficient treatment plan and implementation plan for achieving Tx Goals/pattern change; adequately anticipates challenges; realistic Tx Prognosis

    1   2   3   4   5   6   7   8   9   10

7. *Completeness*: Sufficient number of case conceptualization elements are incorporated and provide a complete case conceptualization

    1   2   3   4   5   6   7   8   9   10

8. *Coherence*: Coherently and logically articulates all the included case conceptualization elements

    1   2   3   4   5   6   7   8   9   10

*** Sperry, L., & Sperry, J. (2020). *Case conceptualization: Mastering this competency with ease and confidence*. Second edition. New York, NY: Routledge.

Index

Page numbers in **bold** denote tables, in *italic* denote figures